JOURNALISM

Exploring the deep transformation that journalism has undergone in the last decade, this book provides students, professors and working journalists with the background on the demise of traditional media in the U.S. and the changes happening in digital newsrooms.

Houston discusses today's changes in journalism in the U.S., comparing and contrasting them with those around the world. Topics discussed include the decimation of the traditional newsrooms, contemporary corporate ownership and investors, the rise of bloggers and digital journalism, finding new audiences, the surge in nonprofit newsrooms and collaborations, investigative centers in the U.S. and globally, new model start-ups, and changing streams of revenue with the expansion of new technologies. The text also looks at the new relationship between journalism professionals and the academy, including the rise in content and stories supplied by university-based newsrooms. Houston, who has been on the frontline of these changes, also discusses the culture clashes and ethical dilemmas in cyber environments accompanied by new challenges to maintaining credibility and creating trust.

To fully explore the rapid-fire changes in news media and online journalism in recent years, this book will be of interest to students of journalism and communications, working journalists, and professors helping prepare budding journalists for their future careers in journalism.

Brant Houston is a Professor and the Knight Chair in Investigative Reporting at the University of Illinois, where he teaches investigative and data journalism. An award-winning journalist for over 40 years, he was a reporter at U.S. newspapers for 17 years and has been an editor of investigative stories for digital newsrooms since. Houston has conducted more than 400 seminars for professional journalists and students in 30 countries, and he is a co-founder of networks of nonprofit newsrooms and educators throughout the world.

CHANGING MODELS FOR JOURNALISM

Reinventing the Newsroom

Brant Houston

NEW YORK AND LONDON

Designed cover image: © Aleksei Derin/Getty Images

First published 2023
by Routledge
605 Third Avenue, New York, NY 10158

and by Routledge
4 Park Square, Milton Park, Abingdon, Oxon, OX14 4RN

Routledge is an imprint of the Taylor & Francis Group, an informa business

ISBN: 978-0-7656-4594-4 (hbk)
ISBN: 978-0-7656-4595-1 (pbk)
ISBN: 978-1-315-71957-3 (ebk)

DOI: 10.4324/9781315719573

Typeset in Joanna
by codeMantra

CONTENTS

Preface vii

Acknowledgements x

Introduction: The fall of traditional media, the rise of nonprofit newsrooms, and the fight to save local news 1

1 What happened to traditional journalism? 23

2 New ways emerge: Blogs, digital start-ups, and the rise of nonprofit newsrooms 50

3 Owners, investors, and donors 74

4 Revenue streams 93

5 Advances in digital tools and innovation for news 119

6 Universities increasing role in journalism 133

7 Public media, collaborations, and digital start-ups 152

8 Advocacy, activists, and solutions 167

9 **Maintaining journalism standards and new ethical challenges and perils** 184

Selected Bibliography 201
Appendix A: Starting up a nonprofit newsroom 204
Appendix B: How to keep up with the changes in journalism 216
Index 221

PREFACE

In 1994, I took what I thought would be a two-year break from daily investigative and data journalism to manage a new on-the-road program at Investigative Reporters and Editors to teach data journalism to reporters, editors, and producers across the U.S.

That two-year plan turned into 14 years of not only teaching but managing and expanding the nonprofit IRE. It meant learning to fund-raise, plan events (workshops and conferences), develop curriculum and write textbooks, oversee a membership program, build and expand a website from the inception just as the commercial web started up, edit newsletters and a magazine, deal with membership concerns and complaints, work with an ever-changing, elected 13-member board of directors, and answer questions every year about whether investigative journalism was dying (it wasn't and hasn't), and start to collaborate with journalists and journalisms around the world. In short, I learned how to be an executive director of a nonprofit organization.

In 2007, I left IRE to become the Knight Chair in Investigative and Enterprise Reporting at the University of Illinois in Urbana-Champaign. I went there with plans to teach classes, work on curriculum, create a community news platform for students and post-grads, delve deeper into data journalism, and start to use machine learning for journalism. But almost immediately I started getting calls from friends and colleagues in investigative journalism who were leaving mainstream media, willingly or unwillingly through lay-offs, and newspaper closures. Inspired by the few existing nonprofit investigative news outlets in the U.S., and in some cases, by the burgeoning global nonprofit newsroom movement, known as the Global Investigative Journalism Network, those journalists were determined to create their own nonprofit newsrooms to do the work they loved to do: watchdog journalism in which they could hold the powerful accountable.

But most of them had little business or fundraising experience and they sought advice from the other existing organization and from journalists who had been managers. All of us with such experience spent hours happily answering their questions, giving the best advice we could, and serving on the boards of directors of many of those organizations. By 2009, however, it was clear that there was a need for an organization – a network – to provide the business training and to collaborate on news stories. Out of the realization of that need in the U.S. emerged the Investigative News Network that later became the Institute for Nonprofit News.

At that point, I turned my attention to helping build INN while still working on the expansion of the Global Investigative Journalism Network, which shared some of the same member newsrooms as INN. It was clear that the road to a successful future in journalism was more collaboration and cooperation than competition. Networks could encourage and support these efforts and networks made more sense to the foundations – such as the John L. and James S. Knight Foundation – that were soon confronted by a wave of nonprofit newsrooms – and even some for-profit newsrooms – seeking funding. Networks could check and verify the authenticity of a newsroom (dark money and political fronts were already starting to infest the nonprofit news world) and help in distributing funds.

That approach paid off figuratively and literally with the number of nonprofit newsrooms in INN growing to more than 400 and the number of newsrooms in GIJN to nearly 250.

Thus, it seems a good moment to chronicle as much as possible of what has happened to models of journalism, what is working, and what might lie ahead even though more significant news about the news business seems to spring up daily. The purpose of this book is to present a brief history of the devastation that happened to the kind of newsrooms that I worked in during the first 17 years of my 45-year career and then show the kinds of efforts and strategies used to reinvent news in the U.S., with some references to what has happened internationally. (The international story is worthy of one or more books.)

All of it is a moving target, but the book is meant collect as much of what I have learned, what has worked, and what hasn't worked. Undoubtedly, the story will change in a short time, but it's worth pausing to see where we are and to offer up a series of recipes and checklists for success

I can also share a perspective from having been fortunate to participate in a series of crucial meetings and talks that led to the formation of networks and newsrooms and to give an insider's view of that effort. I also have been fortunate to continue working with the networks and newsrooms on growing and sustaining their work and to share their optimism and energy with my students, many of whom have started or joined these newsrooms. In addition, I have had the opportunity to participate in maintaining and clarifying the ethical standards for nonprofit newsrooms – standards so necessary in a time of rampant social media misinformation and disinformation.

Thus, this book is intended to provide not only ideas and an overview of recent history but also practical in-the-trenches advice and step-by step guidance on navigating the changing models of journalism, especially those of nonprofits. The book has singled out useful research in the field and has case studies that illustrate successful strategies for producing credible journalism on government, business, and communities. The ten chapters look at the changing models for newsrooms, owners and investors, revenue streams, the role of digital innovation, the role of universities and public broadcasting, the increasing activity of advocates in journalism, and the standards for editorial independence and trust.

The book can be used as a core text or supplement to any introductory or intermediate journalism textbook – and it can also serve as a manual for working journalists. There will also be online supplementary material on the web.

ACKNOWLEDGMENTS

I thank the Institute for Nonprofit News, The Global Investigative Journalism, the Local Independent Online News Publishers, the American Journalism Project, and Report for America for their continued support and research for journalism's emerging newsrooms. I also thank the foundations that have long supported the crucial changes in journalism, including the John S. and James L. Knight Foundation and its long-time president Alberto Ibargüen and former vice president of journalism programs, Eric Newton, the Inasmuch Foundation, The Rockefeller Brothers Foundation, the MacArthur Foundation, the Robert R. McCormick Foundation, and Buzz Wooley and the Girard Foundation, the Ford Foundation, the Open Society Foundations, Arnold Ventures, the Gates Foundation, the Reva and David Logan Foundation, and all the other foundations and donors that have given to the independent newsrooms and networks in the U.S. and around the world.

I particularly want to thank Sue Cross, the Chief Executive Officer of INN, and Mark Horvit, professor of journalism at the University of Missouri, for their observations and suggestions on parts of this manuscript.

I also thank many others who have helped with my guiding my thoughts and writings on this topic over the years including Charles Lewis, Laura Frank, Andy Hall, Lorie Hearn, David Kaplan, Gary Kebbel, James T. Hamilton, Robert Rosenthal, Sue Hale, and Clark Bell.Many thanks, too, to my editor, Emma Sherriff, who patiently supported this book's development and publication.

And, as always, my deepest thanks to my wife, Rhonda, who has encouraged and supported me through the many, many months (years actually) of my work on the book, and to my parents who have always supported my work and transitions in journalism.

Last, I want to thank all the journalists who have taken professional and personal risks over the past two decades to ensure that investigative and public service journalism remains alive and well.

In recounting what has happened, it is important to again note the invaluable role of foundations and donors who have stuck with the nonprofit journalism movement. In a symposium in 2008, journalists and scholars worried that foundations and other major donors would be "fickle" and offer only a few years support. But the foundations have not only maintained their support, but in many instances increased it as they recognized how critical the journalism start-ups were to keeping democracy alive. They also have produced research and reports that constantly offer insights to journalists creating and operating newsrooms.

There is courage in doing journalism and there is courage in running and operating a small newsroom and there is the courage to take the leap in the belief that what you do will matter, that will make a difference, and that you will succeed in sustaining that effort.

This book is for all the journalists who have had the courage to have dared to take the leap into reinventing the newsroom and continuing to practice journalism.

INTRODUCTION

The fall of traditional media, the rise of nonprofit newsrooms, and the fight to save local news

In July 2009, 30 journalists gathered at a conference center at the Pocantico estate near New York City to create a network of nonprofit newsrooms to confront and counter the disintegration of the traditional model of U.S. journalism and the ensuing loss of integrity of the profession.

Over a period of more than two decades, print journalism had been undermined by corporate ownership that emphasized marketing over content, a lack of timely adaption in its editorial and advertising activities to a digital world, an accompanying steady decrease in the audience and advertising revenue, and a desperate, perhaps too late, search for new kinds of revenue.

Researchers and industry critics had seen the problems coming for a long time.

"Readership problems have been evident for 50 years in the newspaper industry", wrote Robert G. Picard, a researcher, professor, and media

DOI: 10.4324/9781315719573-1

consultant, in a monograph for Breaux Symposium in 2008 on New Business Models for News.

> We hit a peak of circulation in 1993, but penetration of newspapers in the population has been declining at one and two percent a year for 50 years. The end result: the penetration in the audience today of newspapers is half of what it was in 1950. That's a dramatic change and a dramatic decline.

Picard also noted that the audience of network television was half of what it was in 1980. Indeed, the content and reach of commercial broadcast journalism also had been in a long decline as a quest for ratings and more advertising revenue led to an emphasis on such approaches as happy feature stories, celebrity news, and local crime and weather coverage. In addition, the broadcast industry, like newspapers, was quickly consolidating into a handful of corporate chains that often produced bland, out-of-the-box journalism without regard to the particular quality or distinction of a particular city or region.

"As of 2018, 25 companies owned one-third of the nation's newspapers. Thirty-four ownership groups control the nation's 1,400+ local television stations. Twenty-eight ownership groups control the majority of the country's local radio stations", reported the research group Digital Third Coast. The consolidations have only increased since then.

A nonprofit part of the industry, public broadcasting, had seen increases in listenership and viewership but was facing its own set of challenges, from the aging demographics of its audience to a need to increase its expertise and volume in news coverage, particularly local and regional.

The journalists at the 2009 meeting in New York were well aware of these bleak developments. Most attending were newspaper journalists, but many had already embraced digital online technology and the field of data-driven journalism. Most were investigative journalists who had left, or been laid off, from failing newspapers and were eager to follow the lead of the few nonprofit investigative newsrooms that had been in existence for the past 30 years.

The nonprofit path seemed to promise a revival of investigative and community journalism, an ability to innovate and diversify newsrooms, and a business model not beholden to the pressures of stockholders, advertisers, or the ruthless tactics of hedge funds that had been buying up newspapers and selling off the assets and reducing staffs.

Together the journalists edited and endorsed a declaration of their intent in creating a network, initially called the Investigative News Network (INN) that included both an editorial mission and a plan to provide business services and training to build sustainable newsrooms. The declaration stated about the network:

> Its mission is very simple: to aid and abet, in every conceivable way, individually and collectively, the work and public reach of its member news organizations, including, to the fullest extent possible, their administrative, editorial and financial wellbeing. And, more broadly, to foster the highest quality investigative journalism, and to hold those in power accountable, at the local, national and international levels.

Proceeding Pocantico were two key gatherings. One was the Breaux Symposium at Louisiana State University in 2008. That symposium, "New Models for News", "looked at a troubling trend, the decrease in newsgathering by journalists". It cited the economic travails of the news industry, the cuts already occurring in print and broadcast, and the resulting reduction flow of news, "especially the kinds of news that underpins the public's reliance on the press as a check on government. The goal of the symposium was not only to talk about the trends, but to find ways to expand news reporting".

Among the participants at the Symposium was Charles Lewis, who had founded the nonprofit newsroom, the Center for Public Integrity, already inspired a handful of journalists to create their own nonprofit newsrooms, and would draft the first version of the Pocantico Declaration. Others included Robert G. Picard, a professor media economics; James T. Hamilton, an economist and professor of public policy and author of "All the News That's Fit to Sell: How the Market Transforms Information into News;" Jim Brady, who was executive editor of washingtonpost.com and would go on to try out different news business models and then join the Knight Foundation; and Benjamin R. Shute Jr., the secretary of the

Rockefeller Brothers Fund who would arrange the Pocantico conference. All of them would continue to be guides, commentators, and advocates for new business models.

The two-day symposium covered many of the issues, questions, and possible solutions about business models for journalism, especially nonprofit newsrooms, that would be debated and toiled over for the next decade and many of which are addressed in this book. Those topics included the benefits and issues of foundation and government funding, the increasing roles of universities and public broadcasting in news coverage, launching a start-up newsroom, new models for advertisers, building communities, and keeping up with changing technology.

For the symposium, Geneva Overholser, a long-time editor and a University of Missouri professor, updated her "On Behalf of Journalism: A Manifesto for Change". She had written in 2006 that "Journalism as we know it is over" and the update she added "and a whole new world has opened up before us".

She referred to nine propositions outlined at a June 2005 gathering of journalists and scholars. Those included a greater role for nonprofit newsrooms, better corporate governance by media companies, the importance of the government in protecting and supporting a free press, and the need to bring the public into the arena with courses in media literacy and stronger education in civics. The propositions also called for journalists to better explain what they do and to have a clearer understanding of ethics and good practices.

In concluding remarks, Jack Hamilton, the Dean of the Manship School of Communications at LSU who led the symposium, said, "First of all, I think all agree there is not a model, but many models, and we have to think in terms of many models". He went on to note that they all needed to get a better sense of what all models are and start looking at them as templates.

The next key gathering was at Duke University in May 2009, when James Hamilton, who was a professor at Duke, invited a similar group of journalists, scholars, foundation officers, and others to a gathering focused on nonprofit newsrooms. From that meeting, emerged a report by Hamilton entitled, "The Road Ahead for Media Hybrids: Report of the Duke Nonprofit Media Conference".

The conference brought together a working group to address two questions: "What are the hurdles to nonprofit or foundation ownership of media outlets? And what are the hurdles to nonprofit or foundation subsidies for the creation of public affairs information?"

Hamilton said the conference did not intend to address nuts and bolts of new business models, but instead wanted to focus on how the nonprofit sector could better support watchdog and accountability reporting.

His report focused on four themes:

- Why is there a problem with sustaining watchdog or accounting ability coverage?
- Why may the nonprofit sector offer one way to support this type of public affairs reporting?
- What is the range of nonprofit media alternatives?
- How specifically can foundations, nonprofits, and government foster greater experimentation in nonprofit media provision?

Even then, he wrote "much of the discussion at the conference centered on the threats to watchdog coverage at the local level precisely because participants believed the market would not adequately sustain this type of journalism" – a concern that has only been exponentially magnified since then.

He wrote that accountability journalism, in the form of watchdog beat reporting or investigative projects, can be highly expensive and that in a world where a story's value is measured by eyeballs attracted (and monetized through subscriptions or advertising), this type of public affairs coverage was at risk: "While most conference participants expressed concern about the levels of watchdog coverage likely to survive in the currently turbulent media markets, the question quickly emerged about why nonprofits might offer a solution to this problem".

Hamilton cited an economics term "positive spillovers" to argue why the support of nonprofits would combat the market failure in watchdog journalism. He defined positive spillovers as "benefits created outside of the revenues that flow to the firm creating the good". He said the nonprofit organizational structure offers a way to increase the provision of the underprovided good.

Put practically, he said watchdog coverage can assist a newspaper in gaining subscriptions and advertising revenues from selling the attention of people reading watchdog stories. Then society can benefit from changes in public policy that "are not reflected in a paper's bottom line". Thus, he concluded that a news organization operated as a nonprofit would increase support for watchdog reporting. His reasons roughly summarized were:

- The tax deductibility of donations to a nonprofit media outlet would lower the cost to readers and listeners of supporting coverage of public affairs.
- If revenues exceeded costs they would go back to the organization and not to government taxes.
- The nonprofit status would signal to potential donors about what the funds will be spent on and would encourage managers to not just maximize profits but to focus on maximizing impact.
- Nonprofit status allows a diverse set of people to pay different prices for the creation of a good they jointly value. The nonprofit status in effect is a way to transfer the burden of supporting extensive levels of accountability coverage from particular owners to a larger set of people who value and benefit from the positive spillovers generated by the reporting.

In analyzing what he called media hybrids, he divided them into four groups: "media organizations run as nonprofits; media companies organized as low-profit limited liability corporations, denoted in conversation by the acronym L3Cs; for-profit media outlets with 'affiliated' nonprofit investigative funds; and for-profit media firms who accepted funds from foundations and nonprofits to support particular areas of coverage". He said they were hybrids because they were involved in taking donations while getting market support such as advertising.

Since his report, three of the four hybrids have grown while the L3Cs did not gain traction.

The report provided details and additional models in the newsrooms current at the time in the different categories. Under standalone nonprofits, the report cited MinnPost, a Minneapolis nonprofit newsroom, which hoped to eventually separate itself from major foundation funding through memberships and earned income, and ProPublica, which hoped to increase both its large and small donor support.

Another model was investigative reporting centers at the university, both independent newsrooms and newsrooms that were part of the university, including the now-defunct New England Center for Investigative Reporting and the expanding Wisconsin Center for Investigative Journalism, which was headquartered at the University of Wisconsin in Madison, but an independent nonprofit and not part of the university.

The third model was the traditional newspaper transitioning to a nonprofit. At the time of the conference, there was proposed federal legislation to allow newspapers to convert to nonprofits so they could combat declining revenues by recognizing they had positive spillover, but it was never passed. However, in recent years, the Internal Revenue Service, which grants nonprofit status, has made the issue moot by quickly granting that status to newspapers that had been for profit.

The fourth model was public media, such as NPR and PBS, and the report cited the increasing audience for NPR and American Public Media. Even then, conference attendees noted that public radio stations were not known for doing watchdog work. However, nonprofit investigative centers viewed public media "as natural partners" and later worked closely with National Public Radio stations and in some cases were acquired by the stations.

The fifth model discussed at the conference was nonprofits that worked on public affairs issues that were creating their own research and news stories. Human Rights Watch, the Pew Charitable Trust, and the Kaiser Network were cited as examples.

The sixth model, which did not gain traction despite appearing to be "tailor-made for news organizations", was the low-profit limited liability company (L3C), which had been created under certain states' legislation and was meant for companies that serve education or charitable purposes. The report noted there were many possible hurdles for L3Cs. Later, the idea of the public benefit corporation appeared to take its place.

The seventh model was a for-profit news organization that had an "affiliated" nonprofit partner. That is, the newsroom would create a nonprofit fund to support investigative work. It cited the Huffington Post

Investigative Fund that could receive tax-deductible donations to produce work that would appear in the for-profit Huffington Post. Eventually, the investigative fund staff became a part of the Center for Public Integrity, which then had to fund the staff.

The eighth model was the for-profit newsroom that receives foundation grants and donations for specific topic coverage or investigative work. In recent years, foundations and organizations funded by foundations have given to for-profit newspapers. For example, the Ford Foundation gave grants to the *Washington Post* and the *Los Angeles Times* to supplement their coverage, but the giving to for-profit corporations striving for profits for their stockholders has been controversial. In recent years, the for-profit *The Seattle Times* has been receiving philanthropic funding directly or through giving to the Seattle Foundation and for-profits are seeking donations from the public, saying they need donations to sustain independent journalism.

The report also examined the need for nonprofit newsrooms to build their audience and for community foundations to increase their support and cited the John S. and James L. Knight Foundation's $25 million challenge program which would provide matching funds to community foundations supporting newsrooms. The Knight Foundation has continued to encourage community and foundation support and holds an annual conference bringing together those funders with national foundations. Indeed, a recommendation from the conference was further encouragement for community foundations to work with newsrooms and newspapers to help with innovation and coverage. With the shocking increase in news deserts in the last few years and only barely staffed newspapers, community and family foundations have significantly expanded their support for local news.

Last, the report discussed suggestions that the participants had for foundations and for the government. Among the suggestions from Joel Kramer of MinnPost and Jon Sawyer of the Pulitzer Center for Crisis Reporting, was for foundations to create a donor collaborative. They proposed that philanthropists and foundations would give a central fund that gave grants to qualified independent, standalone nonprofit newsrooms, thus cutting down on all the grant applications the newsrooms had to do and the foundations had to receive. Since then, pools of foundation funds have been created. They include NewsMatch which matches giving by small donors to nonprofits; Report for America, which partially pays for reporters for newsrooms; the American Journalism Project, which provides funding and business training for nonprofit newsrooms.

Another suggestion, contained in a paper I did for the conference, was to create business support for nonprofit investigative centers. I noted that journalists starting up nonprofit newsrooms needed to learn management, administration, and fundraising, even as they try to develop innovative ways to report using newly available data and analytical tools. I suggested that foundations provide training in management, develop low-cost administrative support that can be shared across sites (at fees lower than currently available), help with legal advice on organizational issues and libel, and fund the creation of centralized databases and analytical support that could be shared across investigative teams.

Much of that recommendation was fleshed out by the Pocantico Declaration and the creation of the INN, now the Institute for Nonprofit News and a network of more than 400 newsrooms and more than 2,700 journalists. While spanning local to global coverage, INN members share a commitment to deep original reporting and accountability journalism. INN organizes the network in reporting collaborations, a research consortium that helps benchmark growth of the field, and in joint funding efforts including NewsMatch. It also develops standards for best practices in philanthropically supported journalism that have expanded news-sharing and collaboration across the field and provides training and services for thousands of nonprofit news leaders each year.

Other organizations are also growing to support segments of the independent news sector: The Local Independent Online News Publishers provide training for hundreds of local news organizations, many of them for-profit. The aforementioned American Journalism Project is deepening the funding of a portfolio of local nonprofits through venture funding and coaching, and the Colorado Collaborative provides network services on a regional level to support and transform media throughout one state.

For changes in government policy, the report suggested more regulatory and legislative support for L3Cs and the conversion of for-profit newspapers to nonprofit status. But as noted the support for L3Cs never emerged and the IRS began granting nonprofit status to newspapers. There was also discussion of more government support for newsrooms, but as the report noted, "Conference participants differed sharply on the desirability of expanding the financial role of government supporting the creation of news stories". That debate has continued even as many journalists have pushed for government licensing fee, like that in the United Kingdom, which provides the funding for the BBC.

Altogether, the Breaux Symposium and the Duke Media Conference were deeply prescient in their discussions and recommendations and provided a partial blueprint for the emerging models for journalism.

Previous global activity

Before journalists were building new models and networks in North America, however, another organization to help the growth of nonprofit newsrooms had been created six years earlier. Known as the Global Investigative Journalism Network (GIJN), GIJN had begun with a mission statement at a global journalism conference in Copenhagen in 2003. GIJN formed a network out of nonprofit newsrooms. Indeed, some of the leaders of the original members of GIJN were at INN's founding.

GIJN laid much of the groundwork for the nonprofit news movement through its push for networking, collaborations, and the sharing of resources. It also encouraged training in business sustainability but only in recent years started to add more training and workshops on that.

And GIJN was not only a response to a failing commercial business model in a long death spiral but also the result of a surge in the free press after the end of the cold war.

"Fueled by globalization, international aid, and the efforts of journalism groups, the worldwide practice of investigative reporting has grown dramatically since the fall of communism began in 1989", wrote long-time journalist David Kaplan in a 2013 report for the Center for International Media Assistance.

The profound political changes had led to independent, investigative reporting, particularly in eastern Europe, so that by 2003 there was enough of a core of 35 nonprofit newsrooms from Europe, the U.S., Africa, and Asia to establish GIJN. Even though the deterioration of the journalism business model built on advertising revenue was not close to fully realized in most countries, the journalists forming GIJN clearly saw both the commercial failings of the business model and the corruption of business ownership in previously Soviet countries. In Eastern Europe, journalists had pushed ahead with the creation of nonprofit investigative centers often because of that corruption.

"A major obstacle, investigative reporters noted, is that local media ownership itself often represents part of the problem, with many owners tied to the same corrosive power structure as corrupt politicians, security forces, and organized crime. Research by the Romanian Center for Investigative Journalism, for example, found that as many as half of all media owners in Bucharest had been under investigation for racketeering or money laundering", according to Kaplan's 2013 study for the Center for International Media Assistance.

But GIJN did not intend to do investigations itself. Its formation was inspired by U.S. and Danish nonprofit journalism associations, Investigative Reporters and Editors and DICAR, which focused on training and promoting cross-border editorial collaborations.

GIJN's organizing statement included these points:

The aim of Global Investigative Journalism Network is to:

- Help organize and promote regional and international conferences and workshops.
- Assist in the formation and continuation of journalism organizations involved in investigative reporting and computer-assisted reporting in all countries.
- Support and promote methods of best practices in investigative journalism and computer-assisted reporting.
- Support and promote efforts to ensure free access to public documents and data in every country.
- Provide resources and networking services for participating groups and for investigative journalists.

Thus, both the GIJN and INN networks, which shared some member newsrooms, began as a part of a battle to preserve and grow investigative reporting. But INN expanded to include many types of newsrooms that had an emphasis on specialty reporting and community reporting that fell under the umbrella of public service journalism. Thus, INN later changed its name to the Institute for Nonprofit News to reflect the inclusion of those other kinds of journalism. INN also moved into creating more editorial collaborations so over time the purposes of both organizations overlap more.

In the years since 2009, despite concerns about the sustainability of nonprofit newsrooms and dissolution of some nonprofits, GIJN increased its membership from two dozen newsrooms to 211 in 82 countries by September 2021. It also held biannual conferences and regional conferences in the Netherlands, Norway, Brazil, Canada, Switzerland, South Africa, the Republic of Korea, and Nepal. Over the past few conferences, it has added training in obtaining grants and running businesses.

Like INN, which has grown to nearly 400 members, GIJN is primarily funded by foundations.

Continuing market failure

In the U.S., the prelude to the symposium in 2008, the conference in May 2009 and the July 2009 meeting at the Pocantico estate was the previously mentioned constant staff cutbacks of editors and reporters, the shrinking of content and quality reporting at newspapers for over a decade and then the dramatic losses in revenue and staff in the Great Recession in 2008.

Participants at the 2008 Breaux Symposium on journalism at Louisiana State University, which was held in the midst of the recession, expressed shock at the recent loss of an estimated 3,000 journalists from newsrooms. Over the next 13 years, the losses would be far greater.

But Philip Meyer, a pioneer in using data for journalism who also studied the business side of newspapers, had already written the second edition of his book in 2009, entitled, "The Vanishing Newspaper: Saving Journalism in the Information Age", that without change in its business model and strategies he suggested, the newspaper industry would publish the last edition in 2043.

In a column in 2008 for the now-defunct American Journalism Review, Meyer recalled that as far back as in his 1995 article "… I predicted the financial turbulence that we are seeing today. The piece urged stakeholders in newspaper companies to accept the inevitability of lower returns and to apply their resources to maintaining their community influence".

He said his recommendation in 2008 was for newspapers to transform into "smaller, less frequently published version packed with analysis and investigative reporting and aimed at well-educated news junkies that may well be a smart survival strategy for the beleaguered old print product".

By the second edition of his book, he wrote, "For some, the apocalypse came sooner than expected".

He said "...the horse has left the barn. The self-destruction of the traditional mass-market newspaper could be irreversible". And he added,

> As this is written, the accountants appear to be guiding the transformation without much thought about the end product. If they continue to slash and burn their existing businesses, all they will end up with are slashed, burned obsolete businesses.

However, newspapers that had profit margins as high as 40 percent in the 1990s were already being further stripped of resources by owners who had taken on enormous debt to purchase the newspapers from families or other companies or to pursue ill-advised Internet strategies. Without the debt and pressure from shareholders, some newspapers were still profitable.

Robert Picard, speaking at the Breaux Symposium 2008, said of the newspaper crisis: "These events stem from managerial choices and issues that were made to take on debt and to create these situations where they have to pull so much money out of the newsroom and the operation to pay these debts".

Laura Frank, an investigative journalist who had lost her job when The Rocky Mountain News closed in 2009, reported in a piece called "The Withering Watchdog" for the *Exposé* series (produced by the Public Broadcasting Service (PBS)) that many newspapers were actually profitable. But, she wrote, those papers were cutting staff and failing to reinvest in operations and training because of pressure from Wall Street to retain high profits.

The collapse of the for-profit newsrooms became more palpable after the recession. The Pew Research Center reported in 2021 that newsroom employees at newspapers had dropped from 73,810 in 2008 to 30,820 in 2020, or by 56 percent. After the Covid-19 pandemic struck in 2020 Pew estimated that one-third of large newspapers had more layoffs while digital newsrooms saw a continued pattern of steady layoffs since had been 2017.

In fact, newspapers themselves were disappearing. The News Desert project based at the University of North Carolina estimated in 2020 that one-fourth of the newspapers in the U.S. had closed since 2004: 70 dailies and more than 2,000 weeklies

The latest news desert?

Internationally, the change from print advertising to digital advertising was slower, but eventually some of the same cost-cutting strategies that emerged with loss in print advertising losses caused some Western European journalists to leave their newsrooms in the early 21st century and start independent newsrooms or investigative projects.

By 2014, The Guardian, a nonprofit itself dependent on a for-profit affiliate in the United Kingdom, published a story looking at the failing state of the business of newspapers in Europe:

> Newspapers are in freefall. Print editions are being discontinued. Editors are being replaced with alarming regularity. Financial losses are mounting. Digital strategies are yet to bear fruit. New readerships are fickle, promiscuous and hard to impress.

It continued

> If that's true of British and American newspapers, then the situation is, if anything, worse in continental Europe. Here much of the traditional media is considered to be several years behind in the digital revolution, still experimenting with paywalls, digital technologies and alternative means of storytelling. Bankruptcy stalks the sector, and staff layoffs are a weekly fact of life.

Quality control and credibility falters

Often the first staff members at newspapers to go were the copy editors, who served as the quality control of content by maintaining high standards of accuracy and context.

In the U.S. the diminishing of editing resources led to a lowering of industry standards and a loss of credibility. In addition, as managers regarded reporters as easily interchangeable and transferable personnel, whether it was switching the beats they covered or hiring them in different geographic regions with which the reporters did not have time to get familiar. Traditional newsrooms gradually lost touch with their communities as reporters routinely came and went and thus, lacked knowledge of the places because they did not grow up there or they moved on before they could build that knowledge.

By the 1990s, the corporately owned newsrooms, and even some family-owned newsrooms, quietly acknowledged the distance from their own communities. They created focus groups to find out what they were not covering or held "town hall meetings" for citizens to talk about issues about which a beat reporter would have already known.

New brands of journalism, often fostered by academic studies and foundation funding, also appeared. Some newsrooms backed citizen journalism and "user-generated" content. That strategy could be a marketing tool to show that a company valued its public consumers, but it also could produce cheap or free content. Two other brands, public journalism and civic journalism, which did not call for more intense and in-depth coverage of communities, tried to address the deepening divide between news organizations and the public. Those brands led to events such as town halls and a revamping of news that would be more pleasing to businesses and the public. Those brands also demeaned the professionalism of journalism by suggesting that "everyone is a journalist" and did not need training or skills.

Inevitably, the loss of much of a newsroom's coverage of a community and the undercutting of the skills required to do meaningful journalism opened up the field for social media organizations that had few, if any, journalism standards. That further led to misinformation, propaganda, and corporate advertising posing as journalism.

By 2016, *New York Magazine* published an article entitled, "Citizen Journalism' Is a Catastrophe Right Now, and It'll Only Get Worse", that looked at the intersection of "citizen journalism" and social media as the U.S. presidential election was ending:

> In theory, crowdsourced "citizen journalism" is a good idea. After all, all it really takes to be a journalist is certain critical-thinking skills and/or access to information that other people don't have. Gather a big enough crowd online and that is a lot of brainpower, a lot of access to information. Of course, that isn't how things seem to work these days at all. Rather, whatever potential the concept of crowdsourced citizen journalism has is getting squandered rather spectacularly.

The article examined the social media conversation over leaks of presidential candidate Hillary Clinton and the Democratic National Committee emails and the paucity of actual journalism.

> And yet this sort of coverage and commentary — sane commentary, originating from a place of basic competence and knowledge and good faith — probably accounts for something like 5 percent of the total online content generated by the leaks. The rest is misunderstanding and innuendo and malicious misrepresentation, and it's doing serious damage to democracy's ability to function.

However, since then, more innovative models of citizen engagement in journalism fostered by organizations such as Chicago's City Bureau and Detroit's Outlier Media have emerged and they differed in that they provide training and join citizen reporting and input with professional editing.

Fact-finding and data-driven journalism

In contrast to the trend toward citizen journalism and amateurism in the 1990s and the early 21st century was data-driven journalism – initially known as precision journalism or computer-assisted reporting. Beginning in the 1980s, a handful of journalists and many investigative reporters began learning how to do basic data analysis and visualization. With the advent of the World Wide Web in 1993 and the relative ease, it provided for journalists to gather information and data, the effort to make data analysis a crucial part of reporting gained speed in both the U.S. and internationally.

The traditional media was slow to understand data-driven journalism and editors in newsrooms, both print and broadcast, were heard to call the web a passing fad. But journalists, who later formed many of the nonprofit start-up newsrooms, were gaining experience in the use of data to improve their stories, to do daily and in-depth stories more quickly and to do stories they could have never done before because of the speed at which they could analyze and contextualize and the amount of data they could scrutinize.

The eager acceptance of technology and data by those journalists allowed the start-up nonprofit newsrooms to be nimble and to adopt the new digital tools that appeared each year. With their data skills, they actually could do more with less and level the playing field with the bigger traditional newsrooms and produced stories the larger newsroom could not easily do.

Cooperation and collaborations

Cooperation and collaboration, most often led by nonprofit newsrooms, were another fundamental change in the journalism business model.

Sue Cross, a long-time Associated Press manager, said in an interview in 2021 that the year 2009 was "a pivotal moment" for journalism. She noted that both the initial founding meeting of INN had embedded a spirit of collaboration and cooperation as the Pocantico Declaration made clear. She also said data and technological skills allowed small newsrooms to report stories more deeply. By combining resources with other newsrooms through collaborations, that meant a wider range of those stories could be done.

"It was a significant milestone", Cross said of the formation of the networks. Cross, who became the chief of executive officer of INN in 2015 after leaving AP, said journalists had set aside competition in favor of cooperation and collaboration. "It fundamentally changed journalism". She also said data and technological skills not only allowed small newsrooms to do better stories but also by combining resources with other newsrooms they created collaborations that meant more stories and a wider range of those stories could be done.

Since 2009, collaborations among nonprofit and for-profit newsrooms have soared. They range from shared information among small newsrooms to modest cross-border investigations among a few news organizations to projects based on huge data leaks such as the Panama and Pandora papers in which dozens of newsrooms and hundreds of journalists worldwide join to analyze and make sense of the leaked documents to produce stories published and aired in their countries and regions.

Some of the collaborations have also involved advocacy groups such as Greenpeace or the other activists' organizations which have led to worries about the blurring of objectivity and credibility and these issues will be explored later in the book.

Donors and owners

The new model of nonprofit newsrooms also heightened the importance and influence of foundations and donors.

Without the support of foundations and wealthy individuals for the nonprofit start-ups, the nonprofit newsroom model would not have grown as quickly. The support was substantial and the Media Impact Funders, an association of foundations and donors, estimated in 2021 they had given 33,000 grants totaling $3.2 billion for news and information entities since 2009.

A key and top funder in the U.S. was the John S. and James L. Knight Foundation, the largest journalism foundation, which made key investments in individual nonprofits, innovation projects, and research that helped redirect government actions that were impeding the creation of nonprofits.

Internationally, the Open Society Foundation was the key funder for many independent newsrooms, giving hundreds of millions of dollars to news. It also made some grants within the U.S., attracting conservative criticism because George Soros, the creator of the foundation, had progressive views and causes.

Individual buyers of newsrooms also surfaced, who donated their own funds to create or support nonprofit newsrooms. Meanwhile, some for-profit owners began to convert their newsrooms into nonprofits as had been suggested in the 2008–2009 gatherings as a possibility.

For example, in 2016 the owner of the Philadelphia Inquirer donated the newspaper to the Lenfest Institute, which meant The Inquirer effectively became a nonprofit newsroom receiving partial funding from the foundation. Also, in 2019, the Salt Lake Tribune converted to a nonprofit organization to bolster its finances as did several weekly chains.

The foundations also played a role in propping up newsrooms still running on the for-profit model. As noted in the 2009 Duke media conference report, for-profit newsrooms began seeking grants from foundations for investigative or community reporting. Critics raised questions on why a foundation would support a company operated by a wealthy family or that was giving dividends to stockholders.

For example, *The Seattle Times*, had an annual gross revenue of more than $200 million a year, but, as noted before, managed to convince foundations to partner with it to create and contribute to an investigative fund. Foundations responded that grants to for-profit newsrooms kept the news alive in a community that would not have news without the foundation's support.

At the same time, the nonprofit newsrooms, under pressure by foundations to raise more revenue from other sources, took on some of the revenue strategies of for-profits – soliciting digital advertising and sponsorships, publishing paid newsletters, holding paid events, and instituting specialized and premium coverage for paying subscribers.

Nonprofit newsrooms perils

The nonprofit model is certainly not without its critics and its perils. Critics have said nonprofits can be pressured to serve the agenda of the donors and foundations. The newsrooms maintain they can ensure their independence and credibility by being transparent about its donors and limiting anonymous giving and by developing multiple revenue streams.

But in the U.S., the Internal Revenue Service, which oversees nonprofits, does not require that donors be publicly disclosed. The rule has allowed some dark money (money whose source is shielded or laundered through other organizations) to support newsrooms with a political agenda. One such organization, The Center for Government and Public Integrity, later renamed the Center Square, took money from a right-leaning foundation to create statehouse newsrooms. That center boasted that all its donors would be guaranteed anonymity.

But because of the lack of transparency, traditional state house reporters refused to let the center reporters have offices in the press rooms of state capitols and eventually the operation was reduced in scope and size.

Government support

U.S. journalists have been concerned about government support or funding of journalism fearing undue control or influence by governments. But western European journalists have been more comfortable with government funding, given the history of large monetary support for public broadcast news in the United Kingdom and the Netherlands and funding and grants for journalism in Norway and other countries.

Despite U.S journalists' concerns, there has been long time, sometimes subtle, significant government support in the U.S. for journalism through such actions as lower postal rates for newspapers and magazines, through public and legal notices that are mandated by law to be placed as paid advertising in local newspapers, through funding for the Corporation of Public Broadcasting, and through tax exemptions for nonprofit newsrooms.

Indeed, during the pandemic there was only sporadic and slight hesitation from U.S. newsrooms to apply for government loans– sure to be forgiven so they did not need to give back – to keep operating and pay for employees.

And there has been increasing interest by U.S. journalists in the nonprofit field and news advocates to consider more direct support from the U.S. government. A group of journalists and journalism advocates pushed for federal legislation in 2021 that would provide a tax credit or voucher of $250 a year to individual citizens to buy local news subscriptions or donate that amount to a newsroom.

Steve Waldman, who served on the staff of the Federal Communications Commission, was leading the effort in 2021 and hoped to raise $2.4 billion for newsrooms.

"Under this approach, it would be consumers, not government officials, deciding who to support. It is strictly nonpartisan and nonideological", Waldman wrote in 2021 in a column for the Poynter Institute of Media Studies.

"Ultimately, this could become even more like a voucher. Given that 90 percent of Americans now file electronically, the government could set up a system in which taxpayers see a list of local newsrooms in their ZIP code, and directly assign the funds to that local newsroom", said Waldman.

He also noted it could be like the postal subsidy that began in the 1790s for newspapers and "jump-started the newspaper industry by providing subsidized delivery of newspapers". By the summer of 2022, however, the outlook for the legislation was bleak.

Tech-savvy and tech giants

Without acceptance of the change from hard copy to digital, it was an open field for the tech-savvy ventures and eventually the tech giants Google and Yahoo to aggregate content for free from newsrooms and produce billions of dollars in ad revenue. A tech-savvy start-up, Craig's List, proceeded the giants by becoming a website of classified ads and was blamed for possibly fatally wounding the newspaper industry by taking away one of the most profitable revenue streams for newspapers.

Over the years, has the news industry tried to persuade the Tech giants like Google and Facebook to invest in newsrooms that have provided the content to the giants. Both companies have created programs to support nonprofit newsrooms but although they have made investments in the tens of millions of dollars in training and newsroom support, their investment is relatively small and Facebook has been accused of actually making it more difficult for newsrooms to post legitimate content on

Facebook. By 2022, it was unclear if Facebook (now known as Meta) would continue its efforts.

But a more confrontational approach had emerged as some governments pushed larger technology companies to get those companies to share profits. One effort began with legislation in Australia requiring tech companies had to compensate newsrooms for the content they used.

Sustainability

Whether nonprofit newsrooms can be sustainable and how some of them have become sustainable has been constantly debated and is a large part of this book. There are also questions about the sustainability of both small and large for-profit newsrooms as they try to adapt, often by seeking more But skeptics in the journalism field have doubted that nonprofit newsrooms can come up with strategic and tactical plans to survive and even thrive year after year. Yet the attrition rate of INN member newsrooms has been estimated at less than 10 percent. Partly that is because nonprofit newsrooms do not have the pressures to become large, scalable (growing) corporations.

The nonprofit newsroom industry has seen many of its businesses to stay smaller and on a narrowly focused mission. The industry also has seen some nonprofits grow to tens of millions of dollars in revenue because they have come up with a way to serve a major need that large foundations want to help fill.

Sustainability has been questioned because a nonprofit continues to need to find donors and foundations to support it year after year. But any business must seek revenue every year, often adapting to the financial environment to ensure the business lasts.

Commentators have also suggested that nonprofit newsrooms are fragile entities. But when comparing one part of an industry that has ruthlessly cut its way to near non-existence to another part of an industry that is adding employees and newsrooms monthly, one would have to ask which part of the industry is truly fragile.

1

WHAT HAPPENED TO TRADITIONAL JOURNALISM?

In May of 2021, a hedge fund notorious for pillaging the staff and assets of newspapers, purchased the Chicago Tribune. The Tribune, like most U.S. newspapers, had been in a long decline, although it had survived recent previous tumultuous ownerships, scandals in its management ranks, and a bankruptcy to reorganize its finances.

Once called the "World's Greatest Newspaper", the Tribune's weekday circulation had dramatically decreased from 448,000 to 118,000 in just seven years. The purchase by the hedge fund, Alden Global Capital through its company Digital First Media, was immediately followed by the buyouts and departures of some of the newsrooms' best-known writers.

In the Atlantic Monthly five months later, McKay Coppin wrote,

> What threatens local newspapers now is not just digital disruption or abstract market forces. They're being targeted by investors who have

DOI: 10.4324/9781315719573-2

> figured out how to get rich by strip-mining local-news outfits. The model is simple: Gut the staff, sell the real estate, jack up subscription prices, and wring out as much cash as possible out of the enterprise until eventually enough readers cancel their subscriptions that the paper folds, or is reduced to a desiccated husk of its former self.

While the actions of Alden, which had become the second largest newspaper chain in the U.S. with the Tribune purchase, might have appeared to be a new phenomenon, the news industry had long been the target of financial predators. In writing the second edition of "The Vanishing Newspaper" in 2009, Philip Meyer described the business strategy as "harvesting:"

"A stagnant industry's market position is harvested by raising prices and lowering quality, trusting that customers will continue to be attracted by the brand name rather than the substance for which the brand once stood". He went on to note, "this a nonrenewable, take the money and run strategy".

A long death spiral

The decline of traditional newsrooms has been a long, painful death spiral, especially for newspapers, and has been more and more chronicled and quantified. Greed, monopolies, mismanagement, the emphasis of marketing over content, the emergence of the tech media giants, and the lack of adapting to changing technologies in a world gone digital all were contributing factors to the continual decimation of the industry.

As Robert Picard pointed out in 2008, readership penetration (the number of people reading a newspaper) had been decreasing since 1950. Furthermore, the percentage of people who said they read a newspaper every day had dropped from about 73 percent in 1967 to about 30 percent in 2008.

Meyer said the readership fall was simple to understand: "It is a matter of generational replacement". He said that for year's supporters of newspapers "comforted" themselves with the expectation that younger people would start reading newspapers as they aged. "It never happened", he wrote.

As recounted in the book "*When MBAS Rule the Newsroom*" by Doug Underwood, in 1989 a consultant Steve Star, "a long-time guru of the subject of the business troubles of newspapers", told a meeting of newspaper publishers "that if something didn't happen to turn around the decline in daily newspaper readership, the future of the industry looked bleak". He called it "an impending crisis".

But according to Underwood, Star had been warning publishers since the 1970s of a perilous future. By 1991, Underwood noted, a study had been done for U.S. editors called "Keys to Our Survival" because of the loss of readership and worries about a drop in profits.

However, it is possible that two media owners saw the vulnerability of newspapers much earlier. In 1977, Thomas Murphy, a Harvard MBA, and a colleague, Daniel Burke, ran the media company Capital Cities. They decided to buy newspapers after Capital Cities had built extensive holdings in broadcast in the U.S. and some print properties. Murphy and Burke said they saw inefficiencies in the operations of newspapers and hired aggressive publishers to cut costs, break up unions and hire young, low-paid staff that managers expected to move on to better paying jobs.

Indeed, they paid such low wages at the Kansas City Star, where I worked from 1981 to 1984, that I discovered while writing stories on social services that "zone" reporters, those who worked in bureaus, qualified for government benefits. Management quickly raised the salaries above the threshold for benefits, but years later when wages again fell low, reporters did not receive sudden raises and it was suggested that reporters get second non-journalism jobs to supplement their wages.

Under Murphy and Burke, Capital Cities' profits grew so much that it was able to acquire the much larger network ABC for $3.5 billion in 1986.

Ellen Clegg and Dan Kennedy, journalists and researchers, have been straightforward about the ravenous desire for profits as a leading cause of the decline and have an upcoming book with details on their view. They wrote in a Nieman Labs article in 2021:

> Our view, though, is that these challenges would be manageable if it weren't for corporate greed. Starting in the 1970s, publicly traded chains began taking over newspapers, extracting massive profits and

> cutting back on coverage, leaving the business unprepared for the deluge that was to come. More recently, hedge funds have moved in, bleeding newspapers of their last remaining revenues rather than investing in the future. Compounding all this is that, in many cases, corporate owners take on massive amounts of debt to build their chains and then extract revenues from their newspapers to pay it down.

Commercial broadcasting itself has also seen decline, but that had less effect on news coverage since the broadcast industry had fewer staff and had relied on recycling print stories for years for much of its coverage.

Leonard Downie and Michael Schudson acknowledged in their 2009 "The Reconstruction of American Journalism" study that some broadcast stations did stellar investigative work, but "Still, even in their best years, most commercial television stations had far fewer news reporters than local newspapers", they wrote.

They cited a 1999 study of 59 local broadcast stations that "found that 90 percent of all their stories reported on accidents, crimes, and scheduled or staged events". They said that "in recent years, with their ratings and ad revenues in rapid decline and their once extravagant profit margins imperiled, many local television stations have made further cuts in already small news staffs". They also noted that at 205 stations, newscasts were now produced by stations in other cities.

Missed opportunities

Rather than taking advantage of the dot.com crash in 1999, when many Internet startups went under, the newspaper industry actually backed away from the Internet in some cases. By 2005 – 12 years after the creation of the commercial web – the industry realized it had to become more digital. That moment was marked by publisher Rupert Murdoch in a speech to the American Society of Newspaper Editors in March of that year.

"Scarcely a day goes by without some claim that new technologies are fast writing newsprint's obituary. Yet, as an industry, many of us have been remarkably, unaccountably complacent", Murdoch said.

He continued:

> In the face of this revolution, however, we've been slow to react. We've sat by and watched while our newspapers have gradually lost circulation. We all know of great and expensive exceptions to this - but the technology is now moving much faster than in the past.

Murdoch said newspapers had enjoyed "a virtual information monopoly". He said that even after the advent of television, a slow but steady decline in readership was masked by population growth that kept circulations reasonably intact and he noted that "even after absolute circulations started to decline in the 1990s, profitability did not".

"But those days are gone. The trends are against us", he said, while he suggested there was hope by adapting to young people's changing ways of reading and getting information.

But the decline continued as the industry still resisted substantial change and was a target for business predators. In fact, it was another four years before the Society accepted the assumption of power by the online news and changed its name to the American Society of News Editors, eliminating the word newspaper. Later, it changed its name ironically to "News Leaders".

In 2010, in his book "*Newsonomics: Twelve New Trends That Will Shape the News You Get*", analyst and journalist Ken Doctor expressed exasperation with trying to persuade the owners and managers of newspapers to adapt to the digital world. He titled his 4th Chapter "The Old News World Is Gone – Get Over It". He gave an example of a company chief operating officer he was consulting with who rejected a digital online idea because the officer "did not know how to think about it".

"The digital transformation was just too hard for newspaper companies to think about, to weigh, and to act on. In failing to restructure their enterprises when had the time and money to do it, they've helped to sow the seeds of their current self-destruction", Doctor wrote.

He called on the reader to think the unthinkable: "A time without a daily newspaper". That time has come in the last few years as daily papers print semi-weekly, weekly, or not at all.

Echoing Murdoch (who had disparaged the Internet in the late 1990s) Doctor said publishers "downplayed the Web".

I can attest to that wide dismissive response. As I constantly trained journalists in the late 1990s and early 21st century in data-driven journalism in the U.S. and abroad I was consistently told that the Web was a passing fad. At a major newspaper in Florida, I was told by reporters there that they could not wait to get home to their own personal computers to try out online research techniques I showed them. They said their management forbid access to the Web because of concerns they would waste time "surfing" or open the newsroom to hackers.

One symbol of the misunderstanding of the overwhelming changes was how the Washington Post created its website. Instead of integrating the staff of the new "WashingtonPost.com" with the regular newspaper staff, it located the website offices across the Potomac River and had its staff compete on news stories with the traditional newsroom.

James Brady, who oversaw the WashingtonPost.com, said later that it was actually an advantage to be in a different newsroom because it was easier to make changes and innovate. Thus, he did not see it as a problem to have two newsrooms at that time.

In any case, it took years before the Post consolidated the two operations. Then, after Amazon founder Jeff Bezos bought the Post in 2013 the online and print journalism newsroom became a completely integrated operation with reporters consistently knowing more about their audience and web traffic.

Building printing presses in a digital age

Another greater symbol of failure to deal with change was the building of a $200 million printing press by the Kansas City Star that opened in 2006 and sold for $30 million in 2020.

"The short history of the press project also encapsulates the story of the industry's financial decline", according to a 2020 article published by the Poynter Institute for Media Studies.

In 2002, the Star was a Knight-Ridder paper, but the article stated, "with more than a bit of hubris, executives remained confident that local newspaper monopolies were a defendable franchise".

By 2006, institutional funders had forced Knight-Ridder to sell itself to the McClatchy chain. The Poynter article said McClatchy then collapsed from the burden of paying interest and principal on the $6.5 billion debt it assumed the purchase and finally defaulting in 2020 on required pension payments as it sought bankruptcy protection. It then was bought by the Chatham hedge fund. Meanwhile, the printing press was sold and the Star began being printed in Des Moines, Iowa by another company.

"The problem is the business of journalism is changing, and the foundation on which we are operating is changing", said Picard in 2008. "The problem really isn't profits, which are good in this industry. The problem is debt, and the problem is capital. This is where the fundamental difficulties of the industry exist today".

Picard points out that the family owners of the *Wall Street Journal* sold the newspaper to Murdoch not only because he paid a good price, but because "the company had so destroyed its working capital that it could not make the kind of investments it needed to make in the coming years to survive".

As Doctor wrote, "Roughly 10 years later after the emergence of online sites, the first war is over, and the newspapers have lost".

In Europe, The Guardian, a nonprofit newsroom highly dependent on a related for-profit ad business and donations, reported that "newspapers are in freefall. Print editions are being discontinued. Editors are being replaced with alarming regularity. Financial losses are mounting. Digital strategies are yet to bear fruit. New readerships are fickle, promiscuous and hard to impress".

It then went on to say, "If that's true of British and American newspapers, then the situation is, if anything, worse in continental Europe". It added, "Bankruptcy stalks the sector, and staff layoffs are a weekly fact of life" and went on to go through the losses of circulation, readership, and staff country by country.

Mainstream newsrooms are "toast"

Robert Rosenthal, a long-time journalist and an executive editor who left mainstream journalism for a nonprofit investigative center, said bluntly in 2009 that most mainstream newsrooms were "toast" and "eviscerated" by cutbacks.

Ken Doctor wrote, "Their failure to acknowledge mounting realities around them doomed their businesses, bringing them to bankruptcy or its edges, and crippling their ability to compete".

For those new owners who thought they could buy news companies and easily make them profitable (as Murphy and Burke had with Capital Cities), "They all thought they were buying distressed companies that had been mismanaged. What they neglected to see is that they were buying into a distressed industry". Doctor wrote.

By 2021, the Pew Research Center reported newspaper circulation dropped from about 63 million in 1990 to 25 million in 2020. By 2020, eight out of 10 people got their news from mobile devices, but only one out of three said they sometimes obtained their news through print.

While newspaper advertising revenue (both print and digital) had climbed to a high of over $49 billion in 2006, it had plummeted to about $8.8 billion by 2020 and circulation revenue for the first time exceeded advertising, coming in at $11 billion.

In an earlier report on March 2010, The Project on Excellence in Journalism (later the Pew Research Center) identified some of the reasons for declining circulation:

> While newspapers may not be disappearing in droves (only half a dozen shut down or cut back print publication last year), the declines in daily newspaper circulation are unprecedented and precipitous.

The report continued, "Some of the drop in circulation is a result of more Americans getting their news online, but continued trimming of circulation to distant geographic areas, limited money to spend on promoting new circulation and the recession are also factors" (Figure 1.1).

Pew noted newspapers were also losing substantial revenue from advertisements. "In the past year newspapers, including online, saw revenues from ads fall 26%. Over the past three years the total loss has been 43%".

But the "trimming" of circulation to distant geographic areas had begun much earlier as the strategy of newspaper chains that were buying smaller, often family-owned newspapers.

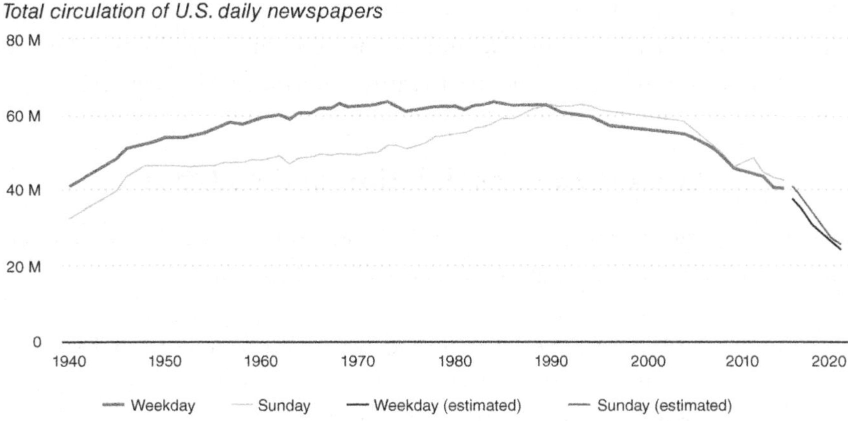

Figure 1.1 Decline of newspaper circulation

Credit: Pew Research Center Newspaper Fact Sheet 2021, https://www.pewresearch.org/journalism/fact-sheet/newspapers/

Trimming and clustering

Starting in the 1960s, many family-owned newspapers began selling themselves to larger companies and chains after being confronted by steep estate taxes and/or intra-family fights. The companies they sold to were mostly controlled by Wall Street and stockholders and were determined to return maximum profits, specifically through consolidation.

One spectacularly unpleasant sale occurred in 1986 when the Binghams, the long-time family owner of the Courier-Journal and The Louisville Times in Kentucky sold its newspapers to Gannett Co. Inc., the nation's largest newspaper group at the time.

"An intense quarrel within the powerful Bingham family resulted in the decision to sell the media empire, which includes broadcast and printing companies as well as the prestigious morning Courier-Journal", reported the Associated Press.

> In announcing his decision to sell the properties, which media analysts had valued between $350 million and $500 million, Bingham Sr. cited tax policies which made it difficult to maintain control of the companies from one generation to another.

Bob Schulman, a retired media critic who was a long-time employee of the Binghams, said the sale "would be viewed nationally as the demise of perhaps the last of the venerated family communications enterprises".

Continued consolidation and collapse

In 1999, the now-defunct American Journalism Review ran an article on the concentration of newspaper ownership and its impact:

> Of the 543 newspaper trades and acquisitions recorded between 1994 and 1998, all but a few have resulted in tighter concentration of ownership within a state or region. Indeed, the idea of building clusters prompted most of those sales in the first place.

The building of clusters meant that some newspapers chains sold papers in their retreat from some geographic areas to focus on other markets. The executives said they wanted to increase the efficiency of operations by having papers in certain areas.

The article quoted William Dean Singleton, CEO of MediaNews and one of the industry's leading practitioners of clustering making a rather paradoxical remark, talking about how to grow the industry while at the same time saying it was not a growing industry.

"Newspaper companies are going to have to find more and more creative ways to keep their companies growing.... Eliminating duplication is one of those things that help do that. This is not a growth industry", he said.

Clustering meant the combining of operations for newspapers that were geographically close to one another – usually in the same or adjacent counties. The strategy led to a trading of newspapers among the chains, which the author of the article likened to playing the game of Monopoly as chains exchanged newspapers to construct their clusters. In fact, Singleton also took advantage of tax rules to do tax-free trades of daily newspapers that had been common in real estate.

While clustering was lauded for cutting costs and keeping profits coming in, it also was prelude to news deserts, in which communities lost their newspapers and news coverage.

Like McClatchy, it was another example of newspaper companies taking on extreme amounts of debt as they purchased newspapers while circulation and revenue fell despite the cost-cutting through consolidation. Singleton, who once predicted that there soon would be only three newspaper chains – and his MediaNews would be one of them – eventually was also crushed by the debt his company had taken on and filed for bankruptcy in 2010.

It was Alden that took a large share of the stock after the company came out of bankruptcy and by 2011 Singleton had effectively removed from the leadership team.

In a prescient article in Nieman Labs in 2011 by Martin Langeveld, headlined, "The shakeup at MediaNews: Why it could be the leadup to a massive newspaper consolidation", Langeveld, who had been a publisher for MediaNews, predicted various mergers involving Alden that eventually took place. He noted that Alden had been building up its newspaper holdings through the Alden Global Distressed Opportunities Fund, "which it launched in 2008 and which is now worth nearly $3 billion. Alden has offices in New York, Dallas, Dubai and Mumbai, along with a tax-haven presence on the Channel Island Jersey".

Langeveld concluded by writing, "It's really the last hope for the newspaper business, but a pessimistic view is possible, of course.... Alden's ultimate interest is in earning a strong return on its investments, not in the future of journalism, so its strategy is at heart a financial one. And, yes, consolidation will come at the cost of jobs".

Absentee ownership

With corporate ownership, the headquarters of the chain was far away from most of the newspapers it owned. As in broadcasting, the chain ownership led to not only a standardization of business practices but also of editorial coverage. The influence of the corporations and MBA managers led also to marketing taking the lead over the content. As documented in his book, *When MBAs Rule the Newsroom* Doug Underwood wrote of a management driven by surveys, focus groups and other marketing tools that made news decisions not on importance of news but of audience and advertisers.

In the 1990s, I witnessed at The Hartford Courant those kinds of editorial decisions (some of which were fortunately later reversed) made based on advertising. Choices of what stories to cover and to run in the newspaper were based on the amount of advertising in a particular town. That meant a major oil spill in one town could be buried in the pages of the paper while a dull city council meeting could get front-page status. In addition, that marketing strategy ignored the fact that many people commuted from one community to another so that their news interest was limited to one town.

At the same time, staff cutbacks at most papers (which at the time had as much as 40 percent profit margins) meant some towns were not getting covered routinely or at all (Figure 1.2). With readers' confidence faltering in the accuracy of news coverage and the lack of reporters, the news corporations concocted strategies to re-engage with an audience they had abandoned or disparaged. Among the strategies were town halls where they invited citizens to come and tell news managers about possible news stories or to come to ill-chosen focus groups where readers ate free pizza and shared their thoughts with group leaders.

The owners also embraced ideas such as public journalism and civic journalism – which were financed by civic-minded foundations – in which citizens were extolled as partners in news coverage. While the movements had some good ideas, on a practical level they often failed and by 2008 the movements were fading fast.

"Some say that its practices have been integrated into the routines of news making without the label attached. Others say that it is simply dying", wrote Joyce Y. M. Nip in a 2008 paper, "The Last Days of Civic Journalism: The case of the Savannah News".

Nip found

> the ideas of civic journalism were instituted in the newspaper through its presentation and routines of discovering community news. However, it was less obvious in the discovery and gathering of news about larger events and issues. The role of the news organization in convening the public for problem solving has continued, but the role of championing particular solutions was not observed.

Figure 1.2 Decline of newspaper staff

Credit: Pew Research Center Newspaper Fact Sheet 2021, https://www.pewresearch.org/journalism/fact-sheet/newspapers/

Around 2010, I attended a gathering of 15 journalists who had tried "citizen journalism", that is, engaging and training citizens in reporting the news. Citizen journalism was yet another way to try to engage the abandoned audience (and get free "user-generated" content). There was a consensus that the group had, at best a 5 percent retention rate, because citizens had regular jobs or found reporting fatiguing.

By the end of the Great Recession in 2009, it appeared news owners were too consumed by finding ways to survive to try out new theories of journalism. In addition, foundations had stopped funding many of those efforts by newspapers.

New competition slashes away at newspapers

Much has been made of the impact of Craig's List on newspaper revenue. Craigslist was a San Francisco-based start-up email list of events in San Francisco in 1995, became a website carrying classified ads in 1996 and then went national in 2000. It was founded by Craig Newmark and Jim Buckmaster and makes money by charging some users low fees to post classified ads for such things as real estate, jobs and services while allowing most people to post for free. For example, there is a one-time $10 to $75 fee for posting a service or a $5 fee for some apartment rentals. It is estimated that Craigslist now brings in about a $1 billion in revenue a year, while changing little in appearance or concept.

But Craigslist's early understanding of the Internet and the easy interpersonal exchange on its web platform deeply undercut newspaper revenue. A 2013 study conservatively estimated that Craigslist has cost US newspapers at least $5 billion in revenue from 2000 to 2007. The study published in the journal *Management Science* found a 20 percent drop in the ad rates but did not account for the lost ads themselves.

Newspaper classified advertising hit a high of $19.6 billion in 2000, the year Craigslist went national. By 2012, the Newspaper Association of America reported classified advertising was $4.6 billion, giving a more overarching picture of how Craigslist and other online classified sites like Monster.com and Realtor.com had seized digital ad revenue.

The Newspaper Association also reported that in 2000 classified ads accounted for about 40 percent of newspaper industry ad revenue, but by 2012 the classifieds were about 18 percent.

The tech giants

As newspapers tried to become more digital and secure more digital advertising the tech giants, Google, Facebook, YouTube, and Yahoo started up. Those startups were willing to endure years of heavy losses to eventually dominate the digital market and reap hundreds of billions of dollars a year in digital ads. By 2020, it was estimated that they took in 70 percent of digital advertising.

The tech giants eventually did enter into agreements with newspaper groups to share in advertising revenue – an ironic move since the giants had made tens of billions of dollars aggregating and linking to newspaper content for free. They also began initiatives to benefit newsrooms and contributed to digital news training for newsrooms, but their investment in news was a very small part of their profits.

As of March 2022, print circulation of newspapers fell further, with the top 25 newspapers dropping by 12 percent in the past six months, according to the Press-Gazette, which based its figures on data shared by the Alliance for Audited Media.

But that average percentage masked how deep a decline that print newspapers had experienced during the pandemic. For example, USA Today's print circulation had plummeted to 159,233 from 486,579 in 2019, or by one-third. The Press-Gazette reported that The Tampa Bay Times, which had become a two-edition a week newspaper in 2020, and the Philadelphia Inquirer were the two worst-performing newspapers in the six-month period. The Tampa Bay Times' average Wednesday circulation was down 26 percent year over year to 102,266, while the Inquirer was down 20 percent to 61,180.

News deserts and ghost newsrooms

Beginning in 2016, journalist, consultant, and professor Penny Abernathy began a project, called the Expanding News Desert, to track and quantify the news desolation created by the failed advertising-based model of the newspaper.

The project found in 2020 that over the past 15 years that the United States has lost 2,100 newspapers, leaving at least 1,800 communities that had a local news outlet in 2004 without any outlet at the beginning of 2020. It noted, "To date, most of losses were weeklies in economically struggling communities".

The report also found, as many other studies have, that the demise of newspapers in the U.S. was especially damaging because newspapers had been supplying 85 percent of the news in the U.S., with much of it repeated by other media such as broadcast, tech giants, and social media.

In its 2020 report, the project stated, "While a fourth of the country's newspapers have vanished since 2004, many of the 6,700 survivors have become 'ghost newspapers' – mere shells of their former selves, with greatly diminished newsrooms and readership".

It said since 2008, "the decline has been relentless, and it appears to have been accelerating in the years leading up to 2020". The project reported that since 2018 about 300 newspapers, mostly weekly, had closed, and that in the spring of 2020, thousands of journalists were being furloughed or laid off.

It attributed much of the decline to reasons given earlier in the chapter, with owners prioritizing profits and "dooming hundreds of news organizations to irrelevance".

In total, the project estimated half the newspapers' editorial staff and half of their readership had disappeared.

It said, "However, much of the decline was inevitable, as the business model collapsed for news organizations and a viable substitute digital model has so far failed to emerge".

A subsequent study, "The State of Local News: The 2022 Report" looked at the situation following more two years of the Covid pandemic.

In her executive summary, Abernathy, now at Northwestern University, opened with "This is a nation increasingly divided journalistically, between those who live and work in communities where there is an abundance of local news and those who don't".

She pointed out that traditionally underserved communities that need local journalism the most are the very places where it is most difficult to sustain either print or digital news organizations.

She also wrote,

> The loss of local journalism has been accompanied by the malignant spread of misinformation and disinformation, political polarization, eroding trust in media, and a yawning digital and economic divide among citizens. In communities without a credible source of local news, voter participation declines, corruption in both government and business increases, and local residents end up paying more in taxes and at checkout.

Some of the key findings of the June 2022 report were:

Vanishing newspapers. The report quantified the continuing loss of newspapers and predicted that a third of newspapers in existence in 2005 would be gone.

- Newspapers are continuing to vanish at a rapid rate. An average of more than two a week are disappearing. Since 2005, the country has lost more than a fourth of its newspapers (2,500) and is on track to lose a third by 2025. Even though the pandemic was not the catastrophic "extinction-level event" some feared, the country lost more than 360 newspapers between the waning pre-pandemic months of late 2019 and the end of May 2022. All but 24 of those papers were weeklies, serving communities ranging in size from a few hundred people to tens of thousands. Most communities that lose a newspaper do not get a digital or print replacement. The country has 6,377 surviving papers: 1,230 dailies and 5,147 weeklies.

Digital news is growing but is not replacing the loss of newspapers.

- Digital alternatives remain scarce, despite an increase in corporate and philanthropic funding. Over the past two years, the number of new digital-only state and local news sites, 64, slightly exceeded the number of sites that went dark. In 2022, there are 545 digital-only state and local sites; most employ six or fewer full-time reporters. Four out of ten local sites are now nonprofit, supported by a combination of grants, sponsorship, and donations. But whether nonprofit or for-profit, the vast majority of those sites are located in larger cities, leaving much of the rest of the country uncovered.

The news deserts – where there is no news coverage or very little – continue to accelerate.

- More than a fifth of the nation's citizens live in news deserts – with very limited access to local news – or in communities at risk of becoming news deserts. Seventy million people live in the 208 counties without a newspaper, or in the 1,630 counties with only one paper – usually a weekly – covering multiple communities spread over a vast area.

Poorer communities are lacking alternative news sources when newspapers disappear.

- Increasingly, affluent suburban communities are losing their only newspapers as large chains merge underperforming weeklies or shutter them entirely. However, most communities that lose newspapers and do not have an alternative source of local news are poorer, older and lack affordable, and reliable high-speed digital service…Instead, they get their local news – what little there is – mostly from the social media apps on their mobile phones.

Circulation and revenue continue to drop at newspapers. (After the report appeared, the Gannett Corporation announced more dramatic losses and staff cuts.)

- The surviving newspapers – especially the dailies – have cut staff and circulation significantly as print revenues and profits evaporated. Since 2005, when newspaper revenues topped $50 billion, overall newspaper employment has dropped 70 percent as revenues declined to $20 billion.

Staff in newsrooms deeply declined.

- Newsroom employment has declined by almost 60 percent, with on-staff photographers declining by 80 percent. Only employees in production and distribution and advertising sales fared worse on a percentage basis than journalists. Accountants and operational managers, charged with making sure expenses did not exceed revenue as profits plummeted, had the most job security.

A few large newspaper chains, mostly controlled by hedge funds, are deciding what news there is.

- The largest chains control the fate of many of the nation's surviving newspapers. Their business strategies and decisions continue to shape the local news landscape. Recent research has shown that, even in their diminished state, newspapers still provide most of the news that feeds our democracy at the state and local levels. So, who owns the country's newspapers has a profound impact on the abundance – or absence – of local news.

Newspaper consolidation has increased with hedge funds and private equity funds leading the charge.

- The number of newspapers has declined, consolidation has increased. The largest chains – most of which are either owned by or indebted to hedge funds, private equity groups, or other investment firms – have been the most aggressive in buying and selling newspapers and in shuttering unprofitable ones when they cannot find a buyer.

- Daily newspapers are turning into weeklies and going more digital.
- Dailies are becoming more like weeklies, and vice versa, but their business models and strategies are diverging. Daily papers used the pandemic and the subsequent economic slowdown to begin aggressively transitioning their readers to digital delivery. The daily newspaper– printed and delivered seven days a week – has already disappeared in many markets. Forty of the largest 100 papers in the country now deliver a print edition six or fewer times a week; 11 publish a print edition only one or two or times a week and e-editions on the other days.

Weeklies are publishing digitally on a daily basis and are profiting in affluent communities.

- Meanwhile, many weeklies and non-dailies have begun supplementing their print editions by publishing daily subscriber email newsletters and routinely updating their websites. While thousands of weeklies have folded since 2005, those in relatively affluent and growing markets maintain strong cash flow and still are able to command multiples of four to five times annual earnings when they are sold.

Weeklies are depending on ads and services revenue.

- In contrast to large dailies, which rely on subscribers for more than half of their revenue, weeklies continue to receive the majority of their revenue from local businesses that buy advertising and services from them and sponsor their various print and digital publications.
- In a part of the report that may not have caught the surge in local digital sites, it said the digital-only news site footprint is small.
- Despite the recent increase in both corporate and philanthropic funds, the footprint of digital-only news sites is small, and predominantly a big-city phenomenon. With staffing levels more typical of weeklies in small and mid-sized markets, successful sites must be very strategic about the issues they choose to cover and how they raise money to support their mission.

For-profit digital sites are mostly locally focused and rely in the traditional revenue streams of subscribers and advertisers.

- Although there continues to be considerable turnover, especially among for-profit sites, approximately 100 of the 525 active sites in 2022 were founded more than a decade ago. Today, the vast majority of for-profit sites are very locally focused and tend to rely on both subscriber and advertiser funding in the markets where they are located.

Nonprofit newsrooms are the majority of state, regional, and topic-oriented sites. The report cited the lack of high-speed Internet in communities, but did not address upcoming government financing to rectify that.

- Most state and regional sites are nonprofit and focus on issues as politics, health, the environment, and education – that attract the support of donors and major community and philanthropic foundations. The lack of access to high-speed Internet in many communities often limits the reach and impact of the journalism produced by both nonprofit and for-profit sites.

The report said strong news organizations are occurring in affluent and growing communities.

- The disparity between communities that have strong news organizations and those that don't is primarily the result of market demographics, ownership structure, and available funding. Whether print or digital, local news organizations that have entrepreneurial owners and are in affluent and/or growing communities with diverse sources of funding are much more likely to establish and maintain a successful for-profit, nonprofit, or hybrid enterprise.

The loss of newsrooms in poor and underserved communities is worsening political and economic divides

- Economically struggling and traditionally underserved communities – where residents need journalists providing transparency and oversight of local government and business decisions – are the ones most likely to lose a news organization and be overlooked by funders looking to invest in both for-profit and nonprofit news operations. That loss of local journalism exacerbates political, cultural, and economic divisions between and within communities.

The cost to a democratic society

The statistics and observations in the 2022 report will be cited in the coming years as will those in other reports that also worry about societal impact. A PEN report in 2019 called "Losing the News: The Decimation of Local Journalism and the Search for Solutions," cited and echoed Abernathy's earlier concerns.

The report stated that at a time when political polarization is growing and fraudulent news is proliferating, "trusted sources of information and analysis are more precious than ever." PEN America, a nonprofit that defends free expression and human rights is made up of writers and artists.

The report said local news outlets "play a vital role in safeguarding community health and welfare by serving as a source of critical information, amplifying local issues, including public health holding local government and corporate actors accountable and building social cohesion by fostering a sense of belonging and shared experience."

It said other studies showed that the loss of local news meant citizens were less like to vote and were less politically informed and showed with the loss of watchdog reporting that government officials conduct themselves with less integrity, efficiency, and effectiveness. At the same time the corruption causes costs such as salaries and taxes to go up and federal funding to decline. In addition, corporate bad behavior, such as creating pollution, increases.

"These costs and benefits are not abstract— they are rooted in the very foundations of American democracy," stated the PEN report.

Like the Abernathy report, the PEN report also found the loss of local news "exacerbates and is exacerbated by systemic inequities in the U.S. media land scape."

Many of the communities that have traditionally been underserved by local media are those most affected by its decline. News deserts are spreading fastest across communities that are poorer, older, more rural, and less well educated than the country overall—in other words, communities with comparatively fewer resources to address the problem.

When ethnic or minority-run outlets shrink or fold, the PEN report said, other media institutions often lack the local connections, trust, resources, or motivation to replace them. The struggle of non-English-language news outlets is sometimes invisible to their counterparts—despite the fact that they serve as a major source of information for millions of Americans.

It noted that news outlets that serve communities of color face the same revenue challenges as other outlets but that there have been long-standing inequities in access and representation:

- The FCC recently found that only 2.6 percent of TV stations, 5.8 percent of AM radio stations, and 2.3 of FM radio stations are owned by people of color.
- Seventy-seven percent of all newsroom employees are non-Hispanic white (compared with 65 percent of all U.S. workers), and 61 percent are men (compared with 53 percent of all U.S. workers).
- The number of American Indian print media sources has shrunk dramatically in recent memory: from 700 media sources in 1998 to only 200 today.

"Even absent today's crisis, these enduring inequities have resulted in imbalanced news ecosystems that serve the critical information needs of some communities far better than others", the report stated. "Finding meaningful, scalable solutions to the local news crisis presents an opportunity to revamp the industry to better represent, reflect, and serve all Americans".

The coming chapters in this book will address in more detail the increasing responses to the concerns over the loss of news through the changing models that seek not to replace the coverage that newspapers have provided – some of which became unnecessary, irrelevant, or even wrongheaded over the past decades – but to reinvent it.

A CASE STUDY FROM THE FRONTLINE OF WEEKLY NEWS: THE ISLAND 360 (BLANK SLATE MEDIA)

Steve Blank has been running his second chain of weekly newspapers, which is known as The Island 360, since 2010. His chain covers six cities on Long Island. He had sold his first chain of weeklies to the News Corporation, the news empire owned by the Murdoch family, in 2008. Before becoming a publisher, Blank had been an award-winning investigative reporter at metropolitan daily newspapers in New York and Missouri.

Despite all the changes in journalism – and a pandemic – his weeklies have survived and grown in number and provided the kind of local news that has been disappearing in other areas across the U.S.

Blank knows the doubts about newspapers and local news well.

"There is a stigma to being print. Everyone thinks you are going out of business", he said.

But Blank said he has 18,689 subscribers and 56,067 readers.

"The distinction between subscribers and readers is very important for advertisers to know", he said. "It's one of the ways that newspapers have shot themselves in the foot - for decades - when competing with television and radio. Broadcasters measure viewers and listeners not televisions and radios".

But Blank noted that he recently had 52,784 unique visitors and 74,409 page views. He said those numbers were low since he had sold his "url" near the beginning of 2022 at a very good profit, when his "domain authority" was based on being a news site and that point pageviews were 440,000 and unique visitors were 220,000. But he said current numbers were rising quickly with the new web address and he expected to hit 150,000 within a short time.

Meanwhile, his "organic" email lists totaled 11,982 and with renewed attention to social media Facebook followers were 3,469, Instagram 935, Twitter 2,325, and a new LinkedIn site was at 176.

A special role

Blank said weeklies have a special role in local news coverage that distinguished their editorial product.

> Weekly newspapers are something unique. People will come to you if they can't get it [news] anywhere else. They will go to

> Washington Post and New York Times for national issues. The larger metro papers were slow to realize that.

For example, Blank said there are 56 school districts in his circulation area that don't get regular coverage from other newsrooms.

"Here, we are on the other side of universe", he said because larger newsrooms like Newsday are not covering the school board and village meetings the way his weeklies do.

> Two-thirds of property tax goes to schools," he said. "So we cover budgets, meetings, and controversies.

Meanwhile, Blank has had to navigate the tremendous shifts in conditions and revenue for weeklies.

Disappearing classifieds

"Over time, classifieds disappeared, and weeklies have disappeared", he said.

He said online startups drew the revenue away: "First, its Craig List, then Indeed and Zip Recruiter and LinkedIn and other "verticals"," meaning topic-driven organizations.

"We are doing a little in classifieds", he said. "We have some home improvements, local professionals, but we had pages and pages in the previous chain".

He said he was now working on a better presentation of "self-serve", that is, where the advertiser can post the ads themselves on his chain's websites. "It has to be done easily and well. We are doing self-serve with legal notices too".

Blank said legal notices are "doing fantastic". The New York Press Service created a self-serve portal for legal notices and self-serve allows how many columns an advertiser wants.

"Most are doing bigger size legal notices and the intent is to get them to spend more online".

The notices are intended to go into print, but they also go online, and Blank said the percentage of legal notices has gone up. "School districts are a big factor".

The importance of legal notice revenue

The importance of revenue from legal notices is significant. Blank estimated that in the first half of 2021 legal notices were 25 percent of his revenue, later dropping to 15 percent to 20 percent, as other revenue rose.

"The big legal notices are tax liens, schools and school budget", he said. He noted that some city governments have seen the importance of legal notices for the press.

"New York City did an interesting thing. They guaranteed that half of ads will go to local media", he said.

Big tech and social media

Blank said there had been challenges with social media such as Google and Facebook. The problem with Google and Facebook, he said, is that the searches that bring audience and revenue to them are based on content created by his reporters. "We pay for the reporters, and they get all the content", he said, adding he has to get libel insurance, but because federal law the "big techs don't have to".

"Congress wanted to give them a chance to grow in 90s and now they are killing us", he said. "Tech is more powerful than government. They are totally unregulated".

Blank recalled that through international advertising, he was getting $3,000 a week and was now down to $500 a week because "Google said we were violating their policies".

He said he moved to brokers for native advertising and that now has restored some of the revenue. He noted, "They signed the contract that said would not violate Google rules".

Of Facebook, he said, "Facebook is working against you. It sends you to the crazies. Finding the most controversial thing is what their algorithm does".

Despite the challenges, The Island has grown. In 2010, he had three weeklies and by 2021 he had six. In 2010, the budget was $300,000 and by 2019 it was $1.6 million. During the pandemic, revenues dropped to $1.1 million. Editorial part of budget went down to 22 percent of the total budget.

"Everything in entertainment ads was gone by March 2020", he said.

He had to cut back from four reporters to two reporters in 2020, but since he added one reporter and was using freelancers more frequently. Over time, he also had to increase weekly reporter salaries to $700 or as high as $800 a week.

He said, based on the authority score of the website, "I was able to sell our 'url' for a very good price that has helped the company's finances considerably. I simultaneously moved our website to another url – theisland360.com".

Blank said he has not gone "all digital" because "I don't want to give up legal notices and there is still an audience that prefers print".

The New York Times and the Washington Post made a lot of money in digital subscriptions, he said, but "I have not seen that much". He did say that he has cut back on the number of newspapers on newsstands and the print news hole (amount of space devoted to news) has been cut back.

Getting printed

One big issue he faced was when the Alden Global Capital bought the Daily News, which printed his weekly, Alden told him in the middle of the pandemic that they would stop printing his papers "unless pay the bill of previous week and 50 percent more". He suggested the price hike might send him into bankruptcy, but he said that did not persuade Alden to stop the increase.

The Daily News, which had spent $50 million on a new printing plant 15 years ago, has since closed its printing operation, forcing him and 20 other publications to find a new printer.

"Most printers were considerably more expensive but I was able to find one that was comparable", he said, "But I, like every other paper had to change the size of the paper – ours is larger – because no other printer in the area used the same web size".

"When you are facing a shutdown, you do a lot of things", Blank said. "You have to become smarter".

Other changes during the pandemic

Blank said the federal government's recovery programs were also very helpful during the pandemic and afterward, allowing him to come out of the pandemic in a stronger condition than he went in.

He said the newspapers went 100 percent remote during the pandemic, which saved quite a bit of money. He said he also found that thanks to the pandemic and improvements in technology many if not all the chain's functions can be handled remotely. He said he planned to go back to a scaled-down office in the future since there are some jobs that no longer require someone to be in the office.

Blank also said The Island had begun to grow its social media presence and was adding followers in Facebook, Instagram, LinkedIn, and Twitter

As for considering changing to a nonprofit newsroom, Blank said he had looked at the possibility but was not doing at that time. As for being a hybrid newsroom that is for-profit and asking for donations, he said, "I have been trying that appeal, but have not seen a lot of money".

Events

Blank said he sees events as increasingly attractive funding opportunities.

> "They have brought in good revenue. We sell corporate sponsorships for events. Sponsors buy tables," he said. "And having a newspaper allows you also to put sponsors on the back page. Having a newspaper allows you also to put it on the back page. We can promote you in a lot of ways."

"Events are becoming a bigger source of revenue", he added.

> I had a news broker who said if 30 percent of your business is not events in seven years, you won't be there.

2

NEW WAYS EMERGE

Blogs, digital start-ups, and the rise of nonprofit newsrooms

By 2022, the Institute for Nonprofit News (INN) reported that it now had more than 400 digital newsrooms as members, an increase of at least 370 newsrooms in 13 years, even with the failure of some and consolidation of some newsrooms over the years.

INN reported that employment had surged to 2,700 journalists within the network and revenues were at $500 million and climbing while mainstream media employment sank. It was estimated that there would be up to 600 nonprofit newsrooms, if not more, within a few years.

Where mainstream newsrooms had been slow to embrace the online world, the nonprofit and small for-profit newsrooms of the 21st century began their lives online, unimpaired by printing presses, delivery trucks, and high overhead. In many ways, it was the culmination of the promise of a changing model of news that began with blogs (Figure 2.1).

DOI: 10.4324/9781315719573-3

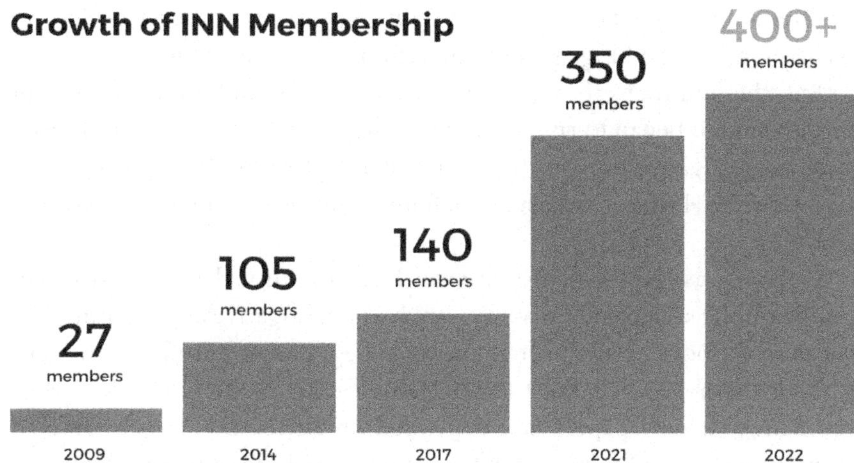

Figure 2.1 Increase in INN membership
Credit: Institute for Nonprofit News 2022

Blogs to newsrooms

The World Wide Web went very public in 1993 and is generally agreed that the first blog appeared shortly after in 1994. Called Links.net, it was a Web homepage in which its creator, college student Justin Hall posted his thoughts and observations.

The event went largely unnoticed by the mainstream press, which only slowly realized how much it would change the industry.

By 1997, the term weblog, created by Jorn Borger, emerged. But the term blog was not used for online diaries and other web pages until 1999, when programmer Peter Merholz shortened the name to blog, the same year that free web publishing tools Blogger and others like it came along.

Journalists finally began using the blog in 1998 when the traditional news site of the Charlotte Observer carried reporter Jonathan Dube's blog about Hurricane Bonnie. Other notable online journalism blogs followed with journalist Andrew Sullivan starting his in 2000, Talking Points Memo publishing a political expose in 2002. By 2002, blogs were proliferating so quickly that the magazine Newsweek enthusiastically and wrongly predicted blogs would replace traditional news sites.

But the number of online journalism blogs and newsletters sent through email began to rise with the conservative Drudge Report, mostly a news aggregator, moving from the Internet forum Usenet to the Web in 1996. The Huffington Post and Talking Points Memo blogs also created websites.

However, as the journalists moved from traditional news and began online public service newsrooms – such as investigative and community-based newsrooms – they often chose to begin as nonprofits with websites. As the news economist James Hamilton has written, public service journalism at newspapers had depended on ad revenue largely derived from other kinds of news coverage so there was little optimism by investigative journalists in a digital world in pursuing ad revenue.

Furthermore, the nonprofit model for investigative reporting had already succeeded at three investigative newsrooms: The Center for Investigative Reporting (now Reveal) in California, created in 1977, The Center for Public Integrity in 1989 in Washington DC, and the magazine Mother Jones founded in 1976. In addition, ProPublica had just begun in 2008 with a massive donation of $30 million over three years by the Sandler family, who had made their wealth in banking and were progressive in their politics.

The older nonprofit investigative newsrooms depended largely on donations from foundations and individuals (More on that in Chapter 3). Smaller amounts of revenue came through payments from large media companies for content, although Mother Jones also earned significant advertising revenue.

In addition, the nonprofit newsrooms received the benefit of federal and state tax breaks on purchases and other items because of their tax exemption status. At the same time, their donors were getting tax deductions on their donations. The tax breaks were based on the newsrooms qualifying for tax exemption under a U.S. tax status known as 501(c)3. The federal government based the exemption for newsrooms on having an educational purpose since there is no specific exemption for journalism.

Some consultants say that being a nonprofit is not a business model, but only a tax status. But running nonprofit demands some different managerial approaches and skills than at a for-profit newsroom. The chapter will largely focus on nonprofits because the largest sustainable growth in newsrooms has been in those that have been nonprofit. However, there also has been a dramatic increase in small, community-based for-profit newsrooms, although they have been less sure about their sustainability.

The rise in nonprofit newsrooms

As noted earlier, the rise in nonprofit newsrooms began in the early 21st century with the founding of the Global Investigative Journalism Network in 2003 by roughly 35 investigative centers and associations. While the network included a few U.S.-based investigative centers, the network involved mostly non-U.S. newsrooms. Some of the non-U.S. nonprofit newsrooms began because the mainstream media was financially faltering in western Europe and others started because mainstream media was owned by corrupt politicians or corrupt individuals and businesses.

The largest increase in nonprofit newsrooms has occurred in the U.S. with the establishment of the Investigative News Network, later changing its name to the Institute for Nonprofit News (INN), in 2009 by 27 nonprofit news organizations. INN quickly developed a membership structure based on the independent non-partisan reporting and transparency of funding. INN then created a task force to review membership applications to ensure its members met the network's standards (see Chapter 9 for more on standards).

The INN membership review process, which is also done by GIJN, did prevent more political and less transparent organizations – and those that are based on promulgating misinformation – from becoming members.

In its beginning, one of INN's major goals was to enable investigative centers to collaborate on stories and share their work with each other. But it quickly became apparent that community or topic-based newsrooms, while not doing investigative work full-time, were providing public service journalism through occasional investigative work and should be included in the organization. INN's other major goal was to teach best business practices to journalists who had mostly been newspaper reporters and editors.

But in the early days of the movement, journalism reviews and critics questioned the nonprofit model, citing potential undue influence by donors and foundation.

Others worried about the "fragile" business condition of nonprofits because of the dependence on philanthropy although public broadcasting in the U.S. had been sustained for decades by foundations and donors. In addition, nonprofits, such as The Christian Science Monitor, Consumer Reports, and the Associated Press, had been operating for decades as had Mother Jones magazine, the Center for Investigative Reporting, and the Center for Public Integrity.

But the concerns persisted, even though traditional newsroom budgets and staff were being badly decimated. In addition, the Internal Revenue Service began slowing the approval of nonprofits as a controversy arose over approvals of more political, activist groups under the 501(c)4 status, which permits tax exemptions for groups that are advocacy related. However, the logjam broke with the intervention of the Knight Foundation, think tanks, and nonprofit associations.

Despite the temporary bureaucratic logjam, the number of nonprofit newsrooms who were members of INN still climbed to 120 by 2015 and few of them had financially faltered during that period.

Summary of previous books

Two thoroughly researched books have previously chronicled the surge of nonprofit newsrooms in the U.S.: Magda Konieczna's *Journalism Without Profit*, published in 2018 and Bill Birnbauer's *The Rise of Nonprofit Investigative Journalism in the U.S.* Both examined the practical and ethical issues of funding nonprofit newsrooms, the importance of the start-ups in keeping government and business accountable, collaborations and news sharing (collaboration and distribution) among commercial and nonprofit newsrooms, and editorial and business practices of nonprofit newsrooms. Each book also has case studies well worth delving into.

Birnbauer's book examined the large nonprofits newsrooms, of which three, as previously mentioned, had been in existence for more than two decades: The Center for Investigative Reporting (now better known as Reveal), The Center for Public Integrity, ProPublica, and Mother Jones. Konieczna did extensive in the field research on the Wisconsin Center for Investigative Journalism (now better known as Wisconsin Watch), MinPost, The Center for Public Integrity and its offshoot, the International Consortium of Investigative Journalists.

Konieczna and Birbauer each addressed the sustainability issues raised about nonprofit newsrooms and reliance of foundation funding, which was primarily national foundations at the time. "This is not a history book", wrote Konieczna. "It is a book about an ongoing evolution and it remains too early to know exactly will emerge".

"In other words", she wrote, "this book tells a story with a trajectory, and the punchline remains a mystery".

Birbauer bluntly titled the final chapter in his book, "Flash in the Pan or a Sustainable Business Model?" but predicted that "The longer-term financial sustainability of the nonprofit model is likely to be found in a combination of foundation support, mergers, increased donor support, and new revenue streams".

Both books aptly and thoroughly caught the nonprofit movement at a time in which many newsrooms were focused on investigative reporting. Since then, the deep concern over the loss of local news coverage in the U.S. and resulting news deserts and "ghost newspapers" (existing but providing little original news) has resulted in the second surge of nonprofits doing local coverage, particularly of underserved communities. Also, there has been an increase in the conversion of for-profit newsrooms into nonprofit newsrooms.

INN Index

Sue Cross who joined INN as its second executive director in 2015 said in that year INN research identified roughly 200 nonprofit news organizations operating in the U.S with roughly 60 percent being INN members.

"Not all of the others meet INN donor transparency requirements. Of those that do, we hope to include many more in membership over the next year", she wrote.

Among those not qualifying were a group of statehouse bureaus under the website watchdog.org. Money for the bureaus came through a nonprofit named The Center for Public and Government Integrity, which refused to reveal its donors although one major source of money was the conservative foundation, the Sam Adams Alliance, in Chicago. Later it was revealed through investigative reporting that wealthy Republican donors had been giving to the foundation to support the center and bureaus.

In 2015, Cross also reported that the INN board approved 11 new members and "more than 10 members are entering transitions from founders to new leadership – a very positive indicator for the health of the sector". In fact, the failure of the new start-ups was estimated at 10 percent or less.

By 2021, Sue Cross wrote

> Perhaps the most striking change over the past few years is that so many more people now get their news from nonprofit sources...Our membership has just about tripled since 2016, and our distribution channels have expanded, to the point that when you add in social media, we can't quantify how many millions of readers the INN network is reaching every day. Cross said, "In sum, INN is growing steadily and we expect a significant increase in independent and nonprofit media through 2017".

2020: the year of nonprofits

By 2021,The Knight Foundation published an enthusiastic article, calling 2020 "the year of nonprofits".

The author, media observer and journalist Mark Glaser, wrote

> In the narrative about the struggling local news business in America, we hear mostly about layoffs, pay cuts and closures of publications this year due to the pandemic. But what we rarely hear about is the resilience, the staying power and the growth of nonprofit local news. In 2020, the membership of the Institute for Nonprofit News (INN) rose by more than 25% — reaching a total of 300 nonprofit news organizations for the first time.

Glaser listed five reasons that nonprofit news had "come of age" in 2020.

Although he repeated the oft-quoted phrase that nonprofits are a tax status, not a business model, his first reason was that nonprofits were "a business model for tough times".

He said that because nonprofits were less reliant on advertising they did not suffer as much as for-profits during the Covid pandemic as small businesses struggled or failed. He observed that community members and charitable foundations kept donating during the pandemic.

A second reason Glaser cited was the existence of a program known as NewsMatch, heavily funded by the Knight Foundation and other foundations and administered by INN:

> "As INN has grown, so has a companion program called NewsMatch which doubles and sometimes triples each donation to a nonprofit newsroom from November 1 to December 31 each year. That funding comes from a growing list of foundations. Some local newsrooms have even tapped into local foundations to triple-match donations," he wrote, adding that the investment in nonprofit news through the program had grown from $2.5 million to $9 million in 2019. Indeed, this was an example of the kind of donor pool that had been called for at the Duke Media Conference in 2009.

In his third reason, Glaser pinpointed a new development. "For-profits are becoming more like nonprofits (or just converting to them)...Many "for profit" publishers in local news are barely scraping by, let alone making huge profits. Most large newspaper chains are owned by extractive hedge funds more interested in stripping away assets than serving the public".

Glaser noted "three interesting threads happening as for-profit newsrooms look more and more like nonprofits". One was that local newspapers had begun running donation campaigns including a Local Media Association Covid Relief Fund that raised more than $1 million for at least 130 for-profit publishers. Also, a nonprofit program, Report for America (see Chapter 4), that provides partial funding for reporters it sends to newsrooms, requires both nonprofit and for-profit newsrooms to fundraise for those reporter positions.

A second thread, he identified, was that for-profit newsrooms had created foundations and funds to attract tax-deductible donations. He noted the family-owned for-profit Seattle Times, which generates more than $200 million in revenue a year, as one newspaper that had created an investigative journalism fund. The creation of the fund had been controversial among some journalists because it was seen as simply a way to increase profits for the family who owned it.

In fact, despite potentially enriching wealthy owners, investors, and stockholders, the foundations and newsroom support groups such as Report for America have made sizeable donations to for-profits in an effort to keep traditional news from disappearing or substantially disappearing from communities.

A third thread, he said, was the outright conversion of a for-profit newsroom to a nonprofit. For example, the Salt Lake Tribune drew attention for how its conversion and the rapid approval it received from the IRS. Other newsrooms such as BerkeleySide in California also converted to nonprofit.

Consideration of that conversion is so prevalent now that INN offers a "Quick Guide to Converting a For-profit to Nonprofit News Outlet" that provides information about "challenges and opportunities presented by restarting their news business as a tax-exempt 501(c)3 corporation". The guide is intended to offer insight, tools, and resources for conversion.

The guide also notes that there are other options for for-profits in business models: "Other legal structures to consider include a Public Benefit Corporation, a subsidiary entity owned by an existing charity, ownership through a nonprofit association, trusts, hybrid for-profit/nonprofit, or a cooperative with employee ownership".

When it became a nonprofit in 2019, the Tribune issued a statement that outlined its reasons:

> For nearly 150 years, The Salt Lake Tribune has been Utah's independent voice. In the last 15 years, our country has lost almost 2,000 newspapers. And The Tribune was nearly one of them. We couldn't let that happen.
>
> That's why we took the bold action to become the country's first metropolitan daily newspaper to transition to a community-funded 501(c)(3) nonprofit. The Tribune is now a news organization funded by the people, for the people. And we're pioneering the way for newspapers everywhere. Our future is in your hands. With your support, we can continue our courageous watchdog journalism and deliver the in-depth stories that inform us, empower us and unite us.

Proposals to make it easier to convert to nonprofit status had been made before. Indeed, in 2009, U.S. Senator Ben Cardin, a Democrat from Maryland had proposed legislation that would allow newspapers to become nonprofits under the education exemption in the 501(c)(3) part of tax code. The legislation did not go through, but other media observers and columnists suggested that large endowments be created for newspapers so they could operate like universities on steady income.

Glaser wrote, "Increasingly, the line is blurring between for-profit and nonprofit newsrooms. However, nonprofit newsrooms that are members of INN are required to abide by designated standards of editorial independence, ethics and transparency".

A fourth reason Glaser gave was that nonprofit newsrooms were becoming more diverse and providing news coverage for communities that were underserved and have large populations of people of color.

While saying nonprofits, like legacy media struggled to be more diverse, he did note that "10 of 24 startups that joined INN from 2017 to 2019 reported that people of color made up 40% or more of the staff".

Glaser's fifth reason was that "collaboration has become a way of life for many nonprofit newsrooms" and then cited decades of collaborations among non-profits with other nonprofits and for-profits.

Collaboration in reporting had been at the root of the nonprofit movement. INN's founding, and that of the Local Independent Online News (LION) Publishers association (which was formed in 2012 and has both nonprofit and for-profit newsrooms as members) not only recognized the importance of collaboration but intended to promote it heavily.

Surge continues in 2021 and 2022

In an otherwise bleak study, In the State of the News report in 2022 from Northwestern University noted that:

> "Troubled by the potential consequences, journalists, policymakers, philanthropists, industry executives, scholars and concerned citizens have stepped up efforts to save local news". It said that philanthropic donors, as well as venture capitalists, are funding more journalistic endeavors and that new government regulations and public subsidies

> are being considered to address the issue. It also said many newspapers and digital organizations are adapting and finding success, especially in larger markets or affluent communities, where there are more funding options.

More optimistic surveys and studies completed in 2021 and 2022 found that the nonprofit movement had continued to surge while at the same time smaller community-based for-profits grew at a rapid pace.

INN, which has been surveying its members annually for the past six years, revealed not only the rapid growth of nonprofits in 2022 since 2008, but also showed the trends and variety of nonprofit newsrooms in their coverage, revenue and expenses, and diversity.

It said 286 member organizations, or 94 percent of the members, responded to the survey. (Since then, INN has grown to more than 400 members by the spring of 2022 and Cross predicted it could increase to 600 in the next several years.)

The INN Index showed the wide array of nonprofits by grouping them into several categories.

Geographically, the groups were local (which was showing the most growth in reaction to increasing news deserts), regional, state, national, and global. In purpose, INN grouped them as investigative, explanatory, and community news.

The data from the survey showed that local nonprofit newsrooms had especially grown with 45 percent of the local newsrooms having begun since 2016 or after. It also showed that the newsrooms had endured with the median age of the newsrooms at six and the average age at 11 years.

The INN Index said,

> The geographic scope of nonprofit newsrooms had shifted strongly to local coverage as traditional newspapers continued their decline and either closed or were left barely staffed. The percentage of newsrooms covering a local area doubled, moving from 23 percent in 2018 to 43 percent in 2022. One third of the local coverage was in a city with about 40 percent in counties and metro editors. About 28 percent was towns and neighborhoods.

The Index said staff sizes hovered around 11 persons on average and six as a median. Full-time employees made up about 80 percent of staff and contractors about 20 percent.

One number about staff was strikingly different. The traditional news industry had difficulty diversifying its staff and white had stayed about 80–90 percent over the years. Among the newer INN members, only about half of the staff was reported as white. And more than half were female.

When it came to the distribution of content about 70 percent of news was published on a website and 10 percent was in print. Newsletters, email, and social media made up the other 20 percent. The percentages reflected that most of start-ups were from those who had been in print or digital media and not in broadcast. It also showed that only a few members of INN were from public broadcasting since public broadcasting has its own network.

Seventy percent said their primary distribution was through its own "channels" while 20 percent said they distributed through third parties despite a heavy reliance early in the growth of nonprofits on third-party distribution, often through legacy media or public broadcasting.

INN measured the performance of a watchdog role as having at least one investigative journalist (78 percent), filing Freedom of Information requests (70 percent), and publishing an online database (35 percent.)

Evolution of nonprofit newsrooms

The INN Index over the years and other studies have traced the evolution of nonprofits in the field and the development of early models and a review of what happened to the early groups and signers of INN's Pocantico Declaration is enlightening to examine.

Several signers were from the Center for Public Integrity, which remains one of the largest centers despite going through changes in management and strategic direction. There were also several signers from the Center for Investigative Reporting, which expanded significantly, and is better known as "Reveal", which now produces audio investigations that are distributed on public radio stations.

Another group of signers included larger nonprofits, who were both investigative and community-based and started with budgets in the hundreds of thousands to $1 million. Those included the Voice of San Diego and MinnPost in Minneapolis, both of which received targeted Knight Foundation funding.

A similar major organization, The Texas Tribune, also a recipient of Knight funding, was not at the meeting but became an integral part of the nonprofit movement. All three organizations are still successfully operating. In addition, Another signer, The Pulitzer Center for Crisis Reporting, is now one of the largest nonprofit newsrooms in the U.S.

The third group included smaller investigative centers that were starting up with modest amounts, often less than $500,000. They included The Watchdog Institute (later named INewsource) of San Diego, The Wisconsin Center for Investigative Journalism (often called Wisconsin Watchdog), and InvestigateWest from Seattle. Despite the challenges of starting small, all three organizations have survived and expanded successfully while winning numerous awards (Figures 2.2 and 2.3).

The fourth group included several newsrooms that took a path that led to acquisition by public media and, in some cases, the loss of their brand and their mission (see Chapter 7). Those included the New England Center for Reporting, based at Boston University, which later became the investigative desk of the public broadcasting station WGBH in Boston.

Another organization like that was Rocky Mountain Investigative News Network which later was acquired by Rocky Mountain PBS and after four years of success there began to have its budget cut and was diminished and gone in the next three years. The third very successful start-up was the St. Louis Beacon, which was acquired by the public broadcasting station in STLPR, and still has a presence there, but the station is facing budget shortfalls and managerial controversy.

However, New Jersey Spotlight, which was at Pocantico, eventually was acquired by large public broadcasting station., WNET in New York City, and has deemed its acquisition a success. WNET was also present at Pocantico and a signer of the declaration.

The fifth group was represented by academics involved in producing news stories and two were the Stabile Center for Investigative Reporting at Columbia University and the Schuster Institute at Brandeis University.

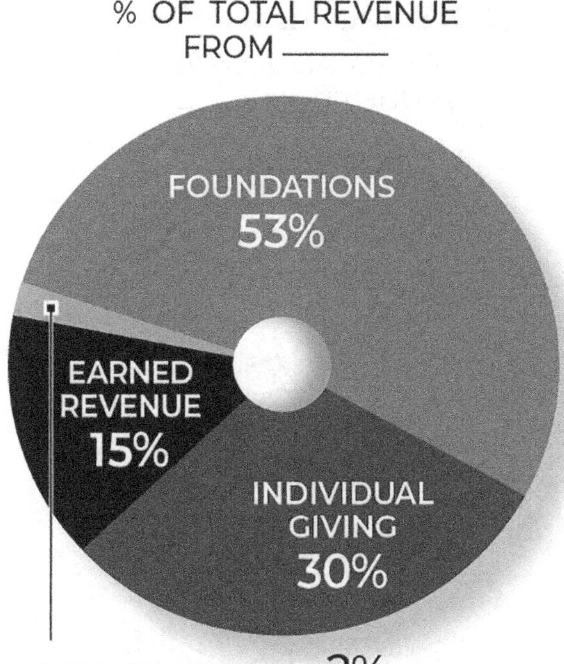

Figure 2.2 Revenue sources for INN members

Credit: Institute for Nonprofit News Index 2022, https://inn.org/research/inn-index/inn-index-2022/executive-summary/

The Stabile Center is still operating, but the Schuster Institute closed when the university could not raise more funds to keep it going (see Chapter 6 for more).

The sixth group was of newsroooms that ended up dissolving. One was Pacific News Service, which had overseen the largest network (1,000 plus) of newsrooms of ethnic media in the U.S. and another was Capitol News Connection, which covered Congress. Both dissolved because they could not obtain continued funding. Huffington Post, which later created a nonprofit investigative team was there. That team and its brand became a part of the Center for Public Integrity, but no longer exists.

The last newsroom was the outlier Watchdog.org, which was rejected for membership in INN because it was not transparent about its funding

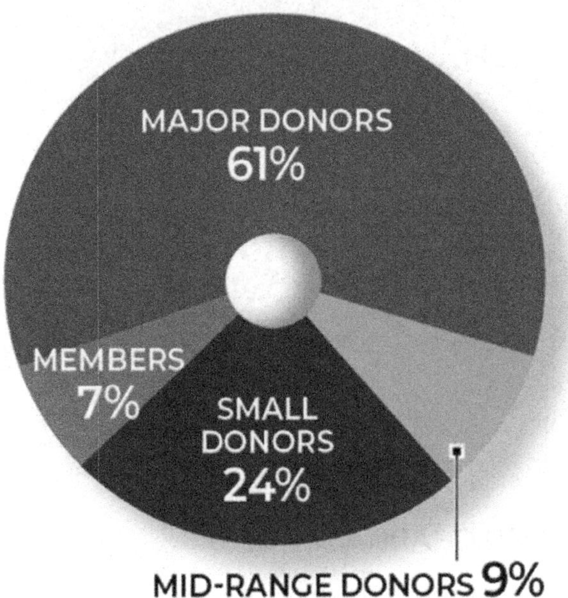

Figure 2.3 Individual giving to INN members

Credit: Institute for Nonprofits, https://inn.org/research/inn-index/inn-index-2022/revenue-growth/

and was part of the network of statehouse bureaus created by the Sam Adams Alliance.

Although the successes, failures, and acquisitions among the Pocantico attendees do not perfectly mirror the overall proportion of the fates of INN members over time, they do represent the variety of paths and perils in the nonprofit model.

LION and the Project News Oasis survey

The LION Publishers association reported that it had more than 400 members in 2021 after having started in 2010 with a handful of online news organizations. According to its website, it became a professional association in 2012 and attained 501(c)3 status in 2019, when it received a $1 million grant from the Knight Foundation to expand its staff and training.

As of 2021, it said about 63 percent of its 400 or so members were for-profit and 37 percent nonprofit. INN and LION's training programs are similar, but LION's program leans toward teaching best business practices that focus more on for-profit revenues such as advertising.

LION co-published a study of its members with a consulting group called Project News Oasis that gave another view of the change in journalism business models.

LION said its study produced insights about the emerging field, saying that "266 organizations started up in the past five years, an increase of nearly 50%, representing an average of more than 50 launches per year". It said an earlier study, which had looked at 1,400 news sites in 2010, "had identified 120 new locals, indicating that the past decade has seen the number of local sites multiply six times over".

Among its findings, the OASIS project found:

- That the outlets rely heavily on social media for visibility.
- Women account for 56 percent of full-time personnel among the 173 organizations that provided demographic data. Only one-fourth are employees of color.
- One in seven of the new locals operates in a news desert, an area where a newspaper has closed or that has traditionally been overlooked.
- About three-fourths operate as commercial businesses, most commonly as limited liability companies. The others, it said, are nonprofits, which tend to be larger in size and to have more funding.

In its introduction, the report said

> digital-native news organizations are gaining a foothold in communities throughout the United States and Canada. Their reach and impact increases every year, as new newsrooms launch, young local startups grow their audience, and legacy news organizations cut back or close.

One-third of the 714 news organizations included in its study had launched in the past five years and two-thirds were 10 years old or younger. At the same time, it said LION Publishers' membership more than doubled in 2020.

Contrary to the optimism in the nonprofit newsrooms found by INN, LION said that "among 255 local outlets surveyed, only one in five publishers considered their operation sustainable. Two in five said they are on a path to sustainability but the rest say they are struggling".

The local news operations surveyed were clearly grassroots efforts and in some ways resembles the early days of blogging in which one or a few people devote time and their own funds to the start-up.

For example, the survey found nine in ten of the newsrooms had ten or fewer full-time employees. The survey also found more than one-fourth of the newsrooms had only one person drawing a salary and one-fourth that had no full-time employees.

Instead, "these organizations often deploy a mix of employees, contractors and volunteers. Some play multiple roles: It is not uncommon for a lone founder to divide her day between covering the news and selling ads". It said among 50 organizations that provided additional details, half use volunteers in some capacity to support their organization.

"The Reconstruction of American Journalism", a 2009 study of changes in journalism models, noted even then, "Many of the startups are still quite small and financially fragile, but they are multiplying steadily".

The Oasis study concluded,

> the explosive growth in the last decade of small, independent digital news outlets serving local communities holds great promise as traditional sources of credible journalism decline. Also encouraging: The emerging field has demonstrated resilience. Two-thirds have emerged from the challenging startup phase of their first few years.

Together, the INN and LION studies show a substantial increase in investigative and community-based newsrooms that seek not to necessarily replace legacy journalism, but to reinvent it.

A SHORT CASE STUDY: TALKING POINTS MEMO – FROM BLOG TO NEWS ORGANIZATION

A start-up that did not take on the nonprofit tax status was the Talking Points Memo. In most ways, its literature, purpose, and operations sound very much like a nonprofit.

Talking Point Memos began in November 2000. It has offices in New York City and in Washington D.C. It is completely transparent that is a "liberal political news and opinion website". Its founder is blogger Josh Marshall and it drew immediate attention for its muck-raking political reporting. In 2008, it won the George Polk Award for its reporting on the scandal of the firing of U.S. attorneys.

It said, "We are particularly focused on reporting on abuses of power and betrayals of the public trust. Our reports have exposed scandals and driven coverage of major news stories across multiple administrations".

It is also fairly transparent about its business model and financials. On its website, it said TPM is funded overwhelmingly by readers' membership fees. More than 70 percent of its income is derived from memberships and the remainder is from advertising. It does not say who donates to it or who its members are or what its budget is.

> As a fully independent organization, TPM has no corporate overlords. TPM is not beholden to or controlled by any outside interests. TPM was founded by a journalist and to this day its "business" side is staffed with former journalists whose primary mission is to create a sustainable environment for our reporters and editors to do great work.

TPM said 74 percent of its revenue goes to salaries, 11 percent to rent, 5 percent to website and tech expenses, and 10 percent to office and legal expenses. Like a nonprofit, it said it takes our profits and uses them to grow its journalism.

It has a range of memberships, saying its most popular is $60 a year. It sells ads at varying rates and it also has had donation campaigns, making clear the donations are not tax-deductible since it is not a 501(c)3 tax-exempt organization. It has a paywall that allowed the viewing on its website of nine articles a month.

But it also said it wants to be accessible to students and those having financial hardships so it has free community-supported memberships.

Members get fewer ads, a newsletter, and access to a forum. A prime ad-free membership costs $120. Its site said that as a member publication, building and maintaining a community is critical to us. We keep close tabs on the political fringe – militias, white nationalists, conspiracy theorists, and more – because we believe they are greater drivers of American politics than mainstream news coverage allows.

It said,

> the goal of our journalism is neither balance nor objectivity but accuracy, fairness and a fundamental honesty with our readers and members at all times. We relish the comedy, folly and absurdity which is so often at the center of the news. Great journalism should jump off the page, unfolding stories that are as compelling as they are important.

Other kinds of models

In 2009, "The Reconstruction of American Journalism" study found other models and ventures in journalism. They included a network of franchised websites in Seattle for neighborhoods, hyperlocal websites, newsrooms covering statehouses, a for-profit newsroom reporting on international issues, and AOL's Patch newsroom which has tried to provide local news but often fallen short.

The study highlighted Politico, a for-profit deeply focused on political news and issues, which has gone onto great success. It also noted successes of blogs and specialized newsletters such as Michele Leder's financial newsletter and website "Footnoted", which provides data and analysis often based on Securities and Exchange Commission public reports.

"Collectively, the newcomers are filling some of the gaps left by the downsizing of newspapers' reporting staffs, especially in local accountability and neighborhood reporting", the study said.

"However, the staffs of most of the startups are still small, as are their audiences and budgets, and they are scattered unevenly across the country. Their growth, role, and impact in news reporting are still to be determined by a variety of factors...", the Reconstruction report said even as far back as 2009.

But since then there have been numerous success stories. Consider two case studies, one a nonprofit and one a for-profit, that look similar in many ways.

A LONGER CASE STUDY: VERMONT DIGGER

VTDigger was founded in 2009 by a laid-off journalist Anne Galloway and became a project of the Vermont Journalism Trust in March 2011. The Vermont Journalism Trust supports journalism employing a nonprofit model and its initial project as a fiscal sponsor was VTDigger.org.

Vermont Digger said it is a statewide news website that publishes daily reports on state government, politics, consumer affairs, business, and public policy. It also publishes in-depth stories with occasional investigative pieces, video, and audio, in addition to raw information in the form of press releases and government documents. It won many awards for its investigation into the financial scandal.

It said it publishes Sunday through Friday and has eight news stories a day and three to four investigative pieces a month and has 14 reporters and six editors, making it the largest news operation in Vermont. It said it has 700,000 monthly readers and we reach another 200,000 readers a month through our AP-style distribution service, which is used by 13 local daily and weekly newspapers across the state. It has no paywall and has a free newsletter.

It is transparent about the amount and percentage of its revenue and reported in its 2020 annual report that it received $467,000 in grants, $369,000 in underwriting, $1.5 million in individual donations, and $135,000 in news revenue for about a total of $2.4 million. It spent about $1.6 million on news, $143,000 on administrative tasks, and $479,000 on fundraising for about a total of about $2.2 million.

Vermont Digger was profiled in an extensive piece for the Institute for Nonprofit News by business consultant Tim Griggs because of Vermont Digger's success as a nonprofit newsroom. Here are excerpts from that piece:

> Griggs noted that the organization's success is far from an overnight sensation. It has toiled for years with the same obstacles faced by peers at local, state, and topic-based nonprofit news sites. They are generally undercapitalized and understaffed ventures, filling a clear gap in reporting vacated by legacy publishers, but with a tenuous at best shot at long-term survival.

"So why has Digger succeeded where others have not? What can we all learn from Digger's accomplishments? What makes it unique and what makes it replicable?" Griggs pointed out several lessons. The first was understanding the market. Using a standard business plan forced Galloway to take her preconceived notions about the need for investigative reporting in Vermont out of the picture and think objectively about a market for that product.

The second lesson was expanding her network. You will find local organizations – a community foundation, a library, a museum, a like-minded civic group – that can help you develop relationships with business leaders, philanthropists, and others. It is important to reach out to people in your community for support. Find the connectors – the people who believe in your work and who are connected to business leaders, philanthropists, and others.

The third lesson was starting small. The classic "foot-in-the-door" sales and fundraising tactic is to ask for a small amount of money or a low commitment first, prove your value, and increase requests over time. Digger has not changed its sponsorship pricing much (about $500 per week for run-of-site display) but over time began creating more custom campaigns.

The fourth strategy was prioritizing business-side investments. Nonprofit news site founders often think they should invest all their time and funding in the journalism in their early years. Early investment in business development is crucial to build and keep momentum around donations, sponsorships, and partnerships, and to create diverse revenue sources.

The fifth strategy was to invest in strong sales people. Good sales people for nonprofit news sites are hard to find because they need to understand mission and the medium. Digger's first sales director, Michael Knight, came out of newspaper ad sales, so he was accustomed to being rejected.

The sixth strategy was to think carefully about quantity. There's a vicious cycle for underfunded news startups: More frequent, high-quality journalism is more likely to attract the right audience, which costs money, and is harder to raise without frequent, high-quality reporting. Being mindful of the role quantity plays here is important. The Digger team made a conscious choice: Go daily as early as possible and encourage readers to develop a habit.

The seventh strategy was, like many nonprofits, to expand through collaboration. Where possible, consider hiring interns and freelancers first, then hire full-time reporters when the budget allows. Most importantly, consider partnerships at every turn to help expand your capacity and capabilities at a lower cost. The eighth strategy was to get the most of out of the board. A nonprofit news board is always responsible for the financial stability of the institution. Beyond that, types of boards vary widely but they're often by nature governance boards (making strategic decisions), advisory boards (providing strategic guidance to the staff), or fundraising boards (the chief development arm of the institution). In Digger's case, the board serves all of these functions.

Over the last couple of years, the Digger team has greatly expanded its products and services. Among them:

- A weekly podcast (started with funds from an INN Innovation Fund grant) called The Deeper Dig, which is sponsored;
- A dedicated mobile app to experiment with push notifications;

- Publishing Facebook Instant Articles to determine if there's an ROI (Return on Investment);
- Topical email newsletters (first up: politics) and a breaking news email;
- A campaign finance database;
- Paid posts (sponsored content);
- A bill tracker for the legislative session

Digger also has planned to start posting classifieds – a job board, obituaries, and legals – as a revenue and audience-building experiment. Galloway said readers were asking for these kinds of services and felt it was an opportunity to provide a service for people who stopped reading the local newspaper or are dissatisfied with Craigslist.

"You have to constantly think of new ways to serve people", she said. "Even with businesses. How do we help them connect with people and improve their business prospects?"

The ninth strategy the study mentions is the diversification of revenue streams, which cannot be emphasized enough.

Don't buy into the notion that there's an ideal number of revenue streams for news organizations. "There's no limit on ideas here", Galloway said. "If you told me tomorrow that there was some idea I'm missing, I'd latch onto it. Then I'd think, 'what's the ROI?'" The reality is that no two markets are the same; what works in one place for one site may or may not work for you. Be wary of silver bullets (they don't exist) and instead constantly and continually experiment and test ideas to generate revenue. In other words, "fail fast, fail cheap".

One last strategy was never stop looking for capital. Most nonprofit news sites have launched without adequate capital to build viable long-term businesses. Digger was no exception. Although its approach to organic, pay-as-you-go growth has worked, the odds of success are much greater with runway in the form of pre-launch funding. A major endowment can help, or in Digger's case, a large infusion of cash to invest in infrastructure and growth (Figures 2.4 and 2.5).

VTDigger 2020 Revenue

Grants | $466,534
Underwriting | $369,456
Individual Contributions | $1,461,863
News Revenue | $135,311
Other | $5,790
Total Revenue | $2,438,954

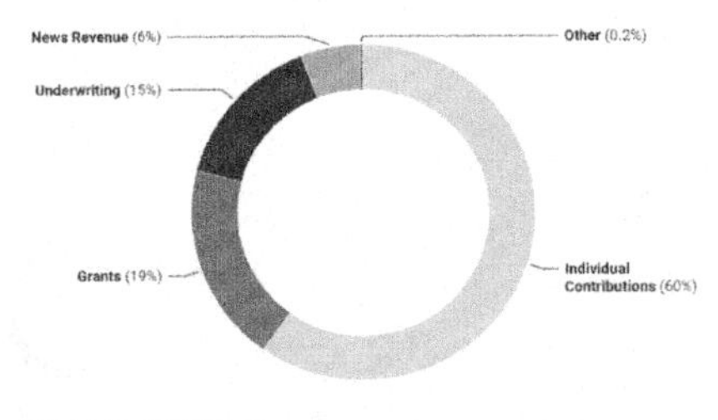

Figure 2.4 VTDigger revenue for 2020

Credit: VtDigger 2020 Annual Report, https://projects.vtdigger.org/annual-report-2020/

VTDigger 2020 Expenses

Program | $1,558,328
General & Administrative | $142,584
Fundraising | $478,362
Total Expenses | $2,179,274

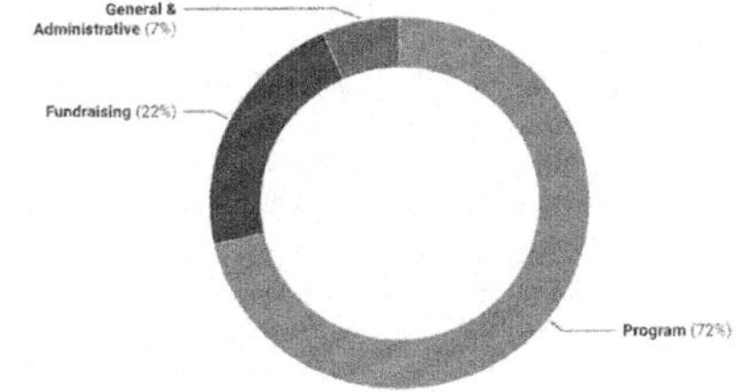

Figure 2.5 VTDigger expenses for 2020

Credit: VTDigger 2020 Annual Report, https://projects.vtdigger.org/annual-report-2020/

3

OWNERS, INVESTORS, AND DONORS

In 2013, Jeff Bezos, the founder of Amazon, purchased *The Washington Post* and invested enough money to allow the Post to become more digital and become profitable.

Another wealthy individual, Carlos Slim, from Mexico had made a sizeable loan to *The New York Times* to shore it up while it became more digital and increased its digital subscribers.

In Boston, a wealthy businessman John Henry bought the Boston Globe and in Minneapolis, another prosperous businessman Glen Taylor bought Star-Tribune Media Company. Both newsrooms are flourishing, having gotten time to shore themselves up with digital subscriptions.

Famed investor Warren Buffett, who had had a small stake in newspapers, bought a group of about newspapers in 2012 for about $142 million, but sold them off 8 years later for $140 million, at one point saying the industry was "toast".

DOI: 10.4324/9781315719573-4

Meanwhile, Marc Benioff, head of Salesforce purchased *Time* Magazine and Laurene Powell Jobs bought the Atlantic Monthly through her charity, the Emerson Collective.

As the media industry experienced consolidation of many newsrooms into corporate chains, the business collapse of those chains resulted in the subsequent purchase of them by hedge funds that found new ways to cut budgets and staff and sell off real estate to wring profits out of what was left.

Confronted with the increasing loss of reliable and consistent journalism and information, new owners and investors had entered the field. It might have appeared that journalism might be returning to a time of only rich magnates who were able to create, buy, and run newsrooms, hearkening back to the 20th-century owners such as William Randolph Hearst and Joseph Pulitzer.

The new owners and investors not only included wealthy individuals – some of them mentioned above – but also international and national foundations, community foundations and local businesspeople, tech giants, and journalists and citizens often starting out with threadbare budgets.

Thus, while those deals by wealthy individuals were being done, the emerging media of nonprofits and small local digital for-profit newsrooms was expanding rapidly and individual entrepreneurs started blogs and newsletters. Universities even began increasing their journalism department's reporting capacity with the help of donors and public media began expanding its local and regional coverage (see Chapters 6 and 7).

The start-ups proliferate

Since then – despite doubts from media pundits – many of those investors and owners are still in the field with more coming in each year.

In the next sections of the chapter, we will look at a series of reports that outline the current ownership in emerging media as compared to mainstream media, at the history of how founders and wealthy owners have pushed emerging media into taking a prominent place in the field. In many ways, it often is what Eric Newton, the former vice president of journalism at the Knight Foundation, has called the return of the journalist-proprietor.

Newton has said that there had been a separation of the newsroom and the business in traditional media – a separation of church and state – that actually hurt journalism. With the owners and operators of the new small newsrooms, there has been a return to a more productive and integrated organization.

As noted in earlier chapters, nonprofit newsrooms and entrepreneurial small newsrooms increased as mainstream media laid off staff and, in many cases, shut their doors. With the loss of the business model of advertising revenue, the start-ups turned to foundations and individual donors to get their operations going.

The foundations

Among the foundations that gave major to the field or increased it were the John S. and James L. Knight Foundation, the largest journalism foundation in the U.S which continues to have the greatest impact.; the MacArthur Foundation; the Open Society Foundations, which gave significant funding internationally, too; the Robert R. McCormick Foundation; The Rockefeller Brothers Fund; the Ford Foundation; the Logan foundations; the Wyncote Foundation; the Ethics and Excellence in Journalism Foundation now known as the Inasmuch Foundation; and the William and Flora Hewlett Foundation; and more recently the foundation, Arnold Ventures. The individual philanthropists and investors included Pierre Omidyar, who financed the newsroom First Look and the Democracy Fund, which often pour money into pools of foundation money for nonprofits newsrooms; John Thornton, a hedge fund veteran who started the successful nonprofit Texas Tribune and then raised $50 million for the American Journalism Project, which has created more pools of funds to finance community start-ups and to teach, like the Institute for Nonprofit News, best business practices to nonprofit newsrooms; The Sandler family, bankers who gave to progressive causes, who decided to pledge $30 million over three years to start ProPublica, now perhaps the largest investigative reporting center in the world; and Craig Newmark of Craig's List, who has given tens of millions through his foundation.

One key businessman and philanthropist has been Buzz Woolley, who started the nonprofit Voice of San Diego and then gave key matching money to the INN that encouraged other funders to give to INN, which has become the largest network of nonprofit newsrooms.

Tracking funding

Despite constant concerns that foundations are fickle in maintaining their giving over time, The Media Impact Fund, which tracks giving the media, collected data that showed foundations gave eight times more in 2020 in the U.S. than in 2009. The fund estimated 591 funders gave 1,712 grants worth $642 million to 861 journalism and news organizations in 2020 in the U.S. compared with 311 funders who gave 910 grants worth $85.5 million to 314 journalism and news organizations.

In the U.S., the Knight Foundation, led by former newspaper publisher Alberto Ibargüen for two decades, spurred the emerging media in a variety of ways. One program was a $25 million innovation fund that was open, not only to journalists but to computer programmers and citizens. While many of the innovations and experiments did not endure, some did, and it demonstrated to journalists seeking funding and throughout the industry that they had to speed up their understanding of digital tools and journalism.

In addition to providing seed money to selected newsrooms such as the Voice of San Diego, MinnPost, and the Texas Tribune, the Knight Foundation also encouraged community foundations to contribute to newsrooms by creating a $25 million challenge program that matched giving by community foundations to journalism projects. Knight also constantly encouraged other foundations not readily identified with journalism giving to join the foundation's efforts.

In the last decade, foundations that became more significant funders were the Gates Foundation and Arnold Ventures. The Gates Foundation especially backed a new brand of news called "Solutions Journalism" and Arnold gave significant support to local, regional, and national newsrooms. The Lenfest Institute in Philadelphia also joined in, supporting journalism in Philadelphia and Pennsylvania and converting mainstream for-profit newspapers into nonprofit.

During the same period, there was also money coming in from wealthy conservatives and libertarians and foundations, but like watchdog.org, a group of statehouse bureaus, the sources and amounts of funding were not disclosed or it appeared directed at specific political and ideological goals. For example, the Mercer family financed Breitbart News and the conservative Adelson family bought the Las Vegas Journal.

Detail and context for ownership and funding

One organization that has produced studies on media ownership is particularly helpful. The project, called the "Future of Media: Truth, Privacy and Power", is headquartered at Harvard University and is a partnership between the Harvard Business School and Harvard's Institute for Quantitative Social Science. Its goal is to research and identify practical solutions "to rebalance truth, privacy and power in the media industry".

It said its

> intention is to understand and address issues related to the media that are impacting society and where it is unlikely that private solutions will emerge due to a lack of trust or neutrality, a lack of resources or low incentives to contribute to the public good.

As a part of its work, it has created ownership indexes: one for U.S. mainstream media and one for U.S. emerging media. The indexes are extremely helpful for giving context to ownership.

The mainstream media index's goal is to "provide radical transparency and a better grasp of the U.S. Mainstream Media by listing publishers (owners, majority voting shareholders, and donors of titles) considered major U.S. daily news sources".

The project said if subsidiaries were counted under parent companies, there are nearly 3,100 newsrooms in America.

This first index is intended to include every traditional media organization in the U.S., where "traditional" is defined as major cable networks, major holding companies of local TV stations, news magazines (both print and digital-only), major public media, major newspapers with over 50,000 digital subscribers, and the seven largest holding companies of U.S. daily newspapers.

It said,

> We do not include podcasts, bloggers, Substack or media columnists or talk radio. To capture a robust index, we focused on parent companies or stand-alone properties with a strong reach (web traffic, prime time news audience, subscribers, or circulation) along with brand recognition.

The project said they use third-party tracking of monthly views unless reported at the source. In the case of cable TV, the project says it combines daily prime-time audiences with monthly views. "Our ranking of traffic is by no means a perfect science. Our focus was on ownership", it said, although it ranks the media by audience. Thus, Wikipedia is listed first in the index with 1.7 billion monthly visitors to its website.

It notes,

> We have, no doubt, missed a few publishers of note and, with dailies, we list the owners of the seven largest newspaper parent companies or standalone dailies with significant paid digital subscribers. We hope this sheds light. It issued a warning: There are some outlets on here that many journalists would deem political propaganda. Thus, the importance of radical ownership transparency.

In the case of Wikipedia, which is a media nonprofit and not a newsroom in any traditional sense, the project lists the tech giant Google as Wikipedia's largest donor in 2020 and the largest donor to its endowment is Arcadia, a charitable fund of Lisbet Rausing and Peter Baldwin. Other major donors include Amazon, the Musk Foundation, George Soros, Craig Newmark, and Facebook (now Meta).

In the index, the next six top listings are all major broadcast companies, including Fox News and CNN. The eighth company listed is Yahoo News, primarily an aggregator of other news outlets. The ninth is MSNBC and the tenth listed by web traffic is the nonprofit NPR.

The rest of the top 50 included more traditional news organizations such as the Hearst family holdings, Gannett, *The New York Times, The Wall Street Journal, The Guardian, Reuters, Associated Press, The Atlantic, Newsweek*, and *New York Post*. It also includes more recent for-profit newsrooms like the Daily Beast, Vox, and the Verge and the hedge funds Alden Global Capital and Chatham Assets, which owns McClatchy newsrooms.

As noted by the project, it is striking how much cross-ownership there is of the top 100 companies – Rupert Murdoch has stakes in companies including *Fox*, the *Wall Street Journal*, and *The New York Post* – and how many different kinds of media some companies own.

The 51st company listed is the Epoch Times, which has a warning label attached to it because the conservative news organization's funding is unclear.

The investor and ownership research in the Harvard is quite detailed, sometimes listing numerous top shareholders in publicly traded companies and dozens of foundations for some nonprofits. The general categories are publicly traded, private/family, and nonprofit.

Pooling funds for journalism

It is important to note the overlap in the indexes.

For example, the nonprofit American Journalism Project, which has played an integral role in emerging nonprofit media, is listed both under mainstream and emerging. The investor information is quite useful in showing how its $50 million funding to help the nonprofit newsroom movement was built through a consortium of foundations and its listing shows how detailed the project's research can be and how funding in the nonprofit news world can be stitched together:

The study showed listed investors are run by VC and Texas Tribune founder John Thornton and giving out over $50M to digital-only nonprofits with Facebook Journalism Project funding along with:

$1.5 million grant from the Boston-based Abrams Foundation
$500,000 grant from the New York-based Horace W. Goldsmith Foundation, Knight Foundation, Arnold Ventures, Emerson

> Collective (Laurene Powell Jobs), Craig Newmark Philanthropies, Pierre Omidyar's Democracy Fund, Christopher Buck and Dr. Hara Schwartz, Lumina Foundation, Erin and John Thornton.

Thornton calls these new digital media outlets, Community News Organizations (CNO). The listing also includes a statement by the organization:

> It quotes the American Journalism Project as saying our "support is designed for nonprofit news organizations with ambitious plans to grow their revenue and programs that support informed communities, plus targeted early stage investments in leaders and communities that present a unique opportunity to change the local news landscape where they operate".

As of 2021, the CNO included The Beacon in Kansas City, MO, Centro de Periodismo Investigativo in San Juan, Puerto Rico, City Bureau in Chicago, IL, Cityside in Oakland, CA, but since then the list of CNO has grown significantly.

The mainstream index is also worth looking through to see the magnitude of those organizations compared to the lesser resources listed in the "Emerging Nonprofit Media and Donors Index".

The project said the emerging media index "provides insights into the emerging digital nonprofit news landscape. With failing revenue models for journalism, many donors have come forward to fund journalism, sometimes around a specific issue or cause". The index highlighted the largest donors at the top of the list and noted that Google and Facebook fund some of the nonprofits listed.

In emerging media, the Harvard index also highlighted:

> The LenFest Institute, which was funded by a major $40 million gift from the late cable TV owner, Gerry Lenfest, and also funding from the Knight Foundation, Facebook, and Google. NewsMatch which matches donations to nonprofit newsrooms and has funders frequently listed include Knight Foundation, Google News Initiative, Facebook Journalism Project, Democracy Fund, Hewlett Foundation, Wyncote.

Another highlighted emerging media group is the Solutions Journalism Network, supported initially by the Gates Foundation. It funds "solutions-driven stories" and includes as its funders a long list that is like a journey through foundations that have been supporting journalism. The funders included a long list that is worth studying to understand the pooling of philanthropic money that was suggested by nonprofit newsrooms in 2009.

The list includes the Barr Foundation, Bill & Melinda Gates Foundation, Catherine Hawkins Foundation, Chan Zuckerberg Initiative, Democracy Fund, Einhorn Family Charitable Trust, Emerson Collective, Enlight Foundation, Fidelity Charitable, Ford Foundation, Google News Initiative, Heising-Simons Foundation, Horace W. Goldsmith Foundation, Knight Foundation, Jonathan Logan Family Foundation, Endowment For Health Novo Foundation, Paul Dosberg Charitable Fund, Ralph C. Wilson, Jr., Rita Allen Foundation, Robert Wood Johnson Foundation, The Kendeda Fund, Tinker Foundation, Town Foundation, William James Foundation, William and Flora Hewlett Foundation.

Another large media group-funder listed is the Fund For Nonprofit News At The Miami Foundation: It is

> a coalition of Democracy Fund, John S. and James L. Knight Foundation, Inasmuch Foundation (formerly The Ethics and Excellence In Journalism Foundation), The Facebook Journalism Project, The Colorado Media Project, The John D. and Catherine T. Macarthur Foundation, The Jonathan Logan Family Foundation, The Rita Allen Foundation, The Wyncote Foundation, and The Present Progressive Fund At Schwab Charitable.

Transparency of funding as a standard

The Harvard index noted the emerging media funders are "incredibly transparent, even if their new donor programs such as AJP, Solutions Journalism, and NewsMatch require another layer of digging for source funding". The Miami Foundation, it noted, "appears regularly with its NewsMatch program, created by many of the same big funders above".

The project also touches on donor-advised funds (known as DAFs), which are funds that often are donated by a third party directed by the actual donor and obscure the donor. In some cases, the donee knows who the donor really is and sometimes not. As the project says, "It is harder to track as it (NewsMatch) is a charity with donor-advised funds".

They also said many of these nonprofits listed are members of the Institute for NonProfit News, whose Index also is included in this book. The Harvard index data for emerging media was collected from March 2021 to March 22 directly from the news websites, according to the index.

Finally, the project noted that

> in comparison, the news orgs, on the Index of Mainstream Media Ownership, where we had the hardest time identifying ownership and funding were right-leaning media organizations such as NewsMax, Brietbart, The Blaze, the Charlemagne Institute's Chronicles, The American Mind, The American Spectator, and Epoch Times.

The emerging media list is alphabetical and not based on web traffic or other audience ratings. Its value is more in the list of donors, which gives an idea of the major players and how the variety of donors has increased. For other details on the nonprofit movement, it is easier to refer to the INN Index since the Future of Media Index relies on some INN data.

Community foundations and the new surge in nonprofits

One of the more recent trends in local ownership of nonprofit news start-ups in major and medium size metropolitan areas that have lost much of their news. National organizations, such as the American Journalism Project and the Knight Foundation, are contributors and catalysts in some cases, but they have strong local support and local donors.

"We are very optimistic about the future of philanthropy and local news", said Sarabeth Berman, CEO of the American Journalist Project, said in an interview with the Knight Report.

> We are seeing more and more philanthropists – especially local philanthropy – stepping off the sidelines to build a future for local news. The rapid decline of commercial local reporting in our country

> combined with an unprecedented year that magnified the essential role local news plays in our day-to-day lives is driving more philanthropists to rise to the moment and ensure the public has the information they need.

The same article highlighted a Media Impact Fund study done in 2021 that looked at community foundation funding that found more support is being directed toward "journalism, news and information".

The fund's study showed that 153 community foundations gave an estimated $124 million to 700 recipients from 2009 to early 2021.

Among the newest nonprofit newsrooms in the recent surge are community-based ones with investors that have been locally or regionally funded with additional national funding. They are listed below with information about their missions and funding. Here is an overview of some of them:

- The Fort Worth Report

  Its mission is a pledge to produce high-quality objective local journalism that informs public decision-making, addresses the quality of life of our community's citizens, holds our policymakers accountable and tells our readers' stories by listening to them and making sure they are valued and understood. In all that we do, earning the trust and respect of our audience is paramount. Our reporting will be free to all who access our primary digital channels.

  It lists in its funding generous donation from The Burnett Foundation.
- The Baltimore Banner

  It states its mission is to be an indispensable resource that strengthens, unites, and inspires our Baltimore community. We accomplish this through trustworthy quality journalism that tells the varied stories of our people, holds our leaders accountable, and delivers local news that readers are willing to support.

  It said its founder, "Stewart Bainum, Jr. provided significant philanthropic seed capital to create a runway for The Baltimore Banner to scale quickly and reach its full potential. We welcome philanthropic support from Baltimore and beyond, from readers, foundations, corporations, and other institutions". The Venetoulis Institute for Local

Journalism is the 501(c)3 nonprofit umbrella and publisher of The Baltimore Banner

- The Ohio Local News Initiative

  It states that it was formed to meet community information needs lacking the media. It said the American Journalism Project had partnered with community organizations and leaders in Ohio to launch a "network of independent, community-led, nonprofit newsrooms" across Ohio, starting in Cleveland, It said it had raised $5.8 million to start and the American Journalism Project will be the fiscal sponsor. The hiring of around 25 employees will take place in the first quarter of 2022, and the newsroom will be funded through a combination of philanthropy, content partnerships, subscriptions, and events.

  The founding organizations were the Cleveland Foundation, Knight Foundation, Sisters of Charity Foundation, Visible Voice Charitable Fund, and Char and Chuck Fowler Family Foundation.

- The Cardinal News in Roanoke, Virginia

  Formed by former staff members of The Roanoke Times, a nonprofit interested in supporting quality journalism approached its founder about starting an online news site. A subsequent $100,000 grant and a matching amount were the seed money to develop The Cardinal News, which launched in September 2021.

- The Local New for Houston Project

  One of the largest start-ups ever, the project said it intends to answer the community's calls for additional news coverage. It said three of Houston's leading philanthropies – Houston Endowment, the Kinder Foundation, and Arnold Ventures – were launching the news site after a two-year research effort, led by the American Journalism Project. It said the American Journalism Project is also serving as a seed funder, along with the John S. and James L. Knight Foundation, and that more than $20 million had been raised.

- The Daily Springfield Citizen in Springfield, Mo.

  It said its goal is not to duplicate the coverage of other local media, as much as it is to fill the gaps left by the persistent reductions made by for-profit media in staff, coverage, and publication schedules. In announcing its launch, it said it needed to make just enough money to sustain – and hopefully expand – our operations. It had raised enough from local donors to have an annual budget of about $1 million to start with.

Its publisher, David Stoeffler, wrote

> We have a five-year plan to reach sustainability. A start-up fundraising campaign is underway and initial gifts and pledges provide us with confidence we will have the funding to maintain or grow our current operations. In the long run, we will rely on support from readers, donations from local individuals and businesses, and grants from foundations for our funding.

- The Beacon in Kansas City and Wichita, KS

  It launched in March 2020 as a regional nonprofit news network serving Kansas and Missouri. It said Beacon stories are issues in health care, education, economics, environment, and civic government. The Beacon in Kansas City Beacon launched in March 2020 and is part of The Beacon, a regional nonprofit news network serving Kansas and Missouri. It said Beacon stories are issues in health care, education, economics, environment, and civic engagement. It listed a wide array of donors that showed all the different possible sources of start-up money, including those who gave $100,000 or more, including the American Journalism Project, the Ewing Marion Kauffman Foundation, Arnold Ventures, and Report for America. Others at the $25,000 to $99,000 level were the Google News Initiative, the Inasmuch Foundation, Solutions Journalism Network, and the William T. Kemper Foundation. At a lower donation level, it received money from the Facebook Journalism Project and the Robert Wood Johnson Foundation among others.
- The Flatwater Free Press, Omaha, Nebraska

  It intends to focus on investigations and feature stories that matter, according to its site. Co-founded by Matt Wynn, who had been working on investigations for the Gannett newspaper in Omaha, it gathered funding from around the state.

THE COMMUNITY-BACKED START-UP

In a question and answer session, Matt Wynn provided more detail on his long-term planning based on the experience of earlier nonprofit newsroom start-ups.

How much did you raise for the start-up of Flatwater?

We raised $750,000, with a match for an additional $1.5 million promised for three years of funding.

How long did it take to raise that money?

We first did a feasibility study that took six months. We used that to structure our asks. All told it took about 14 months.

Where were the largest portions of fund from?

Local family foundations.

(Flatwater also provides an extensive list of those that gave more than $10,000, showing the wide foundation support it received. The list includes these foundations and again it shows the broad support needed for a state or regional start-up:

- Acklie Charitable Foundation
- Annette & Paul Smith Charitable Foundation
- Arnold Ventures
- CL Werner Foundation
- Claire M. Hubbard Foundation
- Cooper Foundation
- Fund for Nonprofit News at The Miami Foundation
- Gilbert M. & Martha H. Hitchcock Foundation
- Good Words Foundation
- Kitty M. Perkins Foundation
- Lozier Foundation
- Mammel Family Foundation

- Nebraska Community Foundation
- Platte Institute
- Rhonda Seacrest
- Sherwood Foundation
- Weitz Family Foundation)

How many editorial staff members did you have initially? How many business side staff members?

We had 3.5 full-time editorial staff and one full-time and one half-time person on the business side. We also have a fundraising part-timer, a business advisor part-timer and an events part-timer.

How did you know it was the right time to do this? The community need and support?

Legacy media made some deep cuts. I kicked the tires on an idea that's long been on my mind and found support. Wynn said he decided to move forward when support went from theoretical to very real – "when we had 18 months of funding in the bank and a strong suspicion we could easily get to three years".

Regional new barons

A new kind of investor and owner has arisen over the past two decades and is being called regional news barons by university researchers.

- CherryRoad Media of New Jersey – a unit of CherryRoad Technologies founded in 2020 – owns 63 papers in 10 Midwestern states plus a publication serving Fort Leavenworth in Kansas.
- The 125-year-old Kentucky-based Paxton Media owns 115 newspapers in 10 Southern and Midwestern states.
- The West Virginia-based Ogden Newspapers – founded in 1890 – owns 101 papers in 18 states stretching from New Hampshire to Hawaii.

In less than a year, with little fanfare, CherryRoad has gone from owning one newspaper to 63 – and counting. One of the investors said, "It was a good time to get into this business. There were some good values to be had".

Researchers said statements by these firms' investment managers described small newspapers, most with circulation of less than 10,000, as reliable and consistent sources of income for their portfolios of diverse business assets. "Small rural markets, they believed, would be relatively insulated in the coming years from competition — either from traditional media, such as television, or the internet, which was then still in its infancy".

Researchers with the News Deserts project have backgrounded three others in the past and published findings in a paper on the "barons". The background was:

- Community Newspaper Holdings Inc. (CNHI) was founded in 1997, as part of a diverse portfolio of investments made by the Retirement Systems of Alabama. CNHI initially acquired papers from Media General and Hollinger International, as well as additional properties from Thomson in 2000 and Ottaway in 2002.
- Liberty Group Publishing, established in 1998, was financed by Leonard Green & Partners LP, a Los Angeles-based private equity firm that specialized in turning around troubled companies. Liberty Group Publishing initially purchased 160 papers from Hollinger International, which was selling 40 percent of its U.S. community group in an effort to pay down debt.
- American Community Newspapers was established in 1998 as Lionheart Holdings with the financial backing of Weiss, Peck & Greer's private equity group and Waller-Sutton Media Partners LP. It quickly grew through the acquisition of E.W. Scripps Co.'s Dallas Community Newspaper Group and three major purchases from families in Minnesota and Kansas. Lionheart Holdings was rebranded as American Community Newspapers in 2002. In 2004, these investment groups held 352 papers – or 20 percent of all the papers owned by the largest 25 companies. But because these companies

> had purchased small papers, they controlled only 7 percent of the circulation among the top 25 groups.

In that report, researchers said all that would change over the coming turbulent decade as other investment groups moved in, displacing the media barons that dominated the charts in 2004.

> For their part, Liberty Group Publishing and American Community Newspapers went through multiple iterations over the course of the decade as the investment firm managers reshuffled their portfolio, making numerous acquisitions and divestitures. After bankruptcy in 2009, American Community Newspapers ceased to exist, its newspapers sold off to other large companies by its creditors.

Meanwhile, the Liberty Group Publishing morphed into New Media Group/GateHouse. In 2014, only Community Newspaper Holdings Inc. existed much as it had in 2004, but with two dozen fewer newspapers.

The University of North Carolina researchers noted that it is difficult to know how the groups operate.

"In this context, the rise of new media barons raises questions of accountability and transparency: Who makes decisions on the overall strategic direction and content of the newspapers these firms manage? What's the structure of these newspaper-owning companies?"

The researchers also noted that publicly traded newspaper companies are required to submit quarterly and annual reports with audited financial statements and management assessments of the business. But private investment companies are required to disclose only the most basic information.

Researchers found during the pandemic privately owned regional chains "have snapped up dozens of newspapers shed by the mega-chains, as well as smaller family-owned operations".

They also found that two-thirds of the 82 papers Gannett sold in the past two years were bought by CherryRoad or Paxton. Six of the ten largest newspaper owners in 2022 are regional chains – with between 50 and 142 papers apiece in their growing empires.

But they also said that among the regional media chains, several experienced considerable churns in their portfolios during the past two-plus years. Paxton bought 55 papers, but also sold five and closed or merged 10. Ogden bought 28 and closed or merged 11.

In 2022, the Editor and Publisher magazine did an extensive article on CherryRoad Media, which gave deep insight to its business strategy. The article said the CEO and founder Jeremy Gulban wanted his technology company to support local journalism. It said Gulban saw the possibility of modernizing local community papers through his technology company. The company has not only purchased newspapers but done startups in news deserts. The business model focuses on hyperlocal content in addition to modernizing technology in newspapers.

The article quoted, Gulban as saying he had found "a niche with rural weekly papers..." He said rural weeklies seem to work best within their goals of keeping local news in communities while modernizing existing technology. He told the magazine that he was planning on seven to ten publications in every state.

"Our business model, right now, is we want to acquire newspapers that are primarily ones that are struggling, bringing efficiency to the print operation and looking to expand digitally", he said.

Push for more government investment and big tech support

Despite the influx of philanthropic money, the years 2021 and 2022 saw a major push for the U.S. government to increase its support of journalism. Although some journalists questioned the influence government money might exert, a large group of journalists, research groups, and foundations sought backing for federal legislation that would give citizens tax credits for taking out subscriptions for newsrooms. The potential revenue from that would be substantial.

Those proponents of government funding pointed out that newsrooms already received discounts on mailings, were assured of getting lucrative legal notices that must be posted in newspapers or on websites, and that nonprofit newsrooms were basically partly subsidized by the government through tax exemptions. In addition, in the U.S., the federal government has given about $400 million to the Corporation for Public Broadcasting a year and public universities give support to many PBS and NPR stations.

However, earlier efforts to get legislation with government support had failed, and the outlook for the newer legislation was uncertain. (For more see Chapter 4.)

Big tech

As mentioned earlier, big tech companies did start giving back to newsrooms, whose content they had used for years to reap huge profits. Google supplied free software useful to journalists, backed training, and gave tens of millions of dollars in grants to newsrooms. Facebook gave money for business practices and Microsoft began supporting local news initiatives. At the same time, the Australian government and European governments started requiring Google to give significant financial support to newsrooms. Microsoft, however, has begun increasing its support for journalism, including local news projects. (For more, see Chapter 4.)

4

REVENUE STREAMS

Block Club Chicago began in 2018 when former DNAinfo Chicago journalists Shamus Toomey, Stephanie Lulay Graves, and Jen Sabella decided to continue to pursue local neighborhood reporting after DNAinfo was shut down by its billionaire owner Joe Ricketts in 2017.

Ricketts also closed another newsroom at the same time, the Gothamist in New York City, a week after employees had voted to unionize. Ricketts did not mention that issue in letter to readers but wrote that his business plan had not worked out.

In the letter he stated:

> I started DNAinfo in 2009 at a time when few people were investing in media companies. But I believed an opportunity existed to build a successful company that would report unbiased neighborhood news and information. These were stories that weren't getting told, and because I believe people care deeply about the things that happen

DOI: 10.4324/9781315719573-5

> where they live and work, I thought we could build a large and loyal audience that advertisers would want to reach.

He wrote that the two newsrooms had delivered the news to hundreds of thousands of people's email boxes and over 2 million, but that DNA is

> a business, and businesses need to be successful if they are to endure. And while we made important progress toward building DNAinfo into a successful business, in the end, that progress hasn't been sufficient to support the tremendous effort and expense needed to produce the type of journalism on which the company was founded.

He concluded, "I'm hopeful that in time, someone will crack the code on a business that can support exceptional neighborhood storytelling for I believe telling those stories remains essential".

Four years later, Block Club Chicago appeared to have cracked the code as a nonprofit newsroom covering the neighborhoods of Chicago.

The three former DNAinfo employees initially considered staying with a for-profit model but decided in the end to form a nonprofit newsroom.

"We went nonprofit because it was the easiest way to communicate to our readers their subscription dollars would be reinvested in our neighborhood news mission. They wouldn't have to worry those dollars would enrich a hedge fund instead", said Stephanie Lulay Graves, co-founder and co-executive editor.

They quickly ran a successful crowdfunding campaign with KickStarter and received a large grant from Civil, which was an organization based on cryptocurrency and later folded. Ricketts also shared DNAinfo's subscriber list with them.

> From there, they embarked on an ambitious plan to fund Block Club Chicago with subscriptions, donations, grants, merchandise and events. Four years later, they have a staff of more than 20 journalists covering 40 neighborhoods, their subscription revenue is more than $1 million from 18,000 paid subscribers and they have a budget exceeding $3 million with an $1.5-million, three-year grant from American Journalism Project grant to increase the organization's business and administrative capacity.

(For more on Block Club Chicago see the case study below).

Not all nonprofits or for-profit startups grow so quickly. Some exist for years on a budget of $200,000 or less a year that pays for an executive director who edits, fundraises, and manages contract reporters with the help of a volunteer board or just volunteers. Nonetheless, over the past decade the many paths to survival, sustainability, and growth for these newsrooms have been mapped out by associations and organizations set up to help journalists raise the money to run their businesses.

Diverse streams of revenue

The first rule whether nonprofit or for-profit is to have diverse streams of revenue, meaning that if one source of funds dries up, others can fill in the budget gap. It can be diverse categories – subscriptions and donations for example – or diverse within a category – several foundations who give to the organization. Among the many kinds of revenue are:

- Foundation grants
- Individual donors
- Memberships
- Subscriptions
- Events
- Fundraisers
- Sales of services (reporting or data and data analysis)
- Sponsorships and Underwriting
- Advertising
- Training workshops
- Crowdfunding
- Government funding, tax breaks, or subsidies

The Institute for Nonprofit News breaks down the revenue sources each year for its members. In its 2022 index, INN said that 53 percent of revenue for its members came from foundations, with the bulk of national foundation money going to the largest organizations. About 30 percent came from individual giving (including memberships), 15 percent was derived from earned income, which could include such sources as ads and events, and 2 percent from other charitable categories. But the proportions of revenue for any organization can vary widely.

For example, VtDigger, as noted in the previous chapter, is a highly successful nonprofit start-up that is a statewide newsroom for Vermont. Its 2020 revenue consisted of grants, underwriting, individual contributions, and revenue from sale of news stories, totaling about a $2.4 million budget. They noted on their website that they offer "a variety of underwriting options, including high visibility leaderboards, email, inline display ads, native content, podcast and video promotions".

Another example of success, The Texas Tribune reported more than $10 million revenue in its 2021 annual report of which about 26 percent came from foundations, 28 percent from individuals, 20 percent from web sponsorships, 13 percent from its highly touted and numerous events, 8 percent from memberships and 4 percent from other earned income.

Inewsource in San Diego, which has had significant growth in the past decade, reported in 2021 that it receives the vast majority of its revenue, nearly $2 million, from contributions and donations from foundations, individuals, and its "spotlight membership program".

Overall, INN reported that among the INN membership, about 70 percent of the organizations had three or more streams of revenue. About 36 percent had revenue of $250,000 or less in annual revenue, 17 percent had revenue from $250,000 to $500,000, 16 percent had annual revenue of $500,000 to $1 million, 12 percent $1 to $2 million, and 20 percent over $2 million. Newsrooms with smaller revenues largely depended on foundation grants and individual donations often supplemented by funds from NewsMatch, and grants from big tech programs.

Small for-profits

The Local Independent Online News Publishing Association has more than 400 members that are mostly small for-profits with some nonprofits that often are also INN members. In a survey report issued in 2021 on newsrooms, they refer to their members as digital natives that are focused mostly on local reporting. Most of the 700 organizations they researched, which included LION members, were for-profits and often limited liability companies (LLCs). The comprehensive report said most were young organizations with small budgets that depended on advertising. Among the report's observations:

- **The field** is experiencing tremendous growth: 266 organizations started up in the past five years, an increase of nearly 50 percent, representing an average of more than 50 launches per year. The earliest study of the emerging field, in 2010, identified 120 new "locals", indicating that the past decade has seen the number of local sites multiply six times over.
- **Publishers operate** in a challenging financial environment, but the field is making progress. One in five publishers believe their organization has reached sustainability and another two in five say they are heading in that direction.
- **Many of these outlets** are bootstrapped. More than half of all publications surveyed bring in less than $100,000 a year. Only one in ten has revenue of more than $1 million.
- **Many rely heavily** on a single source of significant revenue, most often local advertising. Six in ten publishers said advertising sold locally is a major revenue source. (Author's note: In this aspect, they resemble traditional local weeklies.) Outlets in the study that had multiple sources were more likely to be profitable.
- **The founders** tend to be journalists who lack business and sales expertise, and publishers frequently do not have resources to hire staff dedicated to generating revenue. Among 50 outlets that supplied in-depth information, only half have personnel dedicated to the business side.
- **Founders often** turn to personal funds to get started. Two-thirds said they mostly used their savings or other personal funds to launch. (Author's note: In this aspect, they resemble some of the nonprofits that started in 2008 and 2009.)
- **Many operate** with a mix of staff, part-timers, contractors, and volunteers. Half of the organizations that supplied in-depth data use volunteers in some capacity; among these organizations, volunteers make up about a third of the personnel on average.
- **These outlets** rely heavily on social media for visibility. Seven in ten rated social media as one of the top two drivers of traffic to

their websites. At the same time, more direct reader relationships that drive more revenue, such as email newsletters, were often a low source of traffic.

- **One in seven** of the new locals operates in a news desert, an area where a newspaper has closed or that has traditionally been overlooked. The median revenue of these publications is markedly lower than the field at large.
- **About three-fourths** operate as commercial businesses, most commonly as LLCs. The others are nonprofits, which tend to be larger in size and have more funding.
- For its own membership, LION found that 44 percent have annual revenue under $100,000, 33 percent had revenue between $100,000 and $50000, 7 percent between $500,000, and 11 percent over $1 million.

The study noted,

> In addition to improving profitability, having multiple revenue streams is desirable because it enhances the stability of the enterprise. A publication with three revenue streams is more likely to survive if one stream collapses than an organization that loses its sole revenue source.

LION and the Oasis Project also looked at the different streams of revenue for nonprofits and for-profits and what percentage of newsrooms took in certain kinds of revenue. In for-profit, it found 76 percent of the newsrooms took direct-sold ads, 27 percent took membership, and 23 percent had subscription revenue. For its fewer nonprofit members, 74 percent had revenue from philanthropies, 71 percent took small gift donations, 47 percent had major gift revenue, and 25 percent had membership revenue.

Running a business

If having diverse streams of revenue is one business rule for newsrooms, an equally important one is for journalists running newsrooms to accept they are indeed a small business - not only a cause -, whether they are a for-profit or nonprofit. There needs to be audience or customers that want the content. Revenues must come in, bills must be paid, employees and contractors hired, insurance bought, bookkeeping done, and tactical and strategic changes must be made periodically to adapt to the economy.

However, as the surveys and statistics show, there are different approaches and models. Generally, a for-profit newsroom plans to succeed on earned income: advertising sales, subscriptions, and other services. A nonprofit newsroom plans to succeed based on the thought that earned income – such as subscriptions and advertising – will be a smaller portion of its revenue and that tax-deductible donations, grants, and memberships will make up the bulk of its revenue.

Some in the field believe that the difference between the two models of for-profit and nonprofit community and investigative reporting are merging, but the apparent similarities are more likely because the traditional for-profit newsrooms are seeking donations and soliciting grants just as nonprofits are, thus quietly acknowledging that the for-profit business model for community and watchdog news is still failing.

Indeed, at the beginning of the nonprofit newsroom boom, some thought that nonprofit newsrooms were a bridge from an island of failed for-profits to an island of a new for-profit model. But it turned out that nonprofit bridge was actually the next island.

Strategies for running a business for revenue and sustainability

The majority of training programs at different organizations and associations for journalists running community and watchdog newsrooms are often quite similar.

A look at the robust offerings at the INN shows the needs for journalists running newsrooms. INN also offers numerous case studies. LION, the American Journalism Project, the Online News Association, and big tech also have courses and workshops and have elements that promote good practices.

Among the training courses are:

- Creating a start-up that could be a sole proprietorship, a limited liability company or a corporation that is a nonprofit, for-profit, a public benefit company, or cooperative
- Building an audience
- Finding legal, accounting, and human resources services
- Building a membership program
- Building a subscriptions program
- Making money off community events
- Running a fundraising campaign
- Building sponsorships and underwriting
- Selling advertising
- Marketing through social media
- Successful newsletters
- Donor and foundation relations

For-profit training will generally have more training on advertising sales, particularly digital, and a heavier emphasis on paid subscriptions and strategies for paywalls.

Blogs at the beginning

The association networks generally do not train for blogging or solo operations although some of the for-profit starts ups can be, or resemble, blogs – as noted in the last chapter – since blogs laid the groundwork for the digital future of news and the need for digital news models long before traditional media could accept what was happening.

Over the past two decades, the basic revenue stream for for-profit digital news by a single journalist was based on the blog model – the amount of audience traffic to the blog, paid ads based on the traffic, and payments for linking to affiliated blogs and websites. Bloggers have a simple system and show a single journalist can be a profit center. Bloggers build an audience and sell ads through brokers or social media based on the audience traffic they create. In some cases, solo journalists might write a newsletter or blog for a company that carries their work, such as Substack, and split the subscription revenue.

Another strategy for smaller newsrooms is the possibility of adding a focus or expertise on a particular topic or datasets as some commercial and nonprofit newsrooms have. Newsrooms that focus on politics, finance, sports, and entertainment have been among the most successful for-profits.

The freemium model – some content for free, some for pay – has proven successful for a nonprofit like Guidestar (now Candid) that offers a sizeable amount of information from its data and research on nonprofits, but has a paywall for deeper research and information. Michele Leder, who found Footnoted, which is a website, newsletter, and data distributor based on Securities and Exchange Commission data and information, is often cited as a successful revenue model and she has been able to charge higher subscription rates because of her clientele.

INN offers a recipe for success that emphasizes understanding audiences and building on that understanding.

In the LION/Oasis study of members and startups, also emphasized audience and made these suggestions:

- Working aggressively to build and engage a direct audience, ideally with a staff person dedicated to audience growth and prioritizing email newsletters over social media. The more points of connection the news organization owns, the more stable and loyal its readership becomes. As more digital tools become available, experimentation is key.
- Focusing on building a stable paid workforce, starting with a budget and a timeline for paying salaries as revenue grows.
- As INN and others suggested, developing multiple revenue streams and building staff accordingly. "This could mean hiring one person to take the lead on ad sales and another to take the lead on audience development and reader revenue".
- Building diverse and inclusive newsrooms. LION noted, "Not only will this strengthen community connections, but there is ample evidence linking staff diversity to greater profitability and innovation".

LION also called upon support organizations such as foundations and training groups to have a significant role, saying they should expand educational programs and resources to assist digital news founders on the path to sustainability; expand programs that offer modest start-up capital to outlets in key communities such as local news deserts; develop programs to increase diversity and inclusivity in newsrooms; and help find business models that work in small markets.

"With many of the new local outlets operating in news deserts and communities that do not have a strong traditional revenue base, support for innovation will be critical", the report said.

Collaborations: cost-saver and revenue generator

Other studies emphasize the value of collaborations among organizations that can save costs, share resources, expand audience and more recently generate interest and revenue from foundations and donors. However, collaborations do not come in one format.

The Center for Cooperative Media at Montclair State University identified six models in its 2017 report "Comparing Models of Collaborative Journalism", the author and research director Sarah Stonbely, listed those models as:

- Temporary and separate One-time/finite projects in which partners create content separately and share it.
- Temporary and co-creating: One-time/finite project in which partners work together to create content.
- Temporary and integrated: One-time/finite projects in which partners share content/data/resources at the organizational level.
- Ongoing and separate: Ongoing/open-ended collaborations in which partners create content separately and share it.
- Ongoing and co-creating: Ongoing/open-ended collaborations in which partners work together to create content.
- Ongoing and integrated: Ongoing/open-ended collaborations in which partners share content/data/resources at the organizational level.

The study, however, did not delve into how the collaborations might produce revenue through subscriptions or memberships.

But INN has recently turned its attention to great potential through organized collaborations. It has begun building subnetworks of common interests of many members such as those covering rural issues or indigenous communities. INN recently noted that foundations are funding collective journalism that can reshape the economics of local news as well as impact.

It said in a report in 2022 that "a unique holistic approach" to funding collaborations enables foundations to fund critical local and small expert newsrooms at scale. It said that funding injects new revenue into local reporting and creates earned revenue opportunities.

It said INN had received funding for 40 plus newsrooms in 20 states and was building a rural news coverage network. Hearkening back to the Pocantico Declaration, which laid out a plan for network for collaboration for news, INN said it saw itself INN as a platform for collaborative revenue opportunities that would include the issue and place-based funding pools and channels. It also saw creation of earned revenue programs and a sponsorship network. "INN's collaborations are the building blocks of a modern news network" that will create the framework for a newly shaped industry.

INN also noted that it had initial investments from the Knight and Walton foundations and the Google News Initiative for building a $3 million, two-year project

If successful, the INN collaboration money model would add to ongoing international journalism collaborations – such as those run by the International Consortium for Investigative Journalism, the Pulitzer Center for Crisis Reporting, and the Organized Crime and Corruption Reporting Project – that have received significant funding from foundations and governments.

Report for America

Another project that has pooled philanthropy money for newsrooms is Report for America. It has raised money from foundations to pay part of the wages of journalists of small to medium size newsrooms, both non-profit and for-profit.

The organization said in 2022, "A key function of Report for America is to unlock millions of dollars in U.S. philanthropy to help America's decimated local news ecosystems. In 3 years, more than $15 million has been generated for Report for America newsrooms".

The organization pre-screens "emerging journalists who meet the needs of different newsrooms and Report for America pays half their salaries, up to $25,000". The newsroom pays the other half by itself or with the help of local donors split the rest and the Report will assist newsrooms in raising local donations. The Report said its approach "to help unlock a sustainable third revenue stream of philanthropy with the help of our local sustainability and development team".

The amount of money for reporters in the program has increased dramatically going from $861,000 in 2019, to $4,616,059 in 2020, to $7,422,468 in 2021, and $8 million for 2022. It said nearly half the reporters are of color.

The Report listed among its givers of $250,000 to $2 million a who's who of foundations supporting journalism. They included the Conrad N. Hilton Foundation, the Corporation for Public Broadcasting, the Craig Newmark Philanthropies, Google News Initiative, Jon D. and Catherine T. MacArthur Foundation, Joyce Foundation, Just Trust, Knight Foundation, Lumina Foundation, Meta Journalism Project, Microsoft and the Robert Wood Johnson Foundation.

Big tech funding

Over the past decade big tech, such as Google and Facebook (now Meta), who have made tens of billions of dollars in advertising by using unpaid content from news organizations, have been spending hundreds of millions of dollars in business and technology training and grants.

More pressure has been exerted by news organizations and governments for them to share some of the riches that have reaped by using a news content for free. The Australian government passed legislation in 2021 requiring Google there to share some of their profits with news organizations and European governments have been looking at similar legislation. The next three years.

For example, for years, both Google and Facebook have been steering hundreds of millions of dollars toward newsrooms. Those are sums of money that seriously match foundation funding and, in some cases, more than matched.

Some critics say the efforts are self-serving for a better public image and to fend off government regulation. They say the initiatives are also being done to promote their products by training journalists to use them. Critics also say it is ironical and self-serving that the tech companies that seriously damaged the news industry by using its content for free, now are trying to prop up newsrooms.

Nonetheless, many newsrooms have welcomed the assistance and revenue. Recently, Microsoft, which has not received the same kind of criticism because it did generate revenue from using news content for free, also has embarked on initiatives to help newsrooms, especially local ones, so more revenue for newsrooms will be coming from that tech company.

Indeed, in 2021 Facebook announced that it had invested $600 million since 2018 to support the news industry and planned to put at least $1 billion into the industry over the next three years. Google also pledged $1 billion. However, by 2022, it appeared Facebook might be changing its strategy again when it announced the end of a revenue-sharing program with publishers and began cuts in its news staff.

Facebook's journalism initiatives included the Facebook Journalism Project's (FJP) Accelerator Program. It describes the Accelerator Program as providing mentoring and supports to news organizations focused on digital reader revenue business models.

The program was offered by Facebook and administered by the Local Media Association. It defined "reader revenue business models as digital subscriptions or memberships (inclusive of donations, reader contributions, and memberships)".

The program said some initiatives that could be developed based on achieving sustainability include:

- Investing in new technology platforms to customize content for current paying readers
- Developing and promoting new email newsletters
- Building new editorial products supported by reader contributions
- Improving conversion rates by streamlining a site's user experience

The program said it had ten or more weeks of curriculum and include mentoring and online meetings to help to participate publications' business operations.

In 2021, the program announced it had accepted 30 news organizations in North America, and more than half of the 30 were owned or led by Black, Indigenous, Latinx, Asian, and/or other communities of color. It said 75 percent focused on local news

The program was "built on four pillars": (1) virtual workshops where participants listen to experts and participate in hands-on exercises, (2) weekly calls with a dedicated, world-class expert coach, (3) grant funding to execute projects using lessons learned and (4) a community of shared practice in which people work together to support each other's progress. They said there was a mix of subscription and membership revenue models.

Some newsrooms that have received the Accelerator training have praised it. Andy Hall, the executive director of Wisconsin Watch said, the Facebook Membership Accelerator

> played a major role in helping Wisconsin Watch launch its first real membership program, and first significant branding and marketing campaigns, drawing upon a $100,000 Facebook grant to support our hiring of a membership manager and consultants and to pay for a branding campaign as well as digital, print and broadcast marketing efforts.

He added that "it helped sharpen our ability to identify problems, develop strategies for addressing them and moving forward as a team, quickly".

Back in 2017, Facebook announced new initiatives in "The Facebook (now Meta) Journalism Project".

It said wanted to do collaborative development of news products and would connect its product and engineering teams to newsrooms; develop new story-telling formats that would allow newsrooms to present packages of stories to targeted readers. Like so many trying to assist journalism, Facebook said it wanted to support local news and promote independent media on its platform. And it wanted to help with emerging business models such as expanding live "ad breaks" in videos.

Facebook also said it would be working closely with INN, LION, and other groups on training for Facebook products and business tools for journalists.

Google and newsrooms

Google has offered monetary support, business training, and training in Google tools to newsrooms. It has said Google is one of the world's largest financial supporters of journalism and that over the past 20 years, it has "collaborated closely with news partners and provided billions of dollars to support the creation of quality journalism". It also launched the Google News Initiative to expand its work "with journalists, publishers, and industry leaders to help build a resilient future for news around the globe".

Google has partnered with INN and LION, ONA, and other news associations. Among the programs it launched were news labs in North America, "focused on helping small and medium-sized news organizations in the United States and Canada grow their digital businesses".

Google said one lab offered participants customized coaching related to their business goals that included ways to implement specific steps to advance their goals and to learn from peers who face similar business problems. The program was free for accepted participants. Another lab called the North American Sponsorships Lab was set up for "small to medium-sized nonprofit or public service-oriented news organizations that seek to increase revenue from event sponsorships, sponsored content, and other earned revenue sources".

A third lab focused on subscriptions and was meant to help small and medium size newsrooms with subscriptions and increase "sustainable digital reader revenue".

Google said over the years it had more than 7,000 news partners and had provided more than $300 million in funding. It also has run the Google News Initiative Labs, where groups of news organizations come together "to tackle specific business problems, with support from Google and industry experts". In addition, through its Google News Initiative Startups Program, it provides six months of training and capital to create and improve news products that will help with sustainability.

Google said its Startups Lab is a six-month experience that provides a cohort of news founders with coaching and capital to evolve their news products and accelerate their companies on the path to sustainability. And it added a program called "Local News Experiments Project" to help create "The Local News Experiments Project aims to create sustainable, all-digital news organizations in communities currently underserved by local news".

Google had already created the Google News 2018 to fund millions of dollars in training and grants for newsrooms. In its impact report for 2021, it said it introduced the Digital Growth Program to help organizations accelerate growth in advertising and consumer revenue and strengthen their core foundations in audience development, products, and data.

Google also said it created a journalism emergency relief fund that gave $40 million to more than 5,600 local newsrooms for global issues such as COVID-19, which has highlighted the importance of reliable reporting and the trustworthiness of news organizations.

Overall, Google said its News Initiative is to help journalism thrive in the digital age. It said its efforts focus on three pillars: working with the news industry to evolve their business models and drive sustainable growth, elevating quality journalism, and empowering news organizations with new technology.

Wisconsin Watch also has participated in a Google program and Hall said, "Our GNI grant with Milwaukee Neighborhood News Service enabled us to experiment and collaborate (including the hiring of Outlier Media) on the launch of News414, a text news service".

He said it would have not been possible without the Google money. Although there were many strings that were attached to the financial award, and it was a labor-intensive and sometimes confusing process, he was still happy with the outcome of the project. He said, "in the end, well worth it, and News414 continues to evolve as it serves residents of underserved Milwaukee neighborhoods".

Microsoft

In 2020, Microsoft announced a new program to help support journalism. It was called Rebuilding Local News, a pilot program, and Microsoft said it would work "colleges and universities, leaders and organizations, and their wider communities to provide critical support to local newsrooms and help them tell stories in new ways. At the same time, we're experimenting with new revenue streams and funding models".

In October 2020, Microsoft launched its Journalism Initiative to counter the loss of local news. It said the initiative would work to combat disinformation, expand news distribution and pilot a new community-based program that looks at ways to provide journalists and newsrooms new tools, technology, and capacity in order to expand reach and efficiency for local news outlets.

In its announcement, Microsoft said it had expanded its local journalism pilot program to include Northeast Wisconsin. They said they were partnering with Report for America to support five U.S. newsrooms, a majority of which are in rural communities.

The first pilot programs were in Fresno, California; Yakima, Washington; El Paso, Texas and Juarez, Mexico; and Jackson, Mississippi. Microsoft worked with local community foundations to support local newsrooms "with the aim of helping them use the latest tools and technology to tell stories in new ways, experiment with new revenue streams and funding models, and work together with community organizations".

Microsoft touted the cooperative and collaborative approach among the newsrooms it supported. "We're seeing newsrooms that once competed for stories now sharing content". It said also convened sessions among the newsrooms so they could share best practices and also did training in collaborations and data training.

Microsoft also cited its work with and financial support for Report for America to help increase good business practices, provide technology and training in five newsrooms, and to provide salaries for a journalist in each of those newsrooms in addition to mentorship and other help. It also cited a $1 million grant to the for-profit newspaper Seattle Times to create three reporting positions and a collaboration with the American Journalism Project. It also announced a $245,000 grant to offer free legal assistance to small news organizations.

Government revenue

More, and possibly substantial, government funding in the U.S. remains one more possibility. Some media researchers have suggested that as nonprofit local news increases in stature, it may have an opportunity to gain in that area.

"The reality is that across the globe most democratic nations have a robust noncommercial public interest media landscape, mostly publicly funded", said Josh Stearns of Democracy Fund.

> In the U.S. we have far less public funding but we have a much more robust nonprofit and philanthropic sector. As the traditional business model that has supported local news erodes it's critical for philanthropy to help preserve and reinvent journalism as a public good.

A coalition of journalism organizations have been pushing for a tax credit for those who subscribe to a news organization. Furthermore, others, like Susan Minow, author of "Saving Journalism", and media researchers Robert McChesney and John Nichols, have said that only government funding can replace the billions lost in print advertising and resulting loss of reporters and news. They have estimated the amount needed would be $35 billion.

"The history of American communications and news business *requires* focus on private enterprise but for the bulk of American history, governmental involvement has been integral to the structure, financing, and effectiveness of the news industry", Minow wrote.

U.S. governments have assisted newspapers with favorable postal rates and state laws have required hundreds of millions of dollars in legal advertisements to be placed in newspapers, and provided tax breaks to nonprofits. But the coalition has been pushing for ambitious government tax subsidies that would create a massive revenue stream to newsrooms, particularly those that are local.

The effort calls for rebuilding local news and it has been lobbying for support for federal legislation called the Local Journalism Sustainability Act, which proposes a series of tax credits that would encourage news consumers to pay for subscriptions or donate to nonprofit newsrooms, help with payroll costs of keeping journalists and assist small businesses in buying ads in local news media.

In outlining the proposal, the leader of the coalition, Stephen Waldman, who is a co-leader of Report for America, said the proposal:

- Focuses entirely on local news
- Helps local news by amplifying the choices of consumers and small businesses, rather than having the government pick winners and losers
- Is strictly nonpartisan and guards against government favoritism or manipulation of media
- Helps small media as well as larger players, nonprofits as well as commercial models, including communities of color and rural areas.
- Helps a variety of platforms, including digital-first websites as well as newspapers, radio and TV
- Is based on the tax code and is therefore not subject to annual appropriations process or limits
- Would help create a stronger, more inclusive local news system in the future, not merely prop up existing players.

The legislation would provide a tax credit of up $250 a year for a person to subscribe or donate to local news, although a subscriber would have to spend some of their own money. A donation would be a tax credit instead of a deduction.

A donation to a nonprofit news organization mostly becomes a tax credit (which is subtracted, below the line, from your final tax bill) instead of a less-beneficial tax deduction (which is subtracted from your taxable income).

Waldman said the proposal would prevent a government agency from picking newsrooms to support and it could encourage more digital subscriptions which, he said, many local news leaders believe is the only sustainable revenue for local news. He noted the proposal had a payroll tax credit for journalists that give news organizations a tax credit of up to $25,000 in the first year and $15,000 in the second year to help cover salaries of journalists. He said he hoped that would stop the steady loss of journalists in the industry. He noted it's a payroll tax break rather than an income tax break so it could work for nonprofit newsrooms.

The third piece of the proposal was given a refundable tax credit to small businesses to advertise in local news. The proposal would give local small businesses up to $5,000 in tax credits for advertising in local news operations. He said it could include local TV and radio too.

Overall, Waldman said the definition of local news and journalists in the legislation was a bit fuzzy, but acceptable.

Whether the federal legislation or legislation like it eventually passes, it has opened up again a broad discussion of what governments can do to support journalism, and that discussion could lead to broad and substantial government support, as happens in some other countries, rather than a continuing jigsaw puzzle of efforts.

CASE STUDY IN SUBSCRIPTION SUCCESS – BLOCK CLUB CHICAGO

Stephanie Lulay Graves is a co-founder and managing editor of Block Club Chicago, a nonprofit, reader-funded newsroom dedicated to delivering essential coverage of Chicago's diverse neighborhoods. Here is a question and answer with her on Block Club's journalism and business model, especially on its extraordinary subscription growth. I have served on its board since its founding and these questions stem from my first-hand witnessing of its success.

First, how do you decide on your coverage?

Our full-time reporters are geographically assigned to cover a small area – typically two or three neighborhoods – instead of being assigned a traditional beat like cops or courts. Our reporters don't parachute in once to cover a story, only coming in from a Downtown newsroom once a month to write about a crime. Instead, they are embedded in the communities they cover, talking to residents, highlighting new businesses, and attending meetings every day. Thanks to our focus on accessibility and public service journalism, our readership and impact have grown exponentially in the past three years.

How many communities do you cover and what are the demographics?

Block Club is focused on serving 12 key community areas in Chicago. Six of the 12 areas are majority Black or Hispanic neighborhoods on the South and West sides, according to census data.

- Englewood/Chatham/Auburn Gresham: 96% Black
- Hyde Park/South Shore/Woodlawn: 75% Black
- Pilsen/Little Village/Back of the Yards: 77% Hispanic
- Austin/Garfield Park/North Lawndale: 86% Black
- Bronzeville/Douglas/Kenwood: 68% Black
- Logan Square/Humboldt Park/Avondale/Hermosa: 56% Hispanic (26% white, 14% Black, 2% Asian, 2% other)
- Irving Park/Albany Park/Lincoln Square/Ravenswood: 43% white (39% Hispanic, 12% Asian, 3% Black, 3% other)
- West Loop/West Town/Wicker Park/Bucktown: 52% white (20% Hispanic, 17% Black, 9% Asian, 2% other)
- Rogers Park/Uptown/Andersonville/Edgewater: 53% white (20% Black, 18% Hispanic, 9% Asian)
- Jefferson Park/Portage Park/Norwood Park/Edison Park: 63% white
- Lakeview/Lincoln Park/Near North Side: 75% white

One of those beats – Lakeview/Lincoln Park/Old Town – is home to the largest concentration of the city's LGBTQ population. And the Irving Park/Albany Park/Lincoln Square/Ravenswood beat is home to a majority of people of color population.

These neighborhoods have historically been uncovered or maligned by legacy news media.

How do you offer your news?

In terms of our products, our readers are able to access our robust coverage in a variety of ways. Every morning, our free newsletter with stories from across Chicago goes out to about 110,000 people.

Paying members have access to our neighborhood-specific newsletters, which go out twice per week. These hyperlocal newsletters include local event listings, links to stories by other outlets and smaller stories that may not rise to the level of our morning newsletters.

The reporter in each beat also writes a personal note at the top of these twice-weekly newsletters, offering a behind-the-scenes look at how a story came together and asking for tips, suggestions, or other feedback.

In just three years, Block Club has achieved what many in local news have been fighting to accomplish for decades: A sustainable, reader-supported, journalist-run local news operation.

What has the increase in subscriptions been annually? How much did your Kickstarter campaign help?

Before we launched, we had in 2018 we had 2,500 subscribers. We announced we were launching a nonprofit newsroom focused on Chicago's neighborhoods in February 2018 and launched a Kickstarter campaign to court pre-launch subscribers. This was three months after DNAinfo shuttered. We ended up raising $183,700 through that one-month Kickstarter campaign, including more than pre-launch 3,000 subscribers.

What happened when Block Club went live?

The site went live in June 2018. We have six reporters and three editors. One reporter was hired because of the success of the Kickstarter campaign. By December 2019, we had tripled our subscribers to 10,000.

Then by March 2020, because of COVID, more people were reading the news and had a need for reliable information. We immediately dropped the paywall on anything related to COVID-19. Much of our content is free through the duration of pandemic (South and West Side news, breaking news, election news, etc.)

In June 2020, our subscribers had increased to 13,000 on our second anniversary. Revenue from subscriptions had increased to nearly

$1 million. By December we had 15,000 paid subscribers. One year later we were at 18,000 because of a successful neighborhood print campaign.

Your goal has been 20,000 subscribers. How close are you to that? What's the next goal?

We're at 18,500 now. As we grow, we know we'll have to work harder to reach new subscribers and replace subscribers who have "churned" (dropped). Part of that strategy will include expanding our total readership. We still have a very attainable current goal of reaching 20,000 and then 25,000 within several years with the help of our new business team.

How did you decide on the annual price of about $59?

We set the annual subscription price at $59 based on a review of our largest competitors' subscription prices: the Chicago Tribune and the Chicago Sun-Times. We wanted to be competitive with them while being affordable to a wide cross-section of the city. We do offer subscribers higher tiers where they can pay more if they choose. And those are popular. We currently have 1,260 subscribers who pay $100 a year.

What does a subscriber get that the public doesn't? How do you decide that?

At Block Club, we operate under a freemium model. Much of our content is free – our South and West Side coverage, breaking news, public health coverage, and election coverage are free to all readers. Paywalled coverage includes our in-depth features, updates on development, and other neighborhood issues. Readers can read five paywalled stories each month before they are asked to subscribe.

Because of our commitment to underserved neighborhoods on the South and West sides, all of our South and West Side newsletters are free.

Our North Side and Downtown newsletters are available only to subscribers.

We are also planning curated events for subscribers and other perks.

How much more do you get in small donations? What is ratio of small donations to subscriptions?

We received over $500,000 in small donations since we launched. Outside of the Kickstarter, we've had 3,218 different people make donations between $5 and $5,000, with the vast majority under $50.

Our ratio of subscribers (annual and monthly) to donations is about 15 to 1. Some [of our subscribers also donate to Block Club.

How do you ensure low-income residents have enough access to your news?

In short, all of our coverage of the South and West sides, majority Black and Latino neighborhoods that have long been uncovered and maligned by the legacy news media, is free. The corresponding newsletters are free, too. We are grateful to Chicago's foundations who generously support this work so we can embed full-time reporters to serve these neighborhoods.

Our ground-level approach of embedding reporters in communities is the bedrock of Block Club and has led to a more accurate portrayal of neighborhoods since our founding. Over time, it allows reporters and communities to build trust, too.

How did you (the team) convince American Journalism Project to fund Block Club even though it is subscription based?

We made the case that the vast majority of our content is available to people without a subscription, including coverage of the city's underserved areas on the South and West sides. We also do not require a subscription for breaking crime news, COVID-19 coverage, election coverage, and public service reporting. We believe that explanation of our "freemium" model combined with the overall success we've had attracting subscribers made a compelling case.

ANOTHER CASE STUDY: THE SUCCESS OF POLITICO AND ITS SALE

"There have been some success stories when it comes to revenue if a newsroom is what is known as a niche publication such as Politco, which focused from its early days on the drama and minutiae of Washington DC politics".

As Jeff Kaye and Stephen Quinn wrote in their 2010 book, "Funding Journalism in the Digital Age",

> Publishers of newsletters focusing on the latest key facts and figures and analysis about industries and markets, such entertainment, oil and pharmaceuticals have always been able to charge hundreds or even thousands of dollars for subscriptions that give readers must-have proprietary information.

In a 2021 article for Nieman Labs, Josh Benton suggested that Politico's success – and its purchase by a German publishing company for more than $1 billion – could offer lessons to any start-up newsroom.

Calling them smart moves, Benton noted,

> Some of these ideas are available to nearly any news organization; others only make sense for an outlet that's targeting a very particular audience or working a very specific beat. You wouldn't want a world where every media company approached news the way Politico does — but that doesn't mean there's not a ton to learn from their successes.

Among the ideas and practices Benton pointed out while acknowledging Politico (which began in 2007) was a polarizing topic:

- "Politico itself was free but it recognized early on something airlines have known for a long time: It's a lot easier to make a lot of money from a few of your customers than a little from everyone... In 2010, rather than a paywall, Politico launched Politico Pro, an almost completely distinct service aimed at people with *real* money: trade groups, lobbyists, defense contractors, banks, health care conglomerates, and the like. With high-value, minute-by-minute updates — often on inside-baseball subjects too boring for the broader audience to be interested in — Politico Pro took the premium-research business into the digital age".

- It built a standalone, strong newsletter. "Thinking of a newsletter as a distinct, standalone editorial product — not a marketing tool for the website or a glorified RSS feed — was still not very common back then".
- It had an entrepreneurial spirit in the newsroom, so much so that reporters left Politico to form their own news organizations.
- Learning and adapting to the online world as it changes. Benton recalls that Politico built an app for Blackberry phones when they were popular and then retained the idea of a newsletter going into an email inbox when Blackberries faded.

5

ADVANCES IN DIGITAL TOOLS AND INNOVATION FOR NEWS

In 2021, Big Local News, a project at Stanford University, began a project to download and organize agendas of public agencies in California and throughout the U.S. and make them available to journalists and the public.

The idea of automating the downloads and distribution of agendas was straightforward and much needed, especially by smaller traditional newsrooms that had lost staff and small startups.

The project, known as Agenda Watch, advertised its services as "learn about newsworthy public meetings before they happen. Track government action at the city, county, and district levels. Find local stories that matter to readers".

It added, "our software sifts through documents, then sends you an email digest of the agenda items relevant to your region and beat".

This is one of many automation efforts underway. Whether it is a traditional or start-up newsroom, there is a race to solve the challenge of

DOI: 10.4324/9781315719573-6

making use of new technologies to speed up production of stories and actually improve stories and content, especially for small newsrooms.

Eliminating repetitious tasks for journalists and creating interactive and visual stories that are packed with evidence-based content and useful data is one sure way to increase revenue through a broader audiences and methods that are cost-saving. Efforts to do this through data-driven stories and artificial intelligence tools have been ongoing but they have accelerated recently.

What has been lagging is a concerted effort to integrate these approaches with mobile devices.

It seems obvious to start with a mobile device strategy but sometimes, as the great writer Goethe said, "The hardest thing to see is what is in front of your eyes".

But walk into any classroom or across any university campus and almost everyone is looking at their mobile phones. Walk down a city street and the scene is the same. While a mobile phone user may be texting friends, looking up restaurants at which to eat, or how to get from one place to another, that user inevitably will be first viewing and reading news stories and getting news alerts on a mobile phone or other devices.

The conference, MobileMe&You, has been focused on progress and strategies in mobile news since 2015. Conceived of and run by Gary Kebbel, a former professor, Knight Foundation program officer, and newsroom innovator, it bills itself as "an annual journalism and technology conference about storytelling on mobile media platforms. It highlights new and innovative techniques and teaches best practices for communicating to mobile-media audiences".

As a Knight Chair at the University of Illinois at Urbana-Champaign, I assist with the conference planning and operations, along with Jeremy Gilbert, a Knight Chair in digital news at Northwestern University.

The conference offers an array of sessions each year. Included in recent years have been:

- Storytelling with mobile devices
- Using artificial intelligence and machine learning to automate news and machine learning, such as downloading and organizing data sets, and writing short stories

- Using geolocation technology and spatial journalism to guide news
- Implementing augmented and virtual reality in a newsroom
- Using texting to deliver news, data and to crowdsource
- Developing mobile news products
- Keeping up with developing drone technology and drone journalism
- Using bots in the newsroom
- Workshops in using mobile devices for audio and video newsgathering

The MobileMe conference schedules themselves are useful catalogs of the latest developments in mobile news. Other conferences, run by the National Institute for Computer-Assisted Reporting, the Global Investigative Journalism, and the Computation + Journalism Conference offer similar sessions and more hands-on, how-to sessions.

However, as with the advent of the web, journalists and the journalism profession have been slow to fully embrace the mobile world and other forms of technology. But now it is sprinting to catch up. By the time this chapter is published, there will be more technological advances in journalism but here are some of the new approaches thus far for what might be referred to not as newsroom of the future, but the newsroom of now.

Lifestreams and web free

First, however, a conceptual although ultimately practical digression. In 2010, David Gelernter, a visionary computer scientist who first saw the power of computer programs to reflect and augment daily life in his book, "Mirror Worlds", wrote an article in Wired Magazine that said the way we would process information would be less fixed and more a matter of dealing with "life streams". The provocative article was entitled, "The End of the Web, Search, and Computer as We Know It".

He wrote: "It all began with the 'lifestream', a phenomenon that I predicted in the 1990s and shared in the pages of Wired almost exactly 16 years ago". He said the lifestream "arrived in the form of blog posts and RSS feeds, Twitter and other chatstreams, and Facebook walls and timelines".

He said, "Today, this diary-like structure is supplanting the spatial one as the dominant paradigm of the cybersphere. The web will be history".

While the web is not gone, the concept of dealing with streaming (or it might be roughly synonymously called scrolling) is a part of what mobile newsrooms and audiences are dealing with. The mobile newsstream can lead to Web and social media sites, but journalists and news users are often dipping only into the stream itself of information and stories flowing by.

Gerlernter called it a time-based structure. He wrote,

> It is a bit like moving from a desktop to a magic diary: Picture a diary whose pages turn automatically, tracking your life moment to moment ... Until you touch it, and then, the page-turning stops. The diary becomes a sort of reference book: a complete and searchable guide to your life. Put it down, and the pages start turning again.

As with "Mirror Worlds" it took years for some of his predictions to come to fruition but is valuable to keep them in mind as news technology becomes more sophisticated. Of late, the phrase "web free" has pointed at this direction.

Data-driven stories, automation, and text

Over the past three decades, journalists have become more comfortable with analyzing and visualizing datasets and posting the datasets themselves and their analysis and visualizations to the web and social media. Journalists also learned to structure unstructured data such as text, audio, and video so it also could be analyzed and visualized.

Advances in data journalism have led to stories with more context and more detail and award-winning projects that change legislation, improve regulations and cut government waste. Those stories increase audiences and therefore increase revenue through donations, subscriptions, and memberships in organizations. However, few organizations have implemented plans to bring in revenue from data on a freemium model such as Guidestar has with its nonprofit data and document collection on nonprofits. Guidestar offers basic regulatory filings for free, but when it adds value to them through analysis and collation, it sets up tiers of charges.

For years, Investigative Reporters and Editors ran a data library that brought in up to $100,000 per year because it collected government data, often through Freedom of Information requests that could take months, and then cleaned the data to eliminate as many errors in the data as possible. That saved hundreds of newsrooms time and they were willing to pay low charges for the data. The newsrooms were also willing to pay for data library staff to do analysis and visualization of data which reporters in newsrooms could use for the basis of stories.

Most of the data library is with ProPublica now, which it sells data for low prices to journalists and high prices to other professions. But most newsrooms are not taking advantage of the model. Some major publications, like Bloomberg, or Mining News, however, employ this method for financial and corporate data and reaped large amounts of revenue.

However, the move to data-driven stories has laid the foundation for entrance into the field of more coders and training for journalists to code in order to make better use of government and business data. That has resulted in a higher sophistication in the use of technology in journalism and set the stage for better automation in the newsrooms since as journalists became more adept with structured (rows and columns) data and unstructured, they began automating more of their work and routines.

Text for news

One fairly new and developing approach is using text messaging to distribute and gather news. That approach also helps to solve part of the issue of low-income and communities of color being excluded from access to news and information because of the lack of access to broadband Internet.

An excellent example of that approach has been "Outlier Media", a nonprofit news project that started in Detroit that is now part of another innovative nonprofit, MuckRock, which has helped automate and track Freedom of Information requests and acquired "DocumentCloud", a project that allows journalists to upload and analyze government and business documents.

Outlier, founded by a lawyer Sarah Alvarez, first did what has become standard data-driven journalism: found useful government datasets on the web, scraped and downloaded them from the Web, and then put them into an overall database.

Among the initial databases she used were:

- Detroit Parcel Points Ownership Database (Detroit Open Data)
- City of Detroit Building, Safety Engineering and Environmental Department (Detroit Open Data)
- City of Detroit Water and Sewerage Department (FOIA requests)
- The Office of the Wayne County Treasurer (LOVELAND Technologies web scraper)

She then expanded her project into what she called "service journalism", defined as "news consumer-oriented approach to identifying information needs, building trust with news consumers, and creating accountability".

She automated the texting batches of citizens' phone numbers "with an offer to search housing, eviction, and blight ticket data — helping users make decisions about finding new places to live, taking care of neighboring properties, and holding local officials accountable", according to a Nieman Labs article in 2021. Alvarez or a data reporter from Outlier would follow up if the database could not answer the request.

"By drawing on a hefty database of information compiled from city and county public sources and automating initial responses, Alvarez has built the one-woman-show of Outlier Media into a resource for low-income news consumers in Detroit in search of tangible, individualized information", the article continued, In 13 months, Alvarez has sent messages to about 40,000 Detroit cell phone numbers in her quest to reach "as many Detroiters as possible".

But Alvarez, who came to journalism after working as a civil rights lawyer, said, "Even though the journalism was very good, I was not satisfied with covering low-income communities for a higher-income audience. I wanted to cover issues for and with low-income news consumers".

She said "I covered issues that were important to low-income families, but I was not a housing reporter. Using Outlier's method and delivery system, it's such efficient beat development".

Alvarez said Outlier was begun as "an intervention instead of [aiming] to be a longstanding institution — I think a lot of news organizations want to be institutions — what we wanted to do was deliver information, make a difference, and change the ecosystem in Detroit".

Outlier's work also resulted in news stories based on text findings that were published by partner newsrooms including stories on rent, evictions, and a tax auction.

As mentioned in a previous chapter, in 2020, in Milwaukee, Wisconsin, Outlier teamed with Wisconsin Watch, a statewide nonprofit investigative newsroom and the Milwaukee Neighborhood News Service to provide similar service, called News414, in Milwaukee with Google News Initiative News Funding.

The project described itself this way: "The free texting service offers essential information such as where to find food near you and what rights you have as a tenant during the pandemic. And if you have questions or want to share information with us, News414 will connect you with a reporter who will try to track down the information you want", according to an announcement of the project, which said the news project planned to spin off investigative stories from the text news service.

Text news alerts and location

Another recent project involved text alerts based on audience location through a newsroom application.

Writing for the Knight Lab at Northwestern University, Ryan Restivo of Newsday in Long Island, New York, said that as Newsday launched in its new version of its app, "we started thinking about how our app could improve how we interact with our community".

He recalled, "A couple of weeks later, I was at the University of Illinois at the Mobile Me & You conference and saw Amy Schmitz Weiss from San Diego State University present some research she had done".

Schmitz Weiss, who is a leader in spatial journalism research, had done research on location and news and found people want news customized to where they are. In one of her articles, she had written:

> Connecting spaces and places to information might be considered common sense. But the mindset and framework to employ a spatial understanding of the community aren't typical in journalism. This kind of spatial understanding has long been a part of other fields, like architecture, geography, and urban planning — but less so in news.

She said with that approach, "There can be a change to how communities are understood, covered, and connected when we revisit the idea of spaces and places through the creation of spatial narratives, place-based knowledge, and locative data".

Talking with Schmitz Weiss after the conference, Restivo said he realized that we needed to understand what "community" means to people. Restivo then embarked on redesign of the "Alerts" page on the app, did some market research, and conquered with his team a series of design and technical issues.

The result was a system of news alerts that can inform the app users of the issues in the towns that matter most to them and allows the newsroom to build engagement in those towns.

Automation and visualization tools

The texting and alert systems are just a preview of the coming automation of news gathering and distribution. An Associated Press study of the artificial intelligence use or lack of use in newsrooms, especially small ones led to a comprehensive article at Northwestern by those working on the project.

The article noted,

> Different tools match different organizations, and our recommendations depend on your previous experience with automation, computer science, and artificial intelligence. You don't have to be an expert programmer or hire a team of developers to build and use

> these tools—there are plenty of great off-the-shelf solutions available, and we're eager to help you find them.

The article said journalists using AI systems do not have to have a thorough understanding of how the tools work. The article suggested that a baseline for using the tools was to know how to effectively search the web, use online database, or use Google Alerts. A more advanced basis was having an organization that automatically ran a story starting on a website into social media.

Among the tools listed was Otter.ai, a transcription service that can work in real time or can transcribe uploaded videos or audios. It is being more widely used by journalism and professionals. Another was Descript which can match transcripts with audio files and be used for a news story. In alert systems, Meltwater was suggested for tracking trends.

For social media management, Social Pilot was suggested for scheduling content across various media platforms. Other tools included Natural Language Generation, which creates text from data that can be edited.

A popular visualization tool they suggested is Flourish, like another software Tableau, which can make it easy to visualize data in bar charts and story maps. More advanced tools include new/s/leak that permits a user to illustrate relationships between people, organizations, and places.

The article concluded,

> While trusting AI tools to do work without much supervision is essential in some functions, many newsrooms agree that it should not replace the personalized and nuanced work of a journalist. While AI can be used for data sifting, interpretation is still a human task, and the possibility that automation could completely replace the role of a journalist is concerning to many in the industry.

The article also reminded readers that algorithms can have a bias since they are written by humans and indeed some reporters and newsrooms are dedicated to exposing inherent bias in algorithms.

Ongoing projects

With the loss of so many reporters from daily newsrooms, major efforts are underway to routinely, and automatically, if possible, collect and distribute information about local and regional governments' agendas, minutes, and other data and information.

Involving citizens in a way that seems far more effective than trying to create citizen journalism programs is Documenter, a project in which citizens record meetings and feed them into a database. Started in Chicago, by the nonprofit City Bureau, it has been expanded in the past few years. Citizens document meetings, by keeping track of agenda items discussed, attendance including organizations and companies represented, and the tone of the debate room.

The City Bureau also collaborated with ProPublica on a project to scrape data from public meetings, like other projects are doing.

Data-driven news

The data-driven approach noted before has led to an ambitious national project underway to collect, report on, and distribute more local government information is the aforementioned "Big Local News Project" at Stanford University that says it putting together. Data, tools, and collaborations that empower journalists to better cover their community.

Among databases that can be sliced into subsets for local newsrooms are ones on Opioid use, Wildfires, Education, Hospital Bed Capacity, Traffic Stops, School Enrollments, and Rape Clearances. The idea builds on a large scale of the kinds of databases collected at IRE in the 1990s that are now mostly housed at ProPublica's data store. Another early large set of databases was called Transactional Records (or TRAC) at Syracuse University which focused on justice and tax records and is still in existence.

Big Local News, led by data journalist Cheryl Phillips, also has collaboration and partnerships to produce journalism stories. They included a U.S. Census data cooperative, a community law enforcement accountability network that shares police data, data for coverage of Covid-19, and an open policing project that gathers, analyzes, and shares data on millions of police traffic stops in the U.S. One award-winning collaborative project with newsrooms was on how the consequences of Covid-19 on students and schools. The project also works on ways to automate and organize the public agendas of local governments in California.

A separate data project is called The Accountability Project, which has been led by long-time data journalist Jennifer LaFleur at American University and the Center for Public Integrity. Again, the project team is collecting national data that can be used by large and small newsrooms, but its prominent feature is that has a program that allows datasets to be linked together through a flexible search tool so that data from disparate datasets such as politically lobbying records and owners of nursing homes can be compared for stories.

The Accountability Project (TAP) says it gives researchers and journalists "a powerful, but simple tool to search across data that would otherwise be siloed. Our collection includes more than 1.5 billion public records". The data focuses on people, organizations, and locations and a user can start by simply typing a person's name and information about that person could come out of disparate datasets on nonprofit organizations, licenses, public employees, voter registration, property records, business ownership, lobbying, or medical facilities.

Journalists and researchers regularly use TAP to background and draw connections between people and organizations. The data has supported stories on nonprofit donors, bad nursing homes, and government loans to small businesses.

Other useful projects that increase audience is an international project called OpenCorporates which collects corporate information from international, national, and regional governments that regulate public companies. Other huge datasets include the series of terabytes of leaked data on offshore companies and bank records that have led to global investigations by the International Consortium of Investigative Journalists and their hundreds of news partners. Although few have made an effort to routinely monetize data, the use of the data naturally increases audience, subscriptions, and donations for the newsrooms using them.

Journalism labs for better tools

While some international and national datasets for collaboration are being created some journalism research labs are focused on tools for analysis. The Knight Journalism Lab at the Medill School at Northwestern University has worked on software to help journalists easily do timelines, analyze Twitter feeds, tell stories with maps, and make it easier to use sensor data.

The lab states simply, "We build easy-to-use tools that can help you tell better stories".

The lab said their most popular open source software has been TimelineJS, which "has been used by more than 250,000 people to tell stories seen hundreds of millions of times, and is available in more than sixty languages".

They note, "We also develop prototypes of tools for reporting, data management, research, and storytelling, often in connection with Northwestern classes". The Medill School also has created the Local News Initiative to research decline in local coverage and ways it can be bolstered.

Spatial journalism

Journalists also have been using sensors to track insect infestations, the effects of heat waves, flooding, and movement of animals. In the Midwest, a nonprofit investigative center set up sensors near schools and parks to collect information about pesticide drift. In Florida, reporters gathered sensor data from toll booths to show how law enforcement officers were recklessly speeding. As noted in a Nieman Labs article, "As part of a data-driven reporting approach, sensors can broaden the range of stories journalists take on and increase the authoritativeness of their account".

The article continued,

> Though sensor journalism is still in an early stage, newsrooms are beginning to navigate the terrain, with some journalists cobbling together their own measuring devices or, more often, using data collected by existing sensors. ProPublica and The Lens have reported on Louisiana's disappearing coastlines by analyzing satellite imagery of the state's changing land patterns, while The New York Times has used data collected via satellites to bolster their reporting on conflicts and breaking news events abroad.

The article cites a USA Today's investigation where reporters used a handheld device that measures soil contamination to undertake a comprehensive examination of the legacy left by lead factories, while WNYC did "crowdsourced sensor projects to both predict the arrival of cicadas and measure the effects of heat stress in Harlem. In India, the nonprofit IndiaSpend has teamed up with Twitter to monitor air quality in real time".

As the article noted, satellite data has become much easier to access and reporters in Louisiana obtained the Landsat satellite data for free that provide information across the spectrum that showed the loss of land across the coastline.

Amy Schmitz Weiss, the professor at San Diego State University, publishes a newsletter on spatial journalism that keeps track of the innovation and latest uses of digital tools

Visual investigations

Perhaps, the most astonishing use of satellite technology is when it is combined with social media postings of video and audio, interviews, field work, and archived text and images. At *The New York Times*, visual investigations by journalist Malachy Brown and his team used that information to prove that the Syrian and Russian governments lied that they had not bombed civilians and hospitals. Weaving together audio from Russian aircraft, social media postings of the bombings and their carnage, archived video, and placing it on a timeline, the team won major awards for revealing the truth behind bombings by aircraft.

The team has used its forensic approach for stories on assassinations, mass shootings, riots, and other news events. Another similar team at an organization, called Bellingcat, is constantly producing investigations using those techniques and was able to show a year before official investigations did that a Russian rocket had shot down a civilian airliner over Ukraine.

Big tech and creating news products

While Big Tech has nearly destroyed legacy news by dominating digital advertising, it has begun returning some revenue to the news industry through donations, monetary awards, and training to improve and streamline news operations and the creation of news products. As mentioned in the previous chapter, Google, Facebook and Microsoft have increased training and financial support to small newsrooms and engaged in partnerships with larger ones.

Naturally, training newsrooms in the use of a corporation's digital tools and products – even if free – means the newsrooms will be creating content and products that will attract audiences and revenue to the corporation. However, the trade-off so far has been worth it for the beleaguered news industry.

While many journalists favor open source and free software, those without programming skills find the big tech tools and products much easier to use, and big tech has worked with journalists to hone those tools to fit the needs of journalists.

Google offers training in its tools of web scraping, mapping, data visualization, and analysis routinely through journalism associations, workshops, and conferences. But it also has whole programs on its technology to improve newsroom business practices. Its Google News Lab has a team within the Google News Initiative "whose mission is to collaborate with journalists, academics and nonprofits to drive innovation in journalism". It supplies partnerships and training to strengthen digital skills

Another program in the Digital Foundation Lab that develops technology infrastructure within small to medium-sized news organizations to help them operate "a digital-first business". Google said the lab consists of two phases. In one phase of three to four months, newsrooms set up "building blocks" of technology to run operations (digital flows) to smoothly run business operations such as advertising, audience tracking, subscriptions, and marketing. The second phase, another three to four months, has organizations moving into reader revenue or advertising and sponsorship revenue.

Meanwhile, Microsoft has implemented in its local newsroom initiative ways to improve and use data-driven stories and data visualizations, using Microsoft software products. As part of its journalism projects, Meta bought and offered CrowdTangle to journalists that allowed journalists to track stories, measure their social performance and identify influencers.

Facebook said it was creating more digital and analytical tools to help journalists use Facebook live broadcasting and to recognize potential stories in its social media platforms.

6

UNIVERSITIES INCREASING ROLE IN JOURNALISM

For years, university journalism programs have increasingly been supplying statehouse news as traditional newsrooms have slashed coverage of state government.

Mark Horvit, a professor at the University of Missouri and former executive director of Investigative Reporters and Editors, has overseen the journalism school's long-running university statehouse bureau, which is staffed with journalism students. He estimated in 2022 that about 50 news outlets freely subscribe to the school's news service with about 20 to 30 of those outlets running any one story at a time.

The students do both written and audio stories and he said the audio stories are used more often. Many other universities, including those in North Carolina Utah, and Maryland also provide such coverage.

Over time that coverage has increased at those bureaus, but as commercial newsrooms took further financial blows in 2008, universities

DOI: 10.4324/9781315719573-7

were urged to also play a greater role in investigative and community news coverage.

Journalism programs throughout the U.S. had already had been slowly expanding their collaborations with professional organizations and several investigative reporting centers were operating at universities. A national collaboration of students, News 21, was annually producing a major investigative project out of Arizona State University journalism school. And journalism students had not only been staffing statehouse bureaus across the country, but also reporting on Congress, and providing community news in some states.

Journalism students also continued to work in newsrooms as paid or unpaid interns, using the opportunity to learn and make connections. Journalism professors, who had worked in newsrooms, found their way into newsrooms by working on particular projects or helping with editing or producing during the summer.

But given the crisis in traditional news, foundations, deans, and media researchers called for universities to take a greater role as newspapers shrank and disappeared. They noted that a major strength of the university model is that journalism programs and their newsrooms have been seen as part of stable institutions as opposed to start-ups.

Indeed, it is seen as sometimes easier to get initial large donations at universities since a philanthropist can be assured there is usually a sizable infrastructure of an institution to provide administrative support, office space, and a supply of young journalists who will do the work for little or no pay. Of course, that does not assure certain success.

In 2009, Nicholas Lemann, the dean at Columbia University, suggested that journalism programs needed to have more comprehensive goals and to be "teaching hospitals" in which students learn practical journalism techniques in professional newsroom conditions.

"Like teaching hospitals, journalism schools can provide essential services to their communities while they are educating their students", he wrote in the Chronicle of Higher Education as the devastating impact of the Great Recession on journalism grew.

Gunhild Ring Olsen observed in her book *Newsroom-Classroom Hybrids at Universities: Student Labor and the Journalism Crisis* (2020) that "It is no coincidence that the idea of journalism schools as teaching hospitals was launched in 2009, at the height of the financial recession. Due to the change of context, with the profession searching everywhere for solutions to the journalism crisis, practice-oriented training was seen as an opportunity to produce endangered quality reporting". She wrote, "Instead of being somewhat peripheral players in the field of journalism, students suddenly became the potential saviors of a whole profession".

Olsen noted that Leeman also wrote,

> [T]he education sector is just about the only part of journalism whose business model is still in excellent health. [...] what can we do to help change the situation for news organizations, so that journalism schools and the profession might thrive together.

Olsen herself defined the teaching hospital model as "students working with professional journalists, in the context of a university, to produce content for general audiences in partnership with professional media organizations, *with an overall goal of saving professional reporting*".

In their 2009 study, "Reconstructing American Journalism", Leonard Downie and Michael Schudson joined in the push for a sustained effort in the academy to become a crucial part of the new journalistic landscape.

They recommended:

> Universities, both public and private, should become ongoing sources of local, state, specialized subject, and accountability news reporting as part of their educational missions. They should operate their own news organizations, host platforms for other nonprofit news and investigative reporting organizations, provide faculty positions for active individual journalists, and be laboratories for digital innovation in the gathering and sharing of news and information.

Centers of professional news reporting

They also wrote that "In addition to educating and training journalists, colleges and universities should be centers of professional news reporting, as they are for the practice and advancement of medicine and law, scientific and social research, business development, engineering, education, and agriculture".

"It is time for those and other colleges and universities to take the next step and create full-fledged news organizations", they wrote.

They acknowledged, as in many professional fields, integrating such practical work into an academic setting can be challenging but they called for:

- Increased collaboration with other local news nonprofits, including local public radio and television stations, many of which are owned by colleges and universities themselves and housed on their campuses.
- Increased collaboration with local commercial news media, continue and expand providing commercial newsrooms with news coverage and reporting interns and adviser hyperlocal community news sites and blogs.

"Universities are among the nation's largest nonprofit institutions, and they should play significant roles in the reconstruction of American journalism", they concluded.

Other studies followed with similar advice.

One study, "Shaping 21st Century Journalism: Leveraging a 'Teaching Hospital Model' in Journalism Education", a policy paper in 2011 from the New America Foundation said, "As the media industry reshapes itself, a tremendous opportunity emerges for America's journalism programs".

The paper called on all journalism programs within higher education institutions to:

- Redraw the boundaries of journalism education so that programs provide a broader set of skills for the multiplatform (often entrepreneurial) journalist of the future.
- Extend and increase partnerships among journalism programs and other programs within the university and college.
- Increase coverage of local communities outside the university or college in conjunction with local media.

- Collaborate with other journalism schools on state and national news bureaus.
- Collaborate on adoption of open education materials and freely licensed open software platforms.
- Experiment with ways to move aspects of journalism education to the center of undergraduate core curriculums.
- Extend and focus research toward an agenda that clearly locates journalism in relation to its role in local democracy.

Eric Newton, vice president of the journalism program at the John S. and James L. Knight Foundation at the time, also espoused the idea of journalism programs as teaching hospitals in speeches and in an online piece. Olsen noted that Newton said in one speech in 2011 that the work capacity of more than 200,000 journalism and mass communication students could be used "to help underserved communities".

While Olsen suggested in her book that "teaching hospitals" was just another name for the "Missouri Method" (the use of working newsrooms for students to learn professional skills), Newton wrote: "So you might hear after this talk something from the University of Missouri saying, "We are a teaching hospital"".

He wrote "And as much as I admire them, they've been learning-by-doing for a century, I'd say that's not exactly right. They have great learning-by-doing at their television station and newspaper. They have experiments in their Reynolds Institute. They have great professionals and great researchers. But I don't think they've put it all together to create the ultimate teaching hospital for journalism education".

Newton said defined a teaching hospital journalism program as a model of learning-by-doing that includes college students, professors and professionals working together under one "digital roof" for the benefit of a community.

He further argued that

> To duplicate a teaching hospital, a university-based community-news organization would need to combine in one effort six different elements:

- Students doing the journalism;
- Professionals mentoring them to improve the quality and impact of the journalism;
- Professors bringing in topic knowledge and raising issues;
- Innovators pioneering new tools and techniques;
- Academics doing major research projects;
- Everyone works together with an emphasis on not just informing a community but engaging it.
- The sixth element is not a type of person, it's a way of doing things: working with each other and a community.

Newton cited different examples of each of those elements but urged journalism schools to embrace all of the elements.

Newton also said, "University hospitals save lives. University law clinics take cases to the Supreme Court. University news labs can reveal truths that help us right wrongs".

For a business model, Newton acknowledged the prospect of the programs earning revenue from the industry was not promising.

> Practical journalism schools, like the one at San Francisco State University, have, for years and with no resources, offered local reporting classes yielding good student work published in local newspapers. While that doesn't offer the community engagement and research options we want, it's at least a start.

He cited other examples such as The University of Alabama "teaching newspaper" and the now-defunct New England Center for Investigative Reporting, which had a which variety of revenue streams including a profitable high school journalism training program.

But Newton said he was

> convinced teaching newsrooms will never be able to run on revenue from the news organizations they partner with. Even News21's investigations do not receive any revenue from news organizations. In the end, the question is not whether a program is expensive or no-cost, but whether it is the right size for your campus.

The response to the different recommendations was not instant or overwhelming, but over the past decade, universities have created some of those programs, most often with foundation and donor support.

The Missouri method

For decades, the University of Missouri School of Journalism, which has long extolled the virtues of practical work, has provided extensive and increasing local and state coverage of Missouri.

It has housed an independent community newspaper, the Missourian, which is thoroughly integrated into the school's curriculum. As part of the curriculum known as "The Missouri Method", the school has a commercial NBC-affiliated station, a National Public Radio station, and a statehouse bureau that has two dozen or more students when the legislature is in session. Recently, it combined all its newsrooms into run in recognition of uses of multiple media for any news story.

"The Missouri Method remains the guiding light of the curriculum. The Method emphasizes a heavy dose of real-world experience using the school's daily community newspaper, commercial affiliate television station, NPR member radio station and two professional strategic communication agencies, along with a local entertainment tabloid, a statewide digital business newsletter and a documentary film company", wrote Olsen in her book.

In the 1990s, the Missouri School of Journalism further honed its approach by more closely defining its professional non-tenure track for professors, roughly based on the clinical track at the university hospital.

In addition to the school's newsrooms, there was transformational project within the school that had influence both nationally and internationally.

During my time at Missouri and IRE (1994 to 2008), I oversaw the National Institute for Computer-Assisted Reporting (NICAR), which had an international training program in computer-assisted reporting and a data library staffed by professional journalists and graduate and undergraduate students that provided data analysis and training for more than 100 newsrooms throughout the U.S. annually.

It was an innovative lab that demonstrated how universities could effectively assist in newsrooms in learning new techniques and supply them with research and data that not only augmented professional reporting but also supplied analysis and content that the newsrooms could produce themselves. Many of those students wrote or produced data-driven stories themselves that were published in the university newsrooms and the mainstream press. Many went onto professional jobs, doing award-winning investigative and data journalism for newsrooms. Ironically, only one other professor in the school was assigned to assist with the data journalism program and no other professors ever taught at or visited the data library or participated in the training.

But NICAR amply demonstrated one of Downie and Schudson's recommendations could work:

> Journalists on their faculties should engage in news reporting and editing, as well as teach these skills and perform research, just as members of other professional school faculties do. The most proficient student journalists should advance after graduation to paid residencies and internships, joining fully experienced journalists on year-round staffs of university-based, independently edited local news services, Web sites, and investigative reporting projects.

Overall, the Missouri program always served the educational needs of journalism students while providing citizens with credible news. But the loss and shrinkage of traditional news outlets in Missouri have meant the journalism program has become even a more substantial source for news as have other journalism programs across the country.

In Columbia, Mo., for example, in 2016, the other newspaper in the city, the family-owned Columbia Daily Tribune, was sold to the private equity firm, Gatehouse, which was known for making severe staff and budget cuts. Within two years, 20 staff members at the newspaper had been let go, leaving only one reporter in the newsroom. The number of reporters is now three, bringing the news staff to total to only eight, when including three editors, a content producer and a photographer.

At the Missouri statehouse, the reporters routinely outnumbered full-time professional journalists, until the number of students to professionals rose to 26.–17.

Other university programs

Missouri has not been alone in running programs that offer practical, clinical training. The University of Maryland's journalism program offers students experience in covering state of Maryland and its state house and the federal government. It also now has an investigative center.

Arizona State University has expanded its programs over the last two decades so that it has extensive broadcasting programs and statehouse and community coverage and is now one of the largest producers of news content, if not the largest, in the state. It also has added an investigative center to its News 21 program.

Like San Francisco State, many other programs have students who have been providing community coverage. They include Temple University, the journalism programs at Northwestern University and Northeastern University, and independent student newspapers such as the Daily Tar Heel, North Carolina.

Most of these programs are dependent on revenue from tuition with a few receiving consistent donor support or having an endowment although university and student newspapers have subscriptions and sell ads.

Statehouse bureaus

As noted above, one area in which university journalism programs have contributed substantial coverage is in statehouses where full-time coverage by professional newsrooms has decreased significantly.

In 2014, the Journalism Project at the Pew Research Center found the number of full-time statehouse reporters dropped by a third from 2003 and in 2022 the center found a further drop from 904 to 890 while it did find an increase in part-time coverage, particularly by nonprofits newsrooms

As a result, the student journalists, overseen by professional journalists, became a large source of free news coverage on statehouses and state governments, meaning the programs are mostly dependent on tuition.

PLACE: CASE STUDY – QUESTIONS AND ANSWERS ON BUILDING A STUDENT STATEHOUSE PROGRAM

In addition to programs already mentioned, a robust statehouse news bureau was created at Virginia Commonwealth that represents the ongoing trend. The following is an interview with Jeff South, the recently retired professor who oversaw it for nearly two decades:

How much over the past two decades did the Capital News Service grow in a number of client newspapers and newsrooms:

"Virginia Commonwealth University's Capital News Service program grew from about a dozen news outlets (mostly rural weeklies) in 2003 to more than 115 news outlets (including daily newspapers, radio stations, television stations and online/digital-only news platforms) in 2019. In addition, in 2013, the Capitol News program and the University of Maryland's Capitol News Service started selectively distributing each other's content. Moreover, beginning in 2017, The Associated Press started distributing select stories from VCU's program".

South said the service grew to 80 subscribing news outlets in 2010 and started posting stories itself on news websites such at Topix and GroundReport.com

> By 2017, through its Associated Press arrangement, its stories began appearing in the Washington Post, Los Angeles Times and other major news organizations in the U.S. and around the world. In 2019, the university signed a contract with the Associated Press formalizing the relationship. The service also became a formal partner with Patch.com, a platform for publishing local news, which gave the service a more prominent online presence.

When South began as director of the program in 2003 the distribution of stories was by fax and mail. He switched it to an email-only distribution system. The program is a three-credit course for students. He then expanded the distribution, partly through the Virginia

Press Association and other professional contacts. The service is still free for subscribers and clients and they ask their clientele to give a student a byline if they use the story. News editors can also request a story and if they help the student, they can publish the story first.

South added, "We could legitimately promise to be a remote news outlet's "eyes and ears in Richmond" and to provide "localized, customized coverage" from the state capital," but he ended that practice after 10 years because it was too time-consuming. He noted that some subscribers use the service as a tip sheet. Like Missouri's program, only a part of the subscriber may use any one story.

How much would you say the traditional media's coverage shrank?

First, an anecdote: VCU CNS's bread-and-butter coverage focuses on the legislative session that begins in early January and runs to late February or mid-March. To effectively cover the legislative session, we needed space in the press room that, until recently, was located in the basement of the General Assembly Building next to the state Capitol. When I first took over CNS, I would go to the press room in mid-October with police tape, rope off three or four chairs and desks, and hang a sign declaring "VCU CNS".

Back then – in 2005 through 2010 – you had to stake an early claim to real estate in the press room because there was intense competition for space. Not only did the big metro papers (like the Richmond Times-Dispatch and The Virginian-Pilot) have swarms of reporters covering the General Assembly, but even small papers – from Danville, Martinsville, and Lynchburg, for instance – sent reporters to Richmond for the session.

"By 2013, that changed. There was no need to make a scouting trip to the General Assembly Building's press room before the session. Indeed, the chairs and desks in the press room were covered with dust and cobwebs. The VCU CNS reporters had all the room they wanted. Virginia's smaller newspapers had stopped sending reporters to Richmond to cover the General Assembly, and the larger newspapers had cut back on legislative coverage as well".

South estimated that since 2003 the number of reporters covering the General Assembly full-time has been cut by 50–70 percent. He added, "That decline has been partially offset by legislative coverage provided by journalists who are not at the state Capitol full-time. They include, for example, reporters who might parachute in for a day to cover a legislative hearing, or journalists who write stories after watching a webcast of a committee meeting, news conference or House or Senate sessions". He estimated there is about half as much legislative coverage in Virginia as there was 20 years ago. "A lot of those articles are pro forma process stories", South said. He estimated that deeper, more insightful, investigative stories have been cut by two-thirds.

South said the decline in traditional media coverage is an opportunity for student-powered journalism

South produced a chart of the percentage of state house stories each news outlet in 2014 and in 2018 and showed in 2014, for instance, The Virginian-Pilot provided 23 percent of the legislative stories but only 8 percent four years later. However, the share of news stories from VCU Capital News Service climbed from less than 2 percent in 2014 to 7 percent in 2018.

How did you deal with the learning curve for students and the semester system for the Capital News Service?

"That is the big challenge, especially in a large public university where students may have a wide range of journalistic experience, preparation, and motivation. My CNS classes often drew 25 or more students (which fortunately VCU counted as two sections; CNS is considered a skills course, and under our accreditation rules, skills courses must be capped at 20).

In December, before students dispersed for winter break, I met with the students who would be in the spring CNS class and I gave them readings and other preparation materials to peruse over the break. I urged them to monitor bills and issues for story ideas. I invited students to write stories over the break – stories that I promised to include in their CNS quota. Over the course of the semester, students were expected to write 10 stories and do a team project.

In addition, CNS students had to report for duty more than a week before other classes began at VCU. I felt it was crucial for students to start covering the legislative session from the opening day. Our clients/subscribers expected that, and the Maryland CNS program also had a tradition of starting earlier than other courses.

Launching CNS in early January was also a burden on the instructors (I typically team-taught CNS so we could share editing duties). We didn't get any extra compensation for doing so. As a result, after I retired in 2020, my successors decided to have CNS start when other VCU classes begin.

Besides starting CNS earlier than other classes, I used a lot of technology to help students ascend the learning curve:

> In my nearly two decades of working with CNS, I've found that students often have an eye for stories that more experienced (journalists might overlook. For example, on more than one occasion over the years, my CNS students wrote about bills that sought to give local governments authority to ban plastic bags at grocery stores and other retail establishments.

Maybe the students were better able to look down the road and see what issues might matter in the future. CNS students were ahead of their time reporting on bills to lift the tax on feminine hygiene products, for instance, and to create a Student Loan Ombudsman office".

Overall, South said it will require an investment of time for newsrooms to figure out how to collaborate with universities.

> They'll need to answer questions like: Which courses or programs can produce stories that are ready for publication? Will the college journalists provide coverage that doesn't duplicate the newsroom's existing efforts? What is the process for budgeting, editing and delivering the content -- and for ensuring that it will meet professional standards? And what will the college journalists get for their labor? There's no one-size-fits-all solution. But if newsrooms and j-schools can work together, everybody wins.

Rise of investigative centers

Mirroring the rise of nonprofit journalism has been the rise of investigative reporting centers and programs at universities. These programs, mostly run by experienced journalists who have transitioned to teaching, develop and produce stories that often win regional and national awards not only in student contest categories but in categories including traditional newsrooms and new nonprofits.

Olsen studied four investigative centers in her book: The Investigative Reporting Project at the University of California in Berkeley, the Stabile Center (Columbia University), the Workshop (American University), and the New England Center for Investigative Reporting which had been at Boston University and has since dissolved). Her book offers a more detailed look at those centers, which were a sample of those existing at the time.

The Investigative Reporting Project at Berkeley, led by long-time investigative reporter Lowell Bergman, was one of the first university programs to receive widespread notice after starting in 1991. It was largely funded by foundations and donations and support from the university and was well known for in-depth national stories, some of which were in partnership with PBS's Frontline. It became an institution in 2006. It is still thought of as the first investigative center at a university and is now run by former New York Times reporter David Barstow.

Another investigative program, begun in 1999, was at Northwestern University and known as the Innocence Project. It focused on investigating wrongful convictions that freed at least dozen men from prison but had to survive a controversy over its methods a decade ago over its methods.

The Schuster Institute for Investigative Reporting at Brandeis University announced itself in 2005 as the first formal university investigative center with a substantial donation but lasted only for a decade because it was unable to raise more funds.

The Toni Stabile Center for Investigative Reporting at Columbia University in 2006 with a major donation. The Howard Centers for investigative reporting at the University of Maryland and at Arizona State University opened with the support of the Scripps Howard Foundation, which gave a grant of $3 million over three years to each university for their new investigative centers.

Also, in 2018 The Michael I. Arnolt Center for Investigative Journalism at Indiana University started with a $6 million gift from Arnolt, who was an alumnus of the university. A nonprofit, nonpartisan center, it was intended to help fill the investigative reporting gap left by traditional newsrooms and has already teamed with several national news organizations on investigative stories.

In a move that may be replicated by other centers, Arnolt asked that the university "include specific language in the gift agreements ensuring the complete editorial independence" of Center:

> So as to guarantee the journalistic integrity of the activities of the Center, the Donor and Indiana University understand that the Center shall be fully free and independent with respect to journalistic and editorial decisions. Journalistic decisions, based on the principles of Freedom of the Press, shall rest with the director of the Center.

And in 2022, Temple University's Klein College of Media and Communication launched the Logan Center for Urban Investigative Reporting with a $1.2 million funding grant from the Jonathan Logan Family Foundation in Berkeley, California.

Push for university students to do more local news

In recent years, other universities are responding to the recommendations made from 2009 to 2012 for more local news through student work and collaborations with professional media. While some newsrooms such as the Missourian and the Daily Tar Heel (which covers the University of North Carolina, but also includes coverage of Orange County and North Carolina) other programs work with what is left of traditional media.

In a 2022 article "How college students can help save local news" on the Web site *The Conversation*, two professors, Lara Salahi, an Assistant Professor of Broadcast and Digital Journalism at Endicott College, New Hampshire, and Christina Smith, an Associate Professor of Mass Communication at Georgia College and State University, said they surveyed more than

50 university programs. They found through formal and informal collaborations; college journalists were helping to serve the communities where their universities are located by making sustained contributions to local media.

They called the partnerships "news-academic partnerships" – often in areas that have seen local newsrooms suffer the hardest hits, as identified in the University of North Carolina's news desert report.

> For our initial research, we sent surveys to 50 people who are involved in these collaborations, either as faculty members who manage the partnership at a college and university or as journalists at a local news outlet who oversee the partnership. We got responses from more than two dozen of them and learned these partnerships are key ways to sustain local news in places where news coverage is diminishing or critical issues are going underreported, they wrote.

The professors said they could not find a formal comprehensive list of collaborations between local newsrooms and college journalism programs but could find many through their research.

> Some of these collaborations – such as ones between the Franklin Pierce University and the Keene, New Hampshire, Sentinel newspaper – have existed for more than a decade. But our survey found that they have become more common over the past five years with further media consolidation and layoffs.

They cited another partnership that Salahi had created in 2019 with her beat reporting class at Endicott College in Massachusetts and Gannett, the largest newspaper chain serving communities north of Boston. "That year, Gannett bought 21 publications in the North Shore region of Massachusetts with 32 editorial employees serving 22 communities – and downsized them to just 10 publications with 12 editorial personnel, Gannett staff told us".

They said,

> Each week the students are assigned to report on stories in cities and towns surrounding the college, to be published in Gannett's local

> outlets. In many ways, the class runs like a newsroom, with students involved in every stage of news reporting. In addition to the professor, a Gannett editor works with students on each story, so students get the experience of receiving professional feedback as they see their story through to publication.

They said by 2022, there were only nine Gannett publications employing seven full-time journalists serving that same territory. But ten students in the beat reporting class supplemented local coverage by publishing 65 stories in the spring semester, with "the stories ranging from environmental issues to health stories to local sports and to profiling community members with interesting stories to tell".

Although Gannett was getting free stories, the authors said students benefited from the partnership.

"Some are publishing their stories in news sites beyond a high school or college publication for the first time. In past semesters, a few students have stayed on with Gannett beyond the course to either intern or freelance for these local publications", they wrote. "We hypothesize some partnerships, like this one, also benefit the communities that are served by these newspapers and websites, though that has yet to be studied".

They noted students provided coverage that would not have been done and some community members said they had been interviewed for a news story for the first time. In some cases, the stories written by the student journalists would likely not have been covered because of limited capacity of the newsroom. Some community members whom students have reached out to for interviews told the students they were speaking to a journalist for the first time.

> We hope they might also lead to new journalistic endeavors, like the start of a new news outlet, or revival of a dying one. For example, in October 2021, the University of Georgia's Grady College announced it would revive a nearby community newspaper that was slated to close.

In their article, the authors identified issues long known to professors who either do collaborations with local commercial newsrooms or run a newsroom within the university. Those issues include a lack of sufficient compensation for the hours the professors put into the newsroom and the difficulty of challenges for students and professors who both have other courses.

They wrote,

> We have found that faculty members who seek to create or manage sustainable news-academic partnerships often find they face some of the same problems that editors at local news outlets report, such as burnout, high workloads and low pay. For instance, in a follow-up to our initial study, faculty members who oversaw a variety of news-academic partnerships reported receiving little or no additional compensation, nor a decrease in other responsibilities, such as teaching, to balance the workload.

Echoing the previous earlier studies, they wrote "However, academic institutions are theoretically well positioned to sustain meaningful journalism that serves their communities, which are often outside of elite news coverage areas".

They noted many universities were well funded and "provide the physical and mental space for minds to build healthy skepticism and investigate complex issues in society". They also pointed to public radio stations that have been operated at universities "without limits on editorial or financial independence" and that "We think even more universities could be a source for reducing the number and size of news deserts in the U.S., and ensuring communities across the country retain a reliable source of news and information".

As of June 2022, interest in the issue had risen to the level where the Knight Foundation gave $400,000 to the University of Vermont to start a Center for Community News that would track news and academic partnerships throughout the U.S. The announcement cited as examples a student state capitol news service in Nebraska, the Olgethorpe County, Georgia local newspaper produced by a University of Georgia journalism class, and the CalMatters College Beat in California.

"These are all examples of what researchers at the University of Vermont are calling news/academic partnerships — efforts on behalf of universities, journalism schools, individual professors or local media outlets to employ student journalists to cover local news", the announcement said, which said the new center "to inspire and enable collaborations between local media outlets and students".

The announcement said the national initiative will "support the critical role of local news media around the country and aid colleges in their efforts to help solve the crisis facing local news, Among the center's goals are building and maintaining a comprehensive database of academic-news collaborations in the United States and supporting those involved in this work with examples, advice and consulting".

The center was "inspired by the success of its own local Community News Service" that matched student reporters with professional editors to cover local issues and provide journalism to newsrooms around Vermont. They said more than 1,000 stories had been produced since 2019.

Thus, a decade after recommendations from the national studies, it appeared universities were more fully realizing the news needs of its communities were quickly disappearing and the universities could be part of the solution to restoring journalism in their communities.

7

PUBLIC MEDIA, COLLABORATIONS, AND DIGITAL START-UPS

At the beginning of 2022, the station WBEZ, owned by Chicago Public Media, bought the *Chicago Sun-Times*, saying the acquisition created one of the largest nonprofit news organizations in the U.S.

Chicago Public said it made the purchase with $61 million in pledges from almost a dozen philanthropies.

"We are excited about what lies ahead for this unique model of nonprofit news and raising the bar for supporting, preserving, and strengthening local journalism", said Nykia Wright, the CEO of the *Chicago Sun-Times* in the press release.

The Chicago Sun-Times, like most metropolitan newspapers, had been declining for years in budget, staff, and circulation. Circulation had dropped in 2014, it had been shocking when the circulation dropped by 35 percent from about 637,000 to 410,000. But by 2022, circulation of the printed copy was 57,000 and its digital subscriptions were below 10,000.

DOI: 10.4324/9781315719573-8

"We are excited about what lies ahead for this unique model of nonprofit news and raising the bar for supporting, preserving, and strengthening local journalism", said Nykia Wright, the CEO of the *Chicago Sun-Times*.

The press release said philanthropic support from local and national foundations and individuals who "share a belief in journalism's critical role in informing the public, strengthening local communities, and safeguarding democracy".

The Chicago Public Media said it wanted to maintain and build the Sun-Times' print and digital products, as well as covering the financing needed to support collaboration between the two newsrooms.

In an earlier interview, WBEZ's chief executive director Tracy Brown said that the combining of the newsroom is

> something we will figure out over time and probably end up doing a phased-in approach. I would expect that we will be working pretty closely together. Now, what that looks like is still to be determined.... It's just a matter of figuring out what that looks like.

The purchase of the Sun-Times by Chicago Public Media reflected much of what had been evolving in the news industry for more than a decade. While some questioned the wisdom of buying a failing a newspaper for its brand, audience, and staff, the WBEZ purchase of the Sun-Times represented yet one more symbol of the rise of nonprofit newsrooms as a business model and the hope for public broadcasting to have a greater role in hard news, especially local and especially watchdog reporting.

It also represented a pattern of public broadcasting acquiring other news organizations – which up until that acquisition had been digital start-ups - as it sought to increase its news coverage of local communities and issues.

Public media's broad reach

The current system of U.S. public broadcasting was created by Congress in 1967. Currently, there are more than said there are more than 1,500 local public radio and television stations, the vast majority of public broadcasting service (PBS) stations that have the potential of reaching 98 percent of Americans. And another 60 million listen to podcasts created by public media.

The Corporation for Public Broadcasting says it sends more than $400 million a year in federal funds to a large number of public media stations to help with station costs and news programs. The CPB says public media represents the largest, nonprofit news system in the U.S, with more than 4,300 journalists based at local stations. It notes,

> the sharp decline in the number of local newspapers and the growing reliance on revenue-driven social media platforms as news providers makes public media journalism an increasingly critical source of trusted news to combat the firehose of harmful misinformation and disinformation.

CPB said in 2022 that over the past 15 years, it has invested a total of more than $150 million in discretionary funds to journalism, in addition to the money directly allocated annually to more than 1,500 public media stations. It cited public media collaborations including the recent America Amplified and the development of investigative journalism projects through the Local Journalism Project. It has stated that it has invested more than $42 million in 41 local and regional news collaborations.

In 2021, CPB commissioned a survey of 175 public media stations in all 50 states, Puerto Rico, and Guam as the first step in its strategy to increase public media coverage of state.

Criticism of local coverage by public media and a call to arms

The activity since 2009 came after public media came under sharp criticism from "The Reconstruction of American Journalism Report" and a Knight Commission on community information needs, both published in 2009.

In "The Reconstruction of the American Journalism", the author wrote that,

> a growing number of listeners have turned to public radio stations for national and international news provided by National Public Radio.

> But only a relatively small number of those public radio stations also offer their listeners a significant amount of local news reporting. And even fewer public television stations provide local news coverage.

The Reconstruction report noted that,

> the stations, which are owned by colleges and universities, nonprofit community groups, and state and local governments, supplement relatively small CPB grants with fund-raising from individual donors, philanthropic foundations, and corporate contributors. Most of the money is used for each station's overhead costs and fund-raising, rather than news reporting— even though informing the public is a stated central mission of the CPB, according to the legislation that created it.

The report said three-fourths of the CPB's money goes to public television, which overall has never done much original news reporting.

> The Public Broadcasting Service, collectively owned by local public television stations and primarily funded by the CPB, is a conduit for public affairs programs produced by some larger stations and independent producers that consist mostly of documentaries, talk shows, and a single national news discussion program...

The report went on to state,

> But only a small fraction of the public radio stations that broadcast NPR's national and international news accompany it with a significant amount of local news reporting. Those that do tend to be large city, regional, or state "flagship" stations, some of which have accumulated networks of signals, such as those in Minnesota, Wisconsin, Oregon, Alaska, San Francisco, Los Angeles, Boston, and New York.

The report also pointed out that NPR is a nonprofit that supplies national and international news and cultural programming — "but not local news — to about 800 public radio stations", which are owned and managed by 280 local and state nonprofits, colleges, and universities that support NPR with their dues. In 2009, NPR CEO said she hoped to "to step in where local newspapers are leaving".

Overall, the report concluded, "local news coverage remains underfunded, understaffed, and a low priority at most public radio and television stations, whose leaders have been unable to make or uninterested in making the case for investment in local news to donors and Congress".

It recommended,

> public radio and television should be substantially reoriented to provide significant local news reporting in every community served by public stations and their Web sites. This requires urgent action by and reform of the Corporation for Public Broadcasting, increased congressional funding and support for public media news reporting, and changes in mission and leadership for many public stations across the country.

It also noted that the $400 million that Congress currently appropriates for the CPB each year is far less per capita than public broadcasting support in countries with comparable economies — roughly $1.35 per capita for the United States, compared to about $25 in Canada, Australia, and Germany, nearly $60 in Japan, $80 in Britain, and more than $100 in Denmark and Finland.

"The lion's share of the financial support for public radio and television in the United States comes from listener and viewer donations, corporate sponsorships, foundation grants, and philanthropic gifts". The report also called for more funding for CPB and stations by Congress and a dedicated effort to reporting local news. At the same time, outside of a relatively few regional public radio station groups, very little money is spent on local news coverage by individual public radio and television stations.

The report pointed to CPB's on report on its Public Radio Audience Task Force Report which said "claiming a significantly larger role in American journalism requires a much more robust news-gathering capacity — more 'feet on the street' with notebooks, recorders, cameras, and more editors and producers to shape their work" for broadcast and digital distribution by public radio stations. "The distance between current reality and the role we imagine — and that others urge upon public radio — is large", the report concluded. And that distance is immense for the vast majority of public television stations that do no local news reporting at all.

For all its criticism, the Reconstruction report acknowledged some of excellent work the investigative show Frontline had done over the years (and continues to do). It also did not mention some of the deep investigations and data-driven journalism the NPR national headquarters had done. But the focus of the Reconstruction report was on local news coverage.

Adding to that criticism, was the Knight Commission report on community information needs, also published in 2009, that recommended,

> Public broadcasting needs to move quickly toward a broader vision of public service media, one that is more local, more inclusive, and more interactive. This means pursuing greater integration of new technologies and communication practices with traditional forms of broadcasting. It means using digital platforms to engage local institutions effectively in the public sphere. To advance this, government as well as private sector donors should condition their support of public media on its reform. They should support the creating, curating, and archiving of public media content on the community level.

The public media increases local resources

Within a year, the U.S. public media began trying to change its approach to news, with the CPB funding more in-depth news reporting and collaborations among radio stations.

With much fanfare, CPB "sought to recast themselves as part of the solution to the crisis in ad-supported journalism", according to Current magazine, which covers public broadcasting, at a March 2010 event. At the event CPB announced a major initiative on local news-gathering projects in which it would grant $10.5. million to seven regional collaborations. The plan was to be funded not only by CPB but also by a consortium of stations, and the idea was the project would become self-supporting in two years, that is, the stations would fully support the projects and its reporters.

CPB selected five centers — in the Southwest, Upper Midwest, Plains, Upstate New York, and Central Florida) —and solicited proposals from two other geographic regions, the Northwest and the South.

"This collaboration will enable public media stations to pool their resources and enhance their capacity to produce local journalism", said CPB President Patricia Harrison said at the time. However, within a few years, only one of the collaborations remained, Harvest Public Media, based in Kansas City and covering agriculture issues.

Donna Vestal, who led Harvest Public Media, said Public Harvest succeeded because of its sharp focus on agriculture and it built the project into the budgets of stations. "Sustainability was always a question", she said of the projects.

She said it was a challenge to do collaborations because stations are concerned about raising enough money for their own core budget. In addition, with many stations being based at universities, general managers are constantly dealing with the slowness of academic bureaucracy.

Public media rescue sought again

Under the title: "Business Model: A Bigger Role for Public Broadcasting", a less critical article by the University of North Carolina project on News Deserts was published and asked how many public media can replace of what is lost in local news.

"One alternative could be public broadcasting, with its proven record in the news business through mainstays like National Public Radio (NPR), American Public Media (APM) and the Public Broadcasting Service (PBS)", the article stated. It quoted Julie Drizin, executive director of Current, the nonprofit news service covering U.S. public media, who said public broadcasting is "making a difference". But, "Can public broadcasting fill the void left by the shrinking or the disappearance of newspapers? The answer is no, it can't. But it's doing the best that it can".

The article noted that because stations are locally controlled and operated, "the stations have the flexibility to meet the unique information needs of the communities where they are located". But, based on a study by the News Desert project, it said, "the stations are constrained by a number of factors, including available funding and staffing, as well as decades-old federal mandates to entertain and educate, as well as inform".

University researchers collected data on more than 1,400 outlets, including 1,100 radio stations and 350 television stations. The research focused specifically on identifying the public broadcasting stations that provided either national or locally produced news programming. The study found about half of those outlets – 608 – were producing original content, including news shows that focused on either state or local news. The 608 included 406 NPR stations, of which 144 were affiliated with PBS. It found that while each state has multiple public broadcasting stations, many of them simply transmit programming produced by other stations.

The study also cited survey data from the national radio and television association that showed while 69 percent of NPR stations reported that they offer local news, many of these stations don't produce original reporting, but merely gather and read news reported by other outlets. Thus, even after the 2009 criticism, admonitions, and recommendations, public television stations were even less likely than radio stations to produce local and state news programs.

Only 13 PBS affiliate stations offered a daily local news broadcast, and most are in large cities.

However, NPR continues to promote collaboration across stations and within NPR itself. It includes "topic teams", collaborations on particular issues. "Topic teams are truly collaborative journalism in action. Station reporters are working with each other, NPR reporters, and NPR editors to connect dots between local communities and unearth stories..." NPR stated.

But NPR recently tried to address issues about its lack of investigative reporting by creating five regional hubs to do that reporting. One hub is in the Midwest, which is financed by part of a $4.7 million grant from Eric and Wendy Schmidt (Eric Schmidt was CEO of Google). NPR said all 25 public radio stations in Kansas, Missouri, Iowa, and Nebraska, serving some 63 cities, will have access to the Midwest content.

Another hub is Gulf States Newsroom which consists of public media stations in Birmingham, Alabama, Jackson, Mississippi, New Orleans, and Baton Rouge.

A third hub is in California, also financed by the Schmidts, and includes stations in Los Angeles and San Francisco. A fourth is the Texas Newsroom which is collaboration of the four largest public radio stations, which are in Dallas, Austin, San Antonio and Houston. Smaller stations are also expected to participate.

The hubs just began in 2020 so the questions of sustainability remain.

Acquisitions as a solution

While the stations have struggled to do more local and investigative news, their overall business model has sustained them. The business model for the stations is largely based on individuals donations, often linked to memberships, foundation grants, corporate sponsorships, and events.

For the most part, listenership has grown for NPR. Like WBEZ, many stations have had the funds, or ability to raise funds, to work with, and sometimes acquire, some of the digital start-ups that began in 2009. The idea of acquiring a start-up that has experienced reporters who can do community reporting and investigations has seemed such a sensible shortcut to gaining reporting staff that the "Public Media Merger Playbook", an excellent overview of the field, was published in 2021. And from the digital start-up's point of view, becoming a part of a public media station gives its staff an infrastructure of fundraising and administrative support so that the digital newsroom can concentrate on its reporting.

In its introduction, the playbook authors, Elizabeth Hansen and Emily Roseman, state, "We are entering a new era of journalism in which responsive, civically-minded local newsrooms engage with their communities to provide news and information that matters. Public media is an ally and anchor in the new local journalism landscape".

The authors said the playbook drew intense and comprehensive research to highlight one-way public media stations and local, digital newsrooms "can join forces to provide a new level of local service to their communities".

It noted that a building local digital audience for news has been a struggle for many stations, but the number of free-standing digital news outlets had been increasing. It cited at the time that The Institute for Nonprofit News (INN) calculated those local entrepreneurs have been launching an average of one new digital newsroom per month, every year for the past 12 years.

It noted INN had 250 members as of 2020, but the number of newsrooms as of 2022 had increased to more than 400. Even in 2020, the playbook said the INN newsrooms,

> are providing vitally important investigative, daily, and explanatory news coverage to their communities. Public media organizations and digital newsroom organizations clearly have a lot to learn from each other. And some are discovering just how much stronger they can be together.

The playbook observed that in 2013 the first wave of acquisitions began and cited the St. Louis Beacon merging with St. Louis Public Radio and iNews merging with Rocky Mountain PBS. Actually, both organizations and founding INN members were more acquired than merged. The Beacon still is recognized as a newsroom at the St. Louis station, but iNews no longer exists. The founder of the iNews, investigative editor and reporter, Laura Frank said all went well for four years until a new CEO came to the station. Over the next three years, her budget and staff were cut and she left in 2020.

A CASE STUDY – THE ACQUISITION OF THE ST. LOUIS BEACON BY THE ST LOUIS PUBLIC RADIO AS VIEWED BY THE BEACON'S FOUNDER MARGARET FREIVOGEL

One of the examples cited in the playbook was the acquisition of the St. Louis Beacon by St. Louis Public Radio, a station owned by the University of Missouri. After the acquisition, the staffs of both organizations did stellar coverage of the Ferguson, Mo. Civil rights riots, but since then the station has been buffeted by managerial changes. The founder of the St. Louis Beacon, Margaret Freivogel, was not interviewed for the playbook but she agreed to share her thoughts about the acquisitions of nonprofit digital start-ups by public media in response to questions:

"My general reflection on the mergers and collaborations between public media stations and nonprofit digital news organizations is that they have not yet reached their full potential. Whether they will remains to be seen.

From the founding of the St. Louis Beacon on, I saw our primary mission as finding ways to carry forward the best purposes and practices of great regional news organizations. Equally important, we had to recognize the flaws in our journalistic heritage and the opportunities of the digital world. My focus was not just investigative reporting, as it was for some new newsrooms. Rather it was to create a new kind of local news organization that could serve a fractured region like St. Louis even better than the legacy media organizations that were dying.

I see public media stations, and particularly public radio, as potentially the skeleton around which these new local news organizations could grow across the country. Public radio already has a public service mission, though stations can't always do much because their staffs are so small. Public radio stations also have relatively healthy revenue streams, including small donor bases that take years to build and provide stability as grants and ads come and go. When the Beacon merged with St. Louis Public Radio, we felt a full integration of the organizations had the best potential to have the most impact. I became the editor of the combined newsroom.

But there are several stumbling blocks to achieving this goal of a renaissance in local news. Among them:

- In my experience, national leadership of NPR often didn't really see the point of building strong local news organizations with both digital and audio components. Rather, they saw local stations primarily as valuable for contributing to the national news content.
- Getting a newsroom to do digital, audio (and sometimes video) is hard. Audio takes time, and print/digital reporters feel bogged down as they learn and as they produce both audio and digital versions of their stories. The reporters are used to quicker turn-around.

- Stations still see themselves first as radio (or maybe audio including podcasts). But to cover a region well, you have to have a strong digital component. That's where you can get into the detail of investigations and of general coverage. On-air time usually includes mostly national feeds, and that's OK. But vigorous local news coverage can't fit in the usual time allotted.

In my time at St. Louis Public Radio, I feel we made progress toward creating the kind of local news organizations we envisioned. Our coverage of the racial uprising in Ferguson was testament to the good work we were able to do. But it was only a few steps of progress on a long and uncharted path. I can't speak to what's happened since I left. I know there's been a great deal of turmoil and turnover at various points, but I hope the newsroom and the organization can rise to the challenge of creating the kind of vigorous regional news organization St. Louisans need".

The playbook also recounted that in 2015, the Crosscut merged with KCTS nine in Seattle to form Cascade Public Media and in early 2018, New York Public Radio acquired the Gothamist for WNYC, KPCC with LAist, and WAMU acquired DCist in Washington DC. It said the sites of Spirited Media, Denverite, became part of Colorado Public Media, and Billy Penn became part of WHYY in Philadelphia. In 2019, NJSpotlight became part of NJTV and WNET in New York 2019.

One acquisition not mentioned is that of the New England Center for Investigative Reporting by WGBH in Boston. The center faded away and the New England last story archived at the WGBH site is from 2016. However, WGBH maintains an investigative desk as part of the collaboration with Boston University.

Other nonprofit newsrooms, meanwhile, work closely with public media, such as Inewsource in San Diego and WisconsinWatch in Madison, Wisconsin, but have foregone any merger or acquisition.

The Public Media Merger Project's in-depth study of seven of the public media station and digital newsroom mergers across the country wanted to see how they worked or did not work, and to analyze what made some acquisitions successful and "what should be avoided".

The result was the valuable and detailed analysis and guide to questions that should be asked by both a public media station and the digital start-up. The two basic questions it said must be asked are:

- Is an acquisition right for our organization?
- How do we manage our merger effectively to accomplish our shared goals?

For its research, it asked:

- What are the major organizational and governance decisions that should organize period and due diligence of a merger between a public broadcaster and a digital newsroom?
- What factors (organizational, cultural, contextual), make a merger more likely to proceed smoothly?
- What factors (organizational, cultural, contextual), make a merger more likely to encounter obstacles
- What are the key financial and technical performance indicators that should be attended entities that are considering a merger?
- What indicators of revenue (including membership, advertising, and sponsorship) are most important to consider, and what are reasonable estimates for the performance boost attributable to a merger?
- What technical considerations should be weighed in the consideration of a merger?
- What set of technical and financial metrics can best measure the impact of a merger?
- What are the major managerial and leadership dynamics that are likely to emerge in the postmerger period?
- In particular, how should newsroom leadership manage staff, technical, financial, editorial, and marketing integrations?

Some of these questions are clearly for larger organizations, which would usually be the public media station. Nonetheless, the detailed parts of the playbook are not only well-suited for an acquisition but provide a guide on what to think about when planning a start-up.

At several places, the playbook also warned about cultural differences between journalists from digital newsrooms, who tended toward more hard-hitting and do fast-paced news and public media journalists who tended toward longer pieces and the craft of storytelling.

Laura Frank aptly characterized the cultural difference as public media tending to be more "educational" and digital newsrooms as more "controversial".

Sue Cross, CEO of INN, said she had reviewed the acquisitions cited in the playbook and thought the acquisition of NJ Spotlight by WNET was a bright success, as the NJ Spotlight had maintained its coverage and benefited from the added resources of WNET. However, she said some of the digital start-ups acquired did more feature and entertainment reporting than community reporting.

"These can be positive in combining complementary resources, but I'm not as sunny about these mergers saving significant accountability or investigative journalism more widely", she said. "We do see the stations providing broader financial stability -- and there are some strong examples of combined public media and investigative newsrooms, such as Louisville Public Media and the Kentucky Center for Investigative Reporting".

Cross said, however, that she had not yet seen public media broadly take on anywhere near the level of local in-depth or civic reporting done by independents.

"We do see increases in other kinds of partnership or collaboration," she said.

Cross said she was bullish about Chicago, but the acquisition of the Sun-Times by Chicago Public Media creates a different kind of institutional journalism. She said that was different from the neighborhood-level coverage and community engagement that a Block Club Chicago or City Bureau "are so spectacularly developing". She also cited the depth of reporting by an Injustice Watch or the Better Government Association in Chicago.

> What we see in some of these cases is public media merging with more of a lifestyle or a very light or limited news outlet, or the significant journalism being diluted into public media culture over time. That may be a good thing in its own right but may not fill the

> same reporting needs that the independent newsrooms are addressing, Cross said.

She said some takeovers, such as Colorado Public Media's of Denverite or KPCC of LA list "seem most like branding extensions and have been incorporated in public media coverage in varying ways".

Cross also noted,

> As in all mergers, companies can be expected to keep evolving. For example, Cascade Public Media's KCTS acquired independent Crosscut.com, which described itself as a feisty, civic-minded newsroom at the time in 2015. Crosscut has grown significantly since being folded under the Cascade umbrella, but also has been repositioned several times, as a local news and reporting brand within KCTS.

8

ADVOCACY, ACTIVISTS, AND SOLUTIONS

In 2022, *The New York Times* worked with a nonprofit newsroom, Intercept Brasil, and two nonprofit advocacy groups on a project with the headline that "The Illegal Airstrips Bringing Toxic Mining to Brazil's Indigenous Land", saying the Times and its partners had identified hundreds of airstrips that bring criminal mining operations to the most remote corners of the Amazon.

One of the nonprofit groups was Environmental Institute and another was Hutukara, a Yanomami nonprofit that advocated for indigenous people in Brazil in the Amazon and that had reported dozens of airstrips that support illegal mining in their indigenous land.

It was just one more example of how traditional newsrooms and advocacy groups could work on investigations together – a practice that had been widely resisted over time and sometimes hotly debated.

But advocacy and activists, who already are part of the nonprofit world, have not only worked with traditional media but also seen an

DOI: 10.4324/9781315719573-9

opportunity to establish newsrooms staffed with experienced journalists that do their own work or work in collaboration with independent newsrooms that generally disavow an advocacy role.

The American Civil Liberties Union, Green Peace, Human Rights, Amnesty International, Transparency.org, and a host of other nonprofit and non-governmental agencies have long been as open activists and advocates for issues such as social injustices, environmental pollution and climate change, and stopping autocratic regimes from the imprisonment and torture of citizens.

These issues are often covered independently by legacy and emerging newsrooms, but since the beginning of the 21st century, advocacy groups have moved from doing their own studies and sharing them with journalists to hiring journalists onto their staffs and sometimes conducting collaborative investigations with newsroom.

The common approaches and interests have been clear for many decades. Transparency.org investigates abusive governments and corruption, keeps a corruption index, does its own investigations, and even has the language of investigative journalism, holding the powerful accountable, in its purpose statement.

It states on its website that if follows that goal, "From our work with investigative journalists uncovering global financial crimes, to our participatory documentary partnerships with African communities working to end land corruption, our innovative, donor-funded projects focus on tackling the biggest corruption challenges of our time".

Another statement looks very much like that on many nonprofit newsrooms sites,

> We hold the powerful and corrupt to account, by exposing the systems and networks that enable corruption. We advocate for policies and build coalitions to change the status quo. Our vision of a corruption-free world is not an end in itself. It is the fight for social and economic justice, human rights, peace and security.

Amnesty International openly discloses its evolution into the international investigative world on its website.

"After more than 50 years of groundbreaking achievements, Amnesty has been through a major transformation, adapting to dramatic changes in the world. We have shifted from a large London base, to open regional offices in cities in Africa, Asia-Pacific, Central and Eastern Europe, Latin America, and the Middle East. These offices are major hubs for our investigations, campaigns, and communications. The new regional offices strengthen the work of sections who already work at the national level in more than 70 countries. We can now respond quickly to events wherever they happen and be a powerful force for freedom and justice".

But in addition to these a new movement in advocacy newsrooms, new initiatives called Solutions Journalism and Constructive Journalism, has said that journalists should not just expose systemic flaws in society and corrupt governments, but also suggest solutions to problems. Also, a new debate has risen over what objectivity is in journalism, seeing objectivity as used as moral relativism in reporting that gives equal say to people who hold untenable positions such as a belief in fascism. Add to that, the periodic push for amateur citizen journalism has been adding a wider variety of plants in the journalistic garden.

Meanwhile, conservatives and libertarians have openly and sometimes secretly financed newsrooms that lean far right with strong political agendas.

These changing models of journalism coincided with the advent of the web and social media and the slow and steady dissolution of legacy journalism.

As noted earlier, as resources and staff for journalism in the U.S. and Europe were greatly diminished by the Great Recession of 2008, journalists became more open to closer relationships with advocates, especially when the organizations were staffed by former colleagues or journalists from more traditional newsrooms.

Some critics and journalists worry those relationships have crossed an ethical line. Yet investigative journalists have long blurred the line between journalism and advocacy because of their desire, or their newsrooms' desire, for reform.

James Aucoin, an expert in the history of investigative journalism, wrote in his monograph on Investigative Reporters and Editors and U.S.

journalism that the reporter Henry Demarest Lloyd set out in the late 19th century to expose the wrongdoing of the Standard Oil Company.

But Aucoin also wrote that Demarest also

> established new standards for thoroughness, accuracy, and documentation of evidence. He approached his reporting with the zeal of a crusader, but his meticulous extensive collection of documented evidence when reporting and writing Wealth Against Commonwealth between 1889 and 1894 was a milestone in the evolution of modern American investigative journalism.

Since then, magazines such as the nonprofit newsrooms Mother Jones and the Nation have had a clearly progressive agenda but have maintained that their reporting is evidence-based, and they have gone onto to win major journalism awards and accolades.

Other newsrooms and journalists have worked closely with advocacy groups, taken news tips from them, been connected to sources by them, but the newsrooms have distanced themselves and identified the advocacy group as a separate independent entity from the newsroom. By that distancing, the newsroom hoped to separate itself from any political statements the advocacy group might make.

Co-Publishing

But over the past two decades, journalists have entered into co-publishing arrangements with advocacy groups. Kimberly Abbott wrote that former ABC News producer Dan Green said that in past years nonprofit advocacy groups were always helpful, but today they are essential because stretched journalists simply don't have time to do groundwork – finding experts, lining up interviews, researching characters – before parachuting into a foreign country.

But further questions detailed by Abbott in her Nieman Reports article are whether journalists can maintain independence and will "the arrangement undermine the audience's trust in the media, no matter how altruistic the cause?"

Others argue that the newsroom partnerships with non-government organizations may blur editorial lines and put the journalist at risk of losing objectivity – that is, tilting the reporting and writing to a political view, and potentially – and losing credibility. It could also put the NGO at risk of straying from its mission.

"The promise of NGO journalism is that advocacy groups will pick up some of the slack in media coverage, while deepening public engagement on pressing problems. The peril is that it will distract advocacy groups from their core aims and turn journalism into a platform for fundraising or misleading reporting", wrote Matthew Powers, a communication professor at the University of Washington and author of "NGOs as Newsmakers", for The Conversation.

He noted that

> the entrance of NGOs into journalism presents complications. Advocacy groups produce information not just to inform and enlighten but also to boost donations and promote their brands. Sometimes, these latter aims lead organizations to sensationalize their coverage, which can, in turn, distort public perceptions about the nature of social problems.

As Abbott asked in the Nieman Reports, "But is it better to use the resources – staff, expertise or even funding – of a non-profit organization than to not do the story at all? Is the journalist serving the public better by ignoring the story altogether or by using available channels? As news organizations look for new ways to access original, international stories, they are "increasingly willing to bend some of these rules, as long as you don't bend them too far, media ethicist Steve Roberts says".

Abbott continued:

> Critics who suggest that partnerships cross editorial lines fail to acknowledge — or admit — that these professional barriers have long since begun to erode. Military embed programs have become commonplace and are considered acceptable as long as they are openly presented as such and supplemented with balancing material.

But actually working openly together has been resisted and discouraged by some newsrooms because of the belief that the advocacy group starts at a point of collecting information that will prove the group's points as opposed to a journalist starting with a hypothesis, collecting evidence and publishing or airing findings-based evidence and investigation even if it contradicts the original hypothesis. In fact, some journalists feel the counter-intuitive findings are often more valuable than proving what "everyone knows".

Kate Wright, author of *Who's Reporting Africa Now? Non-Governmental Organizations, Journalists, and Multimedia*, which looked at the growth of NGO work published by African media, has been critical of the interactions between journalists and NGOs. She said that "in seeking to justify their uses of NGO content, journalists tend to alter their understandings of what 'good' journalism is and what it is for".

The line between newsrooms and NGOs has been further obscured with organizations like Greenpeace and the Human Rights Organization hiring investigative reporters and creating their own investigative teams who look like and perform like a newsroom investigative team.

UK Greenpeace, for example, funds an investigative journalism project, "Unearthed", that has its own investigative unit (see below). "UnEarthed" says it maintains editorial independence and it publishes

> accurate, honest, change-making stories that illuminate parts of our changing world no one else is looking at. Environmental journalism is getting better, but the media landscape is still lacking in in-depth, sustained coverage of issues that are only increasing in urgency, from climate change to ocean plastic pollution.

But on a more pragmatic level, some worry journalists with Greenpeace or an advocacy group might distract the journalists from a wider range of different sources or preclude interviews with sources that would provide a better understanding, if not a balance, to the investigation.

Or it might preclude an interview with a key source who might deliver valuable information, leads to valuable information, or even self-incriminating remarks. These collaborations are a new direction in bonding with NGOs is the familiar journalism "consequentialism" that emphasizes the eventual news story is the ultimate justification for the collaboration and for any judgment about the rightness or wrongness of the reporting leading to the story.

Journalists and greenpeace

A strong supporter of working closely with NGOs is long-time journalist and professor Mark Lee Hunter, who is based in Europe where some of the U.S. ethical concerns are not mirrored. Hunter has directly addressed the ethical issues involved.

Hunter wrote for the Global Investigative Journalism Network that "the question on the table is no longer whether, but *how* investigative reporters can collaborate with NGOs".

Hunter said he approached the Greenpeace about working on a carbon cap scandal in 2017 and he and other journalists entered into a contract to work together on the project.

Hunter said the minimum criterion for collaborating with NGOs is acceptance of their means and ends. He acknowledged the main hurdles were ethics and credibility because the advocacy groups are considered biased, by their very nature.

He said the groups can provide information to journalists, like any other source. "Taking their money, as opposed to working for and with news media, therefore means risking one's credibility", he said. But Hunter also added a caveat:

> With all respect, I think this is a secondary debate. If we are in "a war," as Drew Sullivan of the nonprofit Organized Crime and Corruption Reporting Project said, we must have allies who share key goals and values. Some NGOs meet those criteria. It would be more useful to treat collaborations with them as strategic alliances, in which partners share resources and risks toward an agreed-upon goal. In strategic partnerships, working methods, standards, and desired outcomes are matters of negotiation.

Hunter said that NGOs including Greenpeace, Amnesty International, and Global Witness emphasize "the accuracy and coherence of their reports" and that he concluded that they embody a new kind of information media. In the case of his alliance with Greenpeace, he said the organization was wanted to include reporting on a methane pollution issue but when the evidence was not there the topic was dropped.

Indeed, Hunter and those who share his viewpoint hearken back to muckraker Demarest's work in the 1800s.

"I wanted to work with people focused on achieving reforms that matter to me. I have lived part-time in a farming region since 2001, and I saw first-hand that subsidies through the EU's Common Agricultural Policy (CAP) had failed miserably to save rural Europe from depopulation, while making agribusiness interests very rich" Hunter wrote. "Greenpeace has a reform platform, and I checked it before undertaking the project".

Matt Ingram, writing for the Columbia Journalism Review in 2018, said,

> There's no question that work like that done by Human Rights Watch, Greenpeace, and Amnesty International around issues like immigration, the environment, and totalitarianism can help fill gaps in traditional media coverage—especially in foreign countries, where few media companies have the resources to invest in on-the-ground reporting.

But, he said,

> These groups are not fundamentally journalistic in nature. Although they may look and behave like modern media organizations, they are advocacy groups, and have an explicit agenda; they're looking for impact. That agenda may coincide with the news, and they may use traditional journalistic techniques to advance it, but in most cases the larger goal of this work is in service of some kind of policy change or other action, and not information or the public record per se.

American civil liberties union takes up investigative journalism

The ACLU mission statement says the organization "dares to create a more perfect union – beyond one person, party, or side. Our mission is to realize this promise of the United States Constitution for all and expand the reach of its guarantees".

Formed in 1920, it is nonprofit and nonpartisan and gets its revenues from grants, donors, and membership fees and takes no government money. It says it "has 500 staff attorneys, thousands of volunteer attorneys, and offices throughout the nation" and that it continues to fight government abuse and defend individual freedoms. For more than 100 years, its fight has been in the courts and one of its battles has been for freedom of the press.

But in recent years, it has embarked on journalistic investigations. As of 2018, the ACLU's newsroom was producing up to 20 stories a week. Its editorial director was Terry Tang, who had been worked as senior editor at the *The New York Times* for two decades before joining the ACLU in 2017, according to a Columbia Journalism Review article. After joining the ACLU, Tang told the Review she was hiring journalists and planned to add podcasts and videos.

"We have the legal expertise and policy expertise for a lot of these kinds of stories–people who have been plowing these fields for a long time and really know those issues", Tang told the review. "So when something happens it's not like they're just reporting the news, they already understand the issues and so they are able to produce analysis as well. It's not terribly different than having a very seasoned beat reporter".

The ACLU did go onto start the "At Liberty" weekly podcast that reports on civil rights and civil liberties and it has been advertising for contract investigative reporters throughout the U.S. One ad for a contract reporter in Indiana read in part:

> The ACLU of Indiana is seeking an experienced, reliable, and highly motivated Investigative Reporter Contractor. The Investigative Reporter will engage in research, documentation, story gathering, and data analysis that will be used to illuminate media, lawmaker, and public perceptions around civil liberties issues. Projects will focus heavily on the criminal legal system in Indiana.

The job description is much like any other that in regular journalism ads. It said the investigative reporter would develop public materials such as "white papers, reports, and fact sheets" and find "compelling narratives about ACLU's work by engaging with community members to highlight personal stories".

Unlike ads from traditional newsrooms, it made the advocacy duties clear, saying it said the reporter would be "personally committed to ACLU's values, mission, goals and programs…" while echoing more traditional ads, saying the ideal candidate would be "a rock-star writer with an established track record for producing clear and compelling content, distilling complicated narratives, issues, and data sets down into values-based, human-centered stories that inspire people to take action".

Some of the ACLU stories were breaking investigations that were followed by the traditional newsrooms. One of the most notable was a ACLU investigation into the presence of lead in the water of the city of Flint, Michigan.

Curt Guyette, who had 30 years of previous experience at traditional newsrooms, had covered the issues for several months and had worked on a short documentary produced by the ACLU of Michigan. He was an investigative reporter for the ACLU, and during his work, he obtained a leaked memo from the U.S. Environmental Protection Agency about how the state's testing system produced artificially low results. The work resulted in the state taking action to ensure safe water for Flint.

Guyette joined the ACLU's Michigan Democracy Watch Project in 2013. At the time, the Michigan ACLU was said to have an investigative reporter on staff. It was a position supported by a Ford Foundation grant.

At the time, the ACLU Michigan office wrote: "So, let's begin this experiment in nonprofit journalism by turning to the traditional five Ws – who, what, when, where, why – and scrambling their order, going straight to the last one first….Why has the ACLU of Michigan hired a reporter to investigate and write about issues involving emergency management and open government in this state?"

The short answer is this: "The suspension of democracy in financially stressed cities and school districts spread across Michigan is an unprecedented occurrence. There have never been laws that go as far as PA 4, which was quickly rejected by voters, and its hastily enacted replacement, PA 436".

A columnist for Free Press in Detroit was quoted as saying, "'What they did [in making the EPA memo public] was critical'. When you look at it now, the memo really laid out all the problems…".

"I was really walking a line in my own role as a journalist and activist", Guyette told the Columbia Journalism Review, "I'm not just observing the story; I'm participating in it. In my mind, I'm just trying to get to the truth".

Guyette told the journal that his team needed to make the lead testing "bulletproof", because "we knew [skeptics] would come after us" he added.

"The bottom line is that as important as credibility is to any journalist, it's even more important when you're pushing things the way we push them", Guyette said. "You cannot be wrong, because you're so easy to discredit as just having an agenda".

Here is an overview of two other progressive organizations that have increased their investigative reporting.

Human Rights Watch

Human Rights Watch says it is an independent, international organization that works as part of a vibrant movement to uphold human dignity and advance the cause of human rights for all. Our staff consists of human rights professionals including country experts, lawyers, journalists, and academics of diverse backgrounds and nationalities.

Human Rights Watch also says "we scrupulously investigate abuses, expose the facts widely, and pressure those with power to respect rights and secure justice".

It issued reports that are detailed, evidence-based, and read very much like investigative journalism. In just the first five months of 2022, it issued meticulous reports that any newsroom would be considered worthy of investigations. The investigations covered topics of gender discrimination, war, and shortage of medications: Among the investigations it listed:

- The Deadly Impact of Failure to Protect: An 86-page report, "Combatting Domestic Violence in Turkey: The Deadly Impact of Failure to Protect", found failure to enforce court orders leaves women open to continuing abuse from current or former husbands and partners.

- Efforts to Ban Gender and Sexuality Education in Brazil. A 77-page report, "'I Became Scared, This Was Their Goal': Efforts to Ban Gender and Sexuality Education in Brazil", that analyzes 217 bills and laws presented between 2014 and 2022 designed to explicitly forbid the teaching or sharing of gender and sexuality education, or ban so-called "gender ideology" or "indoctrination".
- Cluster Munition Attacks in Ukraine: A 26-page report, "Intense and Lasting Harm: Cluster Munition Attacks in Ukraine", details how Russian armed forces have used at least six types of cluster munitions in the international armed conflict in Ukraine.
- Stymied Reforms in the Maldives: A 56-page report, "'I Could Have Been Next': Stymied Reforms in the Maldives", finds that the Solih administration, more than halfway into its five-year term, has not fulfilled election promises to reform the criminal justice system to address threats to free expression.
- United States' Lack of Regulation Fuels Crisis of Unaffordable Insulin: A 92-page report, "'If I'm Out of Insulin, I'm Going to Die:' United States' Lack of Regulation Fuels Crisis of Unaffordable Insulin", describes the human rights impacts of US government policies that make essential life-saving medication like insulin unaffordable for many people.
- Greece's Use of Migrants as Police Auxiliaries in Pushbacks: A 29-page report "'Their Faces Were Covered': Greece's Use of Migrants as Police Auxiliaries in Pushbacks", found that Greek police are detaining asylum seekers at the Greece-Turkey land border at the Evros River, in many cases stripping them of most of their clothing and stealing their money, phones, and other possess
- Killings, Abductions, Torture, and sexual Violence Against LGBT People by Armed Groups in Iraq:" An 86-page report, "'Everyone Wants Me Dead': Killings, Abductions, Torture, and Sexual Violence Against LGBT People by Armed Groups in Iraq", documents cases of attempted murder of LGBT people by armed groups primarily within the Popular Mobilization Forces (PMF), which are nominally under the prime minister's authority.

Greenpeace unearthed

Greenpeace is a well-known environmental activist group that says its goal "is to ensure the ability of the earth to nurture life in all its diversity, meaning it wants to" protect biodiversity in all its forms, prevent pollution and abuse of the earth's ocean, land, air and fresh water, end all nuclear threats and promote peace, global disarmament and nonviolence.

In 2012, Greenpeace in the UK founded Energydesk and later became Greenpeace Unearthed. It started out as a small team of journalists dedicated to open and accurate reporting on energy and climate change. It said it has grown to cover the environment "more broadly, from forests and oceans to bees and air pollution, as well as the politics and economics that underpin them".

The project added an investigations unit in 2015 and it said we

> publish accurate, honest, change-making stories that illuminate parts of our changing world no one else is looking at. Environmental journalism is getting better, but the media landscape is still lacking in in-depth, sustained coverage of issues that are only increasing in urgency, from climate change to ocean plastic pollution.

It has openly collaborated with more traditional newsrooms on large, often global investigations.

Among its investigations it has been noted:

- A collaboration with a newsroom that found the United Kingdom exported thousands of tons of banned pesticides in 2020, with shipments including a wider range of toxic substances than ever previously revealed, a new *Unearthed* and Public Eye investigation has found.
- A collaboration with newsrooms that found a major supplier of animal feed is still buying soya and corn from a farm linked to the destruction of the Amazon rainforest, despite pledging to clean up its global supply chains. It found that Cargill, a giant agricultural multinational that sells feed to British chicken farms, has been buying crops from a farm growing soya beans on deforested land in

the Brazilian Amazon. The collaboration included the Bureau of Investigative Journalism, Repórter Brasil and Ecostorm.

- An investigation that found ExxonMobil continues to fight efforts to tackle climate change in the United States, despite publicly claiming to support the Paris climate agreement, an undercover investigation by Unearthed has found. It said a senior lobbyist for Exxon told an undercover reporter that the company had been working to weaken key aspects of President Joe Biden's flagship initiative on climate change, the American Jobs Plan.
- An investigation into a past peet-burning season, in which it developed a methodology that uses data from three satellite services – including satellites run by NASA and the European Space Agency – to find evidence of grouse moor fires that was overlaid over government maps that was cross referend hundreds of eyewitness reports obtained by Wild Moors, a campaign group in Northern England.

Conservative and libertarian newsrooms

As progressive organizations have entered the field of investigation so have conservative and libertarian groups. As pointed out by the Harvard Business School index, some of these news groups do not disclose the sources of funds. Nonetheless, there is enough money trail and evidence within the news stories to ascertain the influences and directions.

One of the first efforts was the formation of Watchdog.org, which was the website of a group of statehouse bureaus funded by the Center for Public and Government Integrity (which initially created confusion because its name was similar to the longstanding and nonpartisan Center for Public Integrity). The Center for Public and Government Integrity was funded by the Sam Adams Alliance, a conservative and libertarian foundation in Chicago.

None of the organizations disclosed their individual donors, but further investigation found that some donors were wealthy conservatives. Eventually, journalists who had been hired at watchdog bureaus began leaving, saying there was pressure to tilt their stories to politically conservative views. The organization has now changed its name to Center in the Square.

Another conservative newsroom has been Breitbart News, which has become known for its extreme right-wing views, and is funded by the wealthy conservative family the Mercers.

The third openly political investigative nonprofit is Project Veritas, which has performed undercover, ambush reporting of progressive groups and leaders in which the progressives revealed certain biases. In some cases, the work by Project Veritas has led to resignations.

Because the conservative bias of these newsrooms has been revealed, or they have acknowledged it, the accuracy and context of the reporting have often been questioned.

However, the non-disclosure or unclear disclosure of funds has also led to questions about the more progressive news organization, the nonprofit States Newsroom, which has funding from progressive philanthropists, and has been setting up statehouse bureaus across the country.

The move to advocate for solutions

Over the past few years, a new direction in journalism has risen, largely foundation supported, that emphasizes the need to do reporting that also suggests solutions. In the U.S., it is called "Solutions Journalism" and in Europe, it is called "Constructive Journalism".

Solutions Journalism, begun by two former *The New York Times* reporters, says its "mission is to transform journalism so that all people have access to news that helps them envision and build a more equitable and sustainable world". Yet, it says, "journalism is struggling to be the corrective force it can be".

The site suggests by covering solutions, rather than just problems,

> journalists can equip people in all communities with the knowledge to envision and build a more equitable and sustainable world. We aim to ensure, by 2025, that the majority of US news consumers, and increasing numbers globally, have access to solutions journalism, no matter where or how they get their news. To reach that aim, we will engage journalists, educators, other media producers, news organizations and J-schools.

As of 2022, Solutions Journalism said it had more than 500 news organizations and 20,000 journalists worldwide working with the organization and that said "research shows that, across all demographics, audiences find solutions stories more interesting, trustworthy and informative, changing their understanding of issues in a way that makes them more enthusiastic about participating in civic life".

Some long-time investigative journalists have been puzzled or skeptical of their approaches since many investigative stories have suggested solutions by comparing a systemic failure to reforms that have happened in other locations. Nonetheless, the movement, which gives out grants to newsrooms and conducts training, has gained momentum without too much debate on whether journalists may take on more advocacy roles. The journalism upholds the usual standards of being evidence-based while recommending ways a situation or system can be corrected and it continues to receive strong support from foundations who give to journalism in general.

Meanwhile, part of the constructive journalism initiative has decided it has done enough work. The site constructivejournalism.org said that

> after six years of pioneering work, we feel that the Constructive Journalism Project has achieved its mission of raising awareness of constructive journalism and helping it grow into an established field of journalistic practice. As a result, we have decided to wrap up the project.

The group said it had fought the "negativity bias in the news" by forming a collective to promote and train journalists in the movement and said it had collaborated with universities in the United Kingdom to share lessons from the "growing body of research on solutions-focused news on audiences" and then worked with newsrooms globally.

It said other organizations promoting and teaching constructive and solutions journalism have grown new groups have started up.

> Many are now much larger and better resourced than our project, so we end our activity knowing that the field is in good hands. We've

> been particularly inspired by the brilliant work of the Solutions Journalism Network in the US and Europe, as well as the launch of the Constructive Institute and the Constructive Journalism Network.

Indeed, the movement continues and the Constructive Journalism Institute in Denmark has a website of resources and holds Global conferences, and like other such efforts, says its approach will help with "news avoidance" by the public.

9

MAINTAINING JOURNALISM STANDARDS AND NEW ETHICAL CHALLENGES AND PERILS

In 2010, Stephen Ward, a professor of journalism ethics, wrote in the introduction to a report on ethics for nonprofit newsrooms,

> A media revolution is transforming, fundamentally and irrevocably, the nature of journalism and its ethics. Our media ecology is a chaotic landscape evolving at a furious pace. Professional journalists share the journalistic sphere with tweeters, bloggers, citizen journalists, and social media users.

Indeed, the entry into journalism of advocates, activists, political operatives, and propagandists has brought many new challenges to maintaining credibility and creating trust.

There have been the usual ethical and cultural clashes over what is moral and ethical to publish and present, when a reporter should go undercover or do surveillance, how to avoid endangering people through irresponsible publishing, and the proper use of data and leaked information.

DOI: 10.4324/9781315719573-10

But with the omnipresent, error-filled social media, the anonymity the web can allow, the rise of bots and disinformation, the pervasive fake videos and reporting, and the need to establish standards for truth and ethical guidelines for transparency and conduct have vastly escalated.

In addition, fundamental words in journalism such as objectivity have been questioned on both the right and left of the political spectrum.

Originally, objectivity was defined as applying social science to journalism – start with a hypothesis, collect evidence, and produce a story based on the evidence and not the hypothesis. But the concept had been corrupted in corporate newsrooms to mean each side or sides of a story can be allowed to have an equal say even if one side has no facts or is consciously lying.

That approach of moral ambiguity and outright ignoring of the truth had led to an overall questioning of the use of objectivity and justification for reporting on what one believed rather than what the facts were, leading to further erosion of the credibility of the profession of journalism.

Issues on journalism ethics increase

Early on in the nonprofit newsroom movement, the founders of the Investigative News Network, now the Institute for Nonprofit News, recognized new issues that they had not confronted in commercial newsrooms that were present in the nonprofit world. As one journalist observed, "You used to have advertisers, now you have funders". Suddenly, a new nonprofit newsroom leader had to consult standards and guidelines present in public media and in a few existing nonprofit newsrooms.

That same leader also had to recognize that the questions of transparency had to be addressed. An advertisement, through its very nature, identified who was a source of revenue. But a philanthropist might expect anonymity since universities, museums, libraries, and even public media were willing to do that. In addition, philanthropy tax rules in the U.S. allowed donors to nonprofits to be assured of anonymity unless they chose to identify themselves.

Since many of the founders of the first wave of nonprofit newsrooms in the 21st century were investigative reporters, they had spent their careers following the influence of dark money, that is, money whose source was hidden and they understood the potential for corruption through dark money.

And it was not theoretical: Already the network of statehouses known as Watchdog.org had refused to disclose their donors. A member of the group, who had attended the gathering that established INN, was being denied membership in INN because of the refusal to reveal donors. In trying to track the source of watchdog.org funding, it turned out that the source was the Center for Public and Government Integrity (a name very close to the long-established Center for Public Integrity), which in turn had been financed by the conservative and libertarian foundation called the Sam Adams Alliance in Chicago. (Later, it turned out that conservative donors who wanted to hide their involvement in the statehouse newsrooms had given to the Alliance.)

At the same time, there was another progressive group creating statehouse bureaus that would not disclose its donors and so it was denied membership in INN.

So the issues of transparency, nonpartisanship, and editorial independence were very real in 2010 when the number of nonprofit newsrooms in the U.S. began to increase.

Convening on ethical challenges

In response, some of the founders and supporters of the nonprofit movement, of which I was one, gathered with journalism ethics professor and expert Stephen Ward at the University of Wisconsin in Madison in 2010 to address the questions that would arise about the nonprofits financing – and to begin to create standards that would answer those questions.

Out of the two-day convening and our debates born of experience, Ward produced a report called "Ethics for the New Investigative Newsroom: A Roundtable Report on the Best Practices for Nonprofit Journalism".

He began carefully: "This report lays down tentative guidelines for new models of investigative journalism. We are conscious that the report does not provide the final answers. There are no quick fixes, only sustained and thoughtful dialogue", but indeed many of the suggestions made at the convening informed and improved the standards for the Institute for Nonprofit News and its members.

The report said that "Journalism ethics must do more than point out the tensions between old and new media. It needs to re-invent itself for a new media age. It must decide which principles should be preserved. It should provide new standards to guide online and offline journalism".

The roundtable participants recognized that some issues, such as transparency and conflicts of interest, are not new. Nor is nonprofit journalism a new idea, given the history of public broadcasting. However, participants noted that such issues arise in the new arena of nonprofit, online journalism, and require new policies.

The first issue the group confronted was "the reliance of nonprofit investigative newsrooms on a limited number of donors". "From whom will the centers accept funding? Which donors might threaten the center's integrity?"

A look at the standards for funding at public media had already led to some questions on whether that would provide a satisfactory template for the new digital newsrooms, especially investigative ones.

NPR states that all "funding sources, including corporate sponsors are considered under the "access" principle, which means that NPR has no list of sources from which funding will not be accepted. However, potential conflict of interest and problems of listener misperception, confusion, or similar reason regarding the funder's role and/or influence on programming will be considered in accepting or rejecting underwriting". In addition, NPR also takes government funding, which had been a controversial issue among journalists who worried about undue influence, although often journalists did not know the history of tax breaks, postal discounts, legal notice revenue from government, and other favorable regulatory action taken by the government on behalf of journalism.

At that point in the nonprofit movement in 2010, there also were questions about ever accepting non-media corporate funding since investigative journalists often reported adversely on corporations.

The report stated,

> Centers also need to decide whether they will take money from conventional sources, such as corporations, government, and unions. The acceptance of government money sparked an intense discussion. Some participants worried about journalism becoming indebted to government. Others pointed out that government funding is a familiar feature of public broadcasting.

But there was consensus that the first standard must be editorial independence and that independence should be made clear to any donors or supports.

Transparency

NPR also had a policy that started with the assumption of anonymity of donors, an issue already of concern within the nonprofit movement about conservative-based newsrooms not disclosing its donors.

The NPR policy stated:

> NPR generally doesn't disclose information about its donors, except where permitted by the donor, required by law or government regulation, or as otherwise specified when we collect the information. We do publicly acknowledge donors above a certain level, unless a donor has requested anonymity, but do not include contact or other personal information about donors in our public listings of donors. In addition, we may share information about donors with Member stations that are associated with the donor on the NPR Services or that are to the donor, unless the donor has requested anonymity.

But even if a center has a policy on acceptable donors, the group explored how much information on funders will it provide to the public? The roundtable agreed that, in principle, the newsrooms should try to resist anonymity, but it recognized nuances. Some donors want to be anonymous because they want to avoid public recognition or having others solicit donations from them.

Over the years, the Institute for Nonprofit News has had its guidelines on anonymity evolve. Initially, it asked all members to publish all donors who gave $500 or more. When some members balked at that the INN board eventually raised the limit to $5,000 or more and then added a caveat that no more than 15 percent of an organization's donations can be anonymous.

But as time went by, the debate became more complicated as donor-advised funds started coming to newsrooms. Donor-advised funds are held by a third party such as the Fidelity fund and the donor directs that a contribution be made to a certain organization. Sometimes the nonprofit knows who is directing the donation, sometimes it does not. Some centers argued that if they did not know who directed the donation, then how could they be influenced by the donation.

Other issues brought up at the roundtable were: Will the center disclose any conditions placed on the gift by the donor? Will the center explain publicly which money goes for what story? The consensus was that as much openness as possible would increase a center's credibility. At that time, the issue of foundations or donors requesting a non-disclosure agreement had not even come up, although in later years some foundations tried to get newsrooms to sign the agreements, in which the newsroom legally pledged not to disclose the funder in any way.

The roundtable and subsequent discussions about INN membership formed into INN's general standards as stated in the below section.

INN's standards and what it means to be part of the INN Network

Over the past decade, INN's standards have won the respect of its members and also funders. Some foundations ask if an applicant for a grant is a member of INN, indicating the applicant has passed muster on INN's policies. Here is the INN statement on values and ethics:

INN's vision is to build a nonprofit news network that ensures all people in every community have access to trusted news. To that end, we pursue our mission of providing education and business support services to our nonprofit member organizations and promoting the value and benefit of public service and investigative journalism.

To this end, INN supports, leads, and connects a community of nonprofit, nonpartisan newsrooms that do journalism: gathering, assessing, creating, and presenting news and information. This definition and the following purpose and elements are drawn from "The Elements of Journalism", and they are a good place to start in determining if your newsroom would benefit from INN membership or fit INN membership standards.

INN member newsrooms serve the general public and the overall purpose of journalism: to provide citizens with the information they need to make the best possible decisions about their lives, their communities, their societies, and their governments. They are built on these four elements:

- Journalism's first obligation is to the truth
- Its first loyalty is to citizens
- Its essence is a discipline of verification
- Its practitioners maintain independence from those that they cover

We hold these standards so that the public and other media can know the values and practices of these newsrooms, something that's increasingly important in building trust between the free press and the public we serve. These standards also define a community of newsrooms that collaborate and share coverage based on an understanding of their shared practices.

Donor policies

Over the past decade, most INN members have posted their donor policies. One example is Reveal, also known as the Center for Investigative Reporting.

Financial transparency and donor acceptance policy

"We are committed to transparency in every aspect of funding our organization.

We accept gifts, grants, and sponsorships from individuals, corporations, organizations, and foundations to help with our general operations, editorial beats, and special projects. As a 501(c)(3) nonprofit that operates as a public trust, we do not pay certain taxes. We may receive funds from government programs offered to nonprofits or similar businesses. (In 2020, Reveal received a forgivable loan from the Small Business Administration's Paycheck Protection Program.)

Our journalism judgments are made independently – not based on or influenced by donors or any revenue source. We do not give supporters the rights to assign, review, or edit content.

We will accept anonymous donations without restrictions only if they adhere to all the guidelines laid out in this statement.

We make public through our IRS Form 990 Schedule B, all revenue sources and donors who give $5,000 or more per year. We will not accept donations from sources who – deemed by our board of directors – present a conflict of interest with our work, mission, and values or compromise our independence".

Conflicts of interest

The roundtable in Wisconsin found sufficient principles for the journalists at centers for avoiding conflicts in existing codes of ethics at the Society for Professional Journalists, NPR, and other legacy newsrooms. And it was clear that centers must be able to do the stories they thought important, but they also "must be prepared to do stories that involve funders or board members" – as in the later Reveal policy – just as for-profit newsrooms had always had to be prepared to do stories on advertisers.

The roundtable also noted that the centers had to be careful in taking story suggestions from donors or board members because of the possible perception the board members or donors were paying or steering stories in their interest and have a firewall between the newsroom and donor/supporters.

Since then, like Reveal, the nonprofit newsroom Vt. Digger and its parent organization, the Vermont Journalism Trust have publicized a very clear policy on their website and they also added their conflict of interest policy for board members. Here is the policy:

> Board members may not use their position to influence the reporting of the news. Board members are prohibited from using their position as a member of the Board, as a donor, or as a contributor in any other capacity, to influence the reporting of VTDigger.org, a project of the Vermont Journalism Trust, LTD. ("VJT").

"This *Conflict of Interest Policy* seeks to advance and protect the dedication to nonpartisan and unbiased news reporting of VJT and its projects, including VTDigger.org, and establishes principles for recognizing potential and actual conflicts of interest, procedures for disclosing potential and actual conflicts, and guidelines for determining the appropriate course of conduct when a conflict exists. No policy can possibly cover all conflict of interest issues but these guidelines attempt to guide Trustees in dealing with issues that may arise and give confidence to the public that no undue influence is being exercised by Trustees on any news reporting projects.

As a media organization and a guardian of the public trust, VJT and the individuals representing it must conduct their affairs according to the highest possible ethical and moral standards. As overseers and representatives of the organization, Trustees may on occasion be in a position to have conflicts of interest with respect to decisions and transactions involving VJT and/or VTDigger.org. Trustees must carefully adhere to the principles set forth in this Policy".

Roundtable members worried that the Internet had made a shambles of ethics, that even then "misinformation outruns facts, and opinions 'outshout' reporting. Ethics is considered to be 'quaint' and old-fashioned". Because of that the roundtable agreed ethics needed to be institutionalized and policies easy to understand shared with the public.

Guidelines for both those receiving and giving money

Another group, this time of funders and newsrooms, later met in 2017, to hone guidelines both for newsrooms and donors.

Called "Guidance on philanthropic funding of media and news", the American Press Institute reported on "two sets of broad guidelines of best practices for funders and for nonprofits". The guidelines followed a report, "Charting new ground: The ethical terrain of nonprofit journalism".

"The following two sets of broad guidelines of best practices, one for funders and another for nonprofit media organizations, are the product of more than two years of work exploring the question". The guidelines also applied to for-profit newsrooms since many are taking donations and grants.

The institute cautioned that

> the guidelines come issued in the name of API. Informed by all our conversations, they do not necessarily carry the stamp of approval, in full, of an individual organization whose perspective or employee's perspective was shared within the process. But we do hope they carry their wisdom.

The principles for the funders included guidance on transparency, preventing pressure on grantees, support for newsrooms with high standards, and support for editorial independence:

Transparency with the public: Funders should be transparent about the media they are funding, and they should expect media partners to report their sources of funding. Funders should articulate their motivations for funding journalism and explain what would constitute success in meeting their purposes.

Communications with grantees: Funders should be clear about whether they expect measurement of results, and, if they do, funders should support the cost of the evaluation. Funders should engage the media organizations they fund about what was learned from a particular grant and encourage them to share these lessons with the nonprofit news field.

When possible, news organizations, not funders, should initiate conversations about the journalism they wish to produce. In cases where a funder contacts a news organization first, it is better if the coverage areas being discussed should already be part of the news organization's portfolio, or on a list of projects or beats for which the journalists are seeking funding.

Integrity: Funders should support media organizations that strive to achieve the highest editorial and ethical standards of journalism.

Independence: Funders should uphold the principle of editorial independence in the following ways: There should be no pre-publication review or attempts to influence coverage (either as a condition of the grant or in practice). There should be zero to light-touch post-publication editorial feedback. Funders should offer general operating support whenever possible, thereby providing grantees with maximum flexibility.

When supporting specific content areas or projects, the grant should be broad and general. Ideally, any discussion should be no more specific than about beats or general areas of coverage.

When funding more specific topics or series, the funder and grantee should agree in advance on clear parameters of the grant and the work.

To avoid the appearance of undue influence or attempting to buy coverage, funders should try to avoid when possible being the sole underwriters of specific stories or series. They also should avoid conversations about specific expectations related to the conclusions, outcomes, or opinions that will be derived from the reporting.

One guideline acknowledged that for-profits were seeking and receiving funding:

> The principles outlined above apply equally whether a funder is working with a nonprofit media outlet or a for-profit.
>
> Another guideline seemed to suggest support for business capacity and training

Sustainability and organizational health: Funders should focus not only on reporting and content, but also consider what organizations need to be stronger, more resilient, and sustainable over the long term.

Another suggested that funders themselves should get training on best funding practices for newsrooms.

Education: Funders should actively educate others within their foundation (board, leadership, and program staff) about the nature and best practices of funding independent media.

And another suggested that in the interest of transparency both donors and donees should publish their guidelines.

Guidelines: Funders should adopt and publish guidelines to govern their organization's transparent and ethical support of media. Funders should also encourage or require media partners to have written guidelines of their own outlining their methods of editorial independence and journalistic ethics that they publish.

Meanwhile, the guidelines for newsrooms taking grants and donations were quite similar to those developed in 2010 and carried on by INN.

The principles for nonprofits (and for-profits taking donations and grants) included:

Editorial independence: News organizations should retain editorial control. They should not relinquish legal and ethical responsibilities to funders or to the public.

- News organizations should not allow pre-publication editorial review and never accept directed conclusions from funders.
- Journalists should not promise outcomes in advance.
- News organizations should have a review process to determine whether to accept and how to handle funds for limited purposes, such as coverage of a beat or issue, especially if funders have an interest in related policy outcomes.

Transparency: News organizations should aim for the highest practicable degree of transparency regarding editorial, donor, and business standards and operations, both as a matter of journalistic integrity and because of the transparency journalists demand from other institutions.

- News organizations should clearly disclose their ethics policies, mission statements, conflict of interest policies, and fundraising policies on their websites.

- News organizations should clearly disclose their federal tax returns, audited financial statements, and basic information about the staff and board of directors on their website; they should also explain how to contact the newsroom to report errors or make complaints on their websites.
- Donor information should be readily available to the public. The public should know who paid for the journalism. Projects funded by specific funders should include notifications to the public.
- News organizations should consider in advance how funding decisions will be explained to the public, including critics. Avoid acceptance of funding when it would compromise the integrity or credibility of the journalism.
- News organizations should accept anonymous donations, including from donor-advised funds, only under carefully considered conditions. To do so, each news organization should develop criteria before considering donations.
- News organizations should also encourage all donors to be public and should explain the importance of transparency to the credibility and impact their work.

The guidelines noted that the question of impact should be handled carefully by newsrooms.

Communications with funders: Independent journalism is a public good. Journalism can produce impact and change, but news organizations cannot and should not promise specific outcomes. News organizations can, however, summarize what they have learned during the course of their work.

- News organizations should clearly inform funders of the news organization's mission and guiding values.
- News organizations should help funders understand that support for independent media is in their interest and differs from that of PR and advocacy organizations.
- News organizations have a strong preference for general support on the principle that it best preserves independent journalism. Any fundraising policy should clearly state conditions governing acceptance of general support, coverage of issues and beats, and coverage of specific projects and stories.

- When civic or community engagement is part of a grant, journalists and funders should agree in advance what that means.
- When possible, news organizations, not funders, should initiate conversations about the journalism they wish to produce. In cases where a funder contacts a news organization first, it is better if the coverage areas being discussed should already be part of the news organization's portfolio, or on a list of projects or beats for which the journalists are seeking funding.
- News organizations should have written policies that establish these principles of editorial.
- Independence, transparency, and communication will be the starting point of any interaction with funders.

The Trust Project

Another organization has added to move to achieve standards of credibility within the field. It is called the Trust Project, which is working internationally newsrooms. The Trust Project built the trust indicators "by asking people what they value in the news – and what wins and loses their trust. Then we married their insights with bedrock journalism values to come up with eight core disclosures that every reader, listener and viewer deserves to know."

The indicators are actually a set of questions:

Best practices

- Who funds the site? What is its mission?
- What standards and ethics guide the process of gathering news?
- What happens if a journalist has ties to the topic covered?

Journalist expertise

- Who made this?
- Are there details about the journalist, including contact information, areas of knowledge, and other stories they've worked on?

Type of work

- What is this?
- Do you see story labels with clear definitions to distinguish opinion, analysis, and advertiser (or sponsored) content from news reports?

Citations and references

- What is the source?
- Does the site tell you where it got its information?
- For investigative, controversial, or in-depth stories, are you given access to the original materials behind the facts and assertions?

Methods

- Why was it a priority?
- For investigations, in-depth or controversial stories, why did they pursue the topic?
- How did they go about the process?

Locally sourced

- Do they know the community?
- Was the reporting done on the scene?
- Is there evidence of deep knowledge about the local situation or community?

Diverse voices

- What are the newsroom's efforts and commitments to bring in diverse perspectives across social and demographic differences?
- Are some communities or perspectives included only in stereotypical ways, or even completely missing?

Actionable feedback

- What does the site do to engage your help in setting coverage priorities, asking good questions and finding the answers,

holding powerful people and institutions accountable, and ensuring accuracy?
- Do you provide feedback that might provoke, alter or expand a story?

Since being formed, the Trust Project has developed a partnership program with more 200 newsrooms that meet its standards and it lists all of them on its web site.

But as is clear from the previous chapter, ethical decisions and questions continue to be dealt with as new issues emerge about collaborations between newsrooms and NGOs and citizens and about how newsrooms should or should not openly advocate for change.

CASE STUDY – HOW A NEW JOURNALISM ORGANIZATION DEFINES ITS EDITORIAL ETHICS - THE OUTLIER MEDIA EDITORIAL POLICY

"Outlier Media makes decisions about how and where to focus our reporting resources based on where we see information and accountability gaps for Detroiters. We do not make decisions about what to cover based on anything else, including the opinions of our donors or supporters. This "firewall" is part of what keeps us editorially independent.

We accept donations and grants from individuals and foundations but we do not make reporting decisions based on this support. News judgments are made independently. Outlier does not accept donations from government sources, political parties, elected officials, candidates seeking public office, or groups likely to intersect with our reporting as sources or subjects. ***Outlier Media does not accept funding where an NDA is required.***

Outlier journalists do not accept gifts or favors of more than nominal value, nor any special treatment, from any person or group that is or could be a source or the subject of our reporting. We follow the conflict of interest policy of our fiscal sponsor, Investigative Reporters, and Editors".

SELECTED BIBLIOGRAPHY

Abernathy, Penny, *News Deserts and Ghost Newspapers: Will Local News Survive?* Chapel Hill, NC: University of North Carolina, https://www.usnewsdeserts.com/reports/news-deserts-and-ghost-newspapers-will-local-news-survive/, 2020.Abernathy, Penny, *The State of Local News: The 2022 Report*, Evanston, IL: Medill, Northwestern University, https://localnewsinitiative.northwestern.edu/research/stat-of-local-news/report/, 2022

Barton, Hannah, Bradshaw, Helen, Hoeflich, Joshua, Lee, Grace and Pyo, Sammie, *AI, Automation, and Newsrooms: Finding Fitting Tools for Your Organization*, Evanston, IL: Northwestern University, https://studio.knightlab.com/results/2021-12-07-ai-automation-and-newsrooms/

Birnbauer, Bill, *The Rise of Nonprofit Investigative Journalism in the United States*, New York, NY: Routledge, 2019.

The Breaux Symposium, *New Models for News*, James Reilly Center for Media & Public Affairs, the Manship School of Mass Communications, Baton Rouge, LA, Louisiana State University, April 26, 2008.

Clegg, Ellen and Kennedy, Dan, *What Works: The Future of Local News*, Boston, MA: Beacon Press, 2023.

Doctor, Ken, *Newsonomics: Twelve New Trends that Will Shape the News You Get*, New York, NY: St. Martin's Press, 2010.

Downie, Jr Leonard and Schudson, Michael, *The Reconstruction of American Journalism*, New York, NY: Columbia Journalism Review, Columbia University, https://archives.cjr.org/reconstruction/the_reconstruction_of_american.php, 2010.

Frank, Laura, *The Withering Watchdog*, New York: PBS, https://www.imdb.com/title/tt1471358/?ref_=ttrel_rel_tt, 2009.

Hamilton, James T., *All the News That's Fit to Sell: Why the Market Transforms Information into News*, Princeton, NJ: Princeton University Press, 2004.

Hamilton, James T., *The Road Ahead for Media Hybrids: Report of the Duke Nonprofit Media Conference, May 4th–May 5th, 2009*, Durham, NC: DeWitt Wallace Center, Duke University, https://cspcs.sanford.duke.ed publications, 2009.

Hamilton, James, T., *Democracy's Detectives: The Economics of Investigative Journalism*, Cambridge, MA: Harvard University Press, 2016.

Hansen, Elizabeth and Roseman, Emily, *The Public Media Merger Playbook*, Cambridge, MA: Shorenstein Center of Media, Politics and Public Policy, Harvard University, https://publicmediamergers.org/about/, 2021.

Hewson, Chris, *Local Independent Online News Publishers, Summary of Project Oasis*, Chapel Hill, NC, https://www.lionpublishers.com/introducing-project-oasis-a-deep-dive-into-the-fast-growing-world-of-independent-news-startups/, 2021.

Kaplan, David E., *Global Investigative Journalism: Strategies for Support), A Report to the Center for International Media Assistance* (Second Edition), Washington, DC, https://www.centerforinternationalmediaassistance.com/wp-content/uploads/2015/01/CIMA-Investigative-Journalism-Dave-Kaplan.pdf, 2013.

Kaye, Jeff and Quinn, Stephen, *Funding Journalism in the Digital Age: Business Models, Strategies, Issues and Trends*, New York, NY: Peter Lang Publishing, 2010.

Kennedy, Dan, *The Wired City: Reimagining Journalism and Civic Life in the Post-Newspaper Age*, Amherst, MA: University of Massachusetts Press, 2013.

Kizer, Chloe, *Project Oasis Research Report 2021*, Chapel Hill, NC: Produced by UNC Hussman School of Journalism and Media, LION Publishers, Douglas K. Smith and the Google News Initiative, https://www.projectnewsoasis.com (Report), 2021.

The Knight Commission on the Information Needs of Communities, *Informing Communities: Sustaining Democracy in the Digital Age*, Washington, DC: The Aspen Institute, 2009.

Konieczna, Magda, *Journalism Without Profit: Making News When the Market Fails*, New York, NY: Oxford University Press, 2018.

Meyer, Philip, *The Vanishing Newspaper: Saving Journalism in the Information Age*, Updated Second Edition, Columbia, MO: University of Missouri Press, 2009.

Minow, Martha, *Saving the News: Why the Constitution Calls for Government Action to Preserve Freedom of Speech*, New York, NY: Oxford University Press, 2021.

Olsen, Gunhild Ring, *Newsroom-Classroom Hybrids at Universities: Student Labor and the Journalism Crisis*, Abingdon, UK: Routledge, 2020.

PEN: The Freedom to Write, *Losing the Local News: The Decimation of Local Journalism and the Search for Solutions*, New York, NY: PEN America, November 20, 2019, https://pen.org/local-news/

Pew Research Center, *The State of the News (Project)*, Washington, DC: Pew Charitable Trusts, 2022. https://www.pewresearch.org/topic/news-habits-media/news-media-trends/state-of-the-news-media-project/

Pickard, Victor, *Democracy Without Journalism? Confronting the Misinformation Society*, New York, NY: Oxford University Press, 2020.

Roseman, Emily, McLellan, Michelle and Holcomb, Jesse, *INN Index 2022: Enduring in Crisis, Surging in Local Communities*, Beverly Hills, CA: Institute for Nonprofit News, https://inn.org/research/inn-index/inn-index-2022/

Stonbely, Sarah, *Comparing Models of Collaborative Journalism*, Montclair, NJ: Montclair State University, https://collaborativejournalism.org/models/, 2017.

Underwood, Doug, *When MBAs Rule the Newsroom: How the Marketers and Managers are Reshaping Today's Media*, New York, NY: Columbia University Press, 1995.

Appendix A

STARTING UP A NONPROFIT NEWSROOM

There is plenty of advice and guidance for starting up a nonprofit newsroom and this appendix covers some of the basics. But I also wanted to touch on a few points that sometimes do not get enough attention: creating boards of directors, the basic rules of the road for an executive director dealing with a board, and thinking long term – sustainability and succession plans – at the beginning.

More than a decade ago, I and long-time investigative journalist and nonprofit newsroom founder Andy Hall wrote a 12-step guide to launch a nonprofit. We wrote the guide based on the experience of Hall in starting Wisconsin Watch and about a dozen other nonprofit newsrooms that had recently begun operations. We began the guide with an alert, with encouragement, and with a note that there were tips that would work for someone starting a for-profit newsroom:

> Here's a word of caution: You won't just be doing journalism. You will be an employer, a manager, a grants writer, a negotiator and

> sometimes a bookkeeper. You'll have a steep learning curve. But if you decide to go ahead, you'll be in good company: Scores of enthusiastic and dedicated people have gone before you and formed journalism nonprofits that are carrying out good work. This sets out to identify the hurdles you'll face and guide you through the process of creating a nonprofit newsroom. Even if you ultimately decide that you want to create a for-profit business, you'll find some useful tips in this module.

We also cautioned,

> While you're defining your mission, you also need to take stock of your capacity to carry it out. If you've worked as a journalist, you know how to interview people and gather information. But that's no preparation for developing a business plan, managing your cash flow or supervising staff. Moreover, in the past you've had the support of assigning editors, copy editors, producers and lawyers. As a nonprofit, you probably won't have that kind of safety net.

The 2010 guide broke the 12 steps into:

- Step One: Assessing Yourself and Your Mission;
- Step Two: Determining Your Structure;
- Step Three: Building Your Board;
- Step Four: Filing Documents to Create Your Organization;
- Step Five: Establishing Sound Policies;
- Step Six: Bringing In Revenue, Budget, and Business Plans;
- Step Seven: Connecting with the Community;
- Step Eight: Collaborating with Others;
- Step Nine: Building Your Digital Presence;
- Step Ten: Measuring Your Impact;
- Step Eleven: Building Your Staff;
- Step Twelve: Going for It!

Since then the number of start-up guides have proliferated with organizations such as the Institute for Nonprofit News, offering extensive resources including "a start-up kit" and many case studies. This book offers some case studies and two books, Bill Birnbauer's *The Rise of Nonprofit Investigative Journalism in the United States*, and Magda Konieczna's *Journalism Without Profit: Making News When the Market Fails*, offers other case studies, too, and Ellen Clegg and Dan Kennedy will have another book on another set of case studies in 2023. The Local Independent Online News Publishers also offers start-up resources than can work for for-profits and nonprofits.

Comparing the guide that Hall and I did to the more recent INN guide https://inn.org/research/guides/startup-guide/ reveals what continues to be true about creating a newsroom and what has been learned since 2010.

The INN startup guide describes the process this way:

Chapter 1: Where to Start introduces readers to the business model canvas and the vocabulary of running a nonprofit news business used throughout the rest of the guide. It explains the qualities of entrepreneurship and the demands upon an entrepreneur. It explains the need for market research and having a truly user-centered business.

Chapter 2: Nonprofit News Mission addresses what needs to be in a mission statement, with examples, and how to develop a brand. It explains what an impact model is and how to measure output, outcomes, and ultimately impact. It explains how and why to do a competitive analysis.

Chapter 3: Audience Strategy and Development covers market assessment and what it takes to fulfill a nonprofit's mission. It discusses strategies for building both a direct audience and distributed audiences, which are reached through syndication and redistribution of content. It offers resources on building an email list and creating newsletters to develop an audience willing to support the organization.

Chapter 4: Revenue Models for Nonprofit News introduces the most common revenue streams for nonprofit news, with examples. It offers templates for forecasting revenue based on the kind of revenue a news organization chooses to pursue.

Chapter 5: Fundraising and Partnerships explain how and why journalists need to be asking for money in an ethical and transparent way, the benefit of up-front fundraising, and the role and limits of grants. It introduces the basic tools and tracking used in fundraising.

Chapter 6: The Business Plan covers the basics of forecasting revenue and costs, management and board structure, building a budget, and how to align costs with projected revenue to make sure cash flow will cover expenses.

Chapter 7: Making the Go/No-Go Decision presents a cost-benefit analysis of starting a nonprofit news organization and helps readers decide whether they are prepared to do so.

Chapter 8: The Board Is Your Strategic Partner explains how governance is a pillar of success and the community connector for a nonprofit operation. It provides advice on building a strong board of directors.

Chapter 9: Setting up Operations offers practical information about incorporating, charity registration and taxes, the fiscal sponsorship option, financial controls, insurance, legal support, and human resources and employment issues.

Chapter 10: Trust and Ethics briefly recaps the crucial role nonprofits play in restoring public trust in news media.

Both guides stress the demands and workload a journalist will undergo creating a nonprofit newsroom. Both guides talk about the importance of defining the mission and building a good board of directors and give practical advice on incorporating, registering with the state, and getting nonprofit status. The 12-step guide emphasized collaborations while the INN guide has more details on the ethics of fundraising and running a nonprofit newsroom. Both call for identifying the right audience and doing marketing.

One big difference is that the INN guide jumps right into the need for more in-depth and methodical market research for determining what news needs are being fulfilled for what audience. In the early days, some journalists started with the idea that if they did solid investigative and public service stories, they would naturally have an audience. But with a story distribution that often relied on third parties (mainstream newspapers for example) that obscured the newsrooms identity and brand and a with limited and sporadic publishing schedule, it was difficult for a new organization to distinguish itself and find and build its own audience.

But the biggest difference between the INN guide and earlier guides is that the INN Startup Guide provides an extraordinary amount of detail and nuts and bolts information that many journalists wish they had when they began in the early days of the nonprofit movement.

For example, INN's guide has a chapter on "Audience strategy and development: What does it take to fulfill your mission?" and writes

> This chapter covers market assessment and what it takes to fulfill a nonprofit's mission. It discusses strategies for building both a direct audience and distributed audiences, which are reached through syndication and redistribution of content. It offers resources on building an email list and creating newsletters to develop an audience willing to support the organization.

It then has seven different sections on the topic. One section focuses on matching your mission with the audience and uses the successful Texas Tribune as an example:

> A real-life example: Nearly 28 million people live in Texas.
>
> The Texas Tribune, however, declares that its *core* audience comprises those people who care passionately about public policy, politics, government and statement issues. Sure, the Trib will *gladly* take traffic (and donations) from any of the 28 million … but it *focuses* on reaching and serving the 4 million or so who fit their target "job to be done."
>
> Marketers call that the "total addressable market." (You can read more about it in the customer research chapter of "Media Innovation and Entrepreneurship," an excellent, and free, textbook.)
>
> The Texas Tribune got to that 4 million number through looking at its current audience; U.S. Census and other public data about population and demographics; and finally by conducting some private market research. You don't need to go to those lengths – at least not at first. But start by pulling together any and all information you can get about the number of people who have that *job* that you can do.

Board of directors

One area most guides now delve deeply into is unfamiliar to most journalists unless they have covered the nonprofit world: The board of directors. If a newsroom incorporates, it will need articles of incorporation and bylaws and those documents will describe the number of board member and the terms they will serve. Unlike a journalism association, where journalists are elected to the board, the original board members of a nonprofit will choose other board members and then the entire board will then select future board members.

Do not underestimate the importance of a board and if there is a universal rule for an executive director it is: "No surprises". That is, seek the board's counsel and never delay in giving them the good news and especially the bad news. Failure by an executive director of a nonprofit newsroom to respect the board and keep the board informed has often led to the early exit of an executive director.

In 2010, Hall and I provided details and strategies for having a good and supportive board of directors:

> If you decide to apply to become a 501(c)(3), you'll need to appoint a governing board whose members are responsible for such areas as compensation, policy, practices, fundraising and strategic planning.
>
> At a minimum, you'll begin with a three-person board. It's often best to start small and expand as your needs grow. The number of board members will be set in your bylaws, which also govern issues like the duties of the board and of the executive director, the number of meetings and other areas of operations. (We should have added that It is often recommended that the executive director/chief executive officer not be a member of the board because of the conflicts and politics that may arise.)
>
> Your board should have energy, expertise and passion for the new enterprise. You don't need micromanagers who wonder if you remembered to lock the office doors each night but, rather, members who are intensely interested in what you're doing, actively helpful and able to devote some regularly scheduled time to the organization.

You don't want a board composed entirely of journalists, but you do need at least one top journalist for advice and credibility.

Say that you have seven board members by the end of your first year. Your dream team could look like this:

- A couple of esteemed journalists – and it's a big plus if they have experience managing a nonprofit newsroom.
- If you are located at a university, a respected journalism professor.
- A lawyer (however, you will probably still need the services of an outside lawyer to handle most legal work and to avoid conflicts of interest that could arise).
- An accountant or financial adviser.
- An experienced fundraiser with contacts at major foundations or community donors.
- A business person who loves journalism or has been successful as a digital entrepreneur.
- A tech expert who might guide your software and hardware needs.

If you're lucky, some of your board members will wear two or more hats. Ideally, they will also:

- have experience running or overseeing nonprofits.
- have strong community ties.
- be racially and socially diverse, so they can provide a bridge to underreported stories and issues.

Be clear about what you expect from your board. Your members should:

- Give practical advice and set sound policies and goals.
- Have a strong sense of ethics consistent with your new venture.
- Help market the project, raise money, and oversee incoming funds.
- Support you during some of the rough times that inevitably occur and work with you to problem-solve.
- Be available to meet at least once a year in person, possibly paying for their own travel and lodging.
- Define ways to measure the success of your performance and of the organization.

Some board members may be friends or acquaintances you trust, but you need independent thinkers, too. They should be able to tell you gracefully when they think you are headed in the wrong direction. And you should respect their opinion. You want your board to look at issues from every angle. It should not serve to rubberstamp your decisions – that defeats the purpose.

In fact, in setting up your newsroom, you will have traded one boss for a governing board of many bosses. They may start out as your friends and supporters, but may end up disagreeing with you – and they have the power to fire you.

Most of all, you need a strong board president who can keep the board engaged and running efficiently. Of course, it should be someone with whom you can work one-on-one as you think through issues and strategic directions.

Once you have your startup board, you need to begin thinking about individuals who would be good additions, down the road. Building and keeping a good board is a task that never ends.

The INN guide also emphasizes the crucial importance of a board of directors:

> The board is not a nicety or an auxiliary thing — it is the both the soul and the backbone of your nonprofit, and absolutely critical to its success. It is more central to the operation of a nonprofit than boards are for most for-profit companies.

The functions of the board: A board is an ensemble, and boards vary quite a bit in their function. In most nonprofits, board members are critical fundraisers. They typically are expected to "give or get" – to directly donate or get others to donate to the cause. Other boards may have more policy orientation, guiding the direction of an organization.

Check state requirements: State law may set a minimum number of board members, often three people, and we recommend that number not include the executive director. Some states do not even allow the executive director to be an ex-officio board member. Regardless of the requirements, it is useful to have more than three board members because you need the expertise, guidance, financial support, and connections of a larger group. In a nonprofit, the founder is not the owner because the organization is responsible to the public, and the board serves as the trustees for the public. The founder, executive director or CEO, is the leader but the board ultimately holds the legal and financial responsibility for the nonprofit. The buck stops with the board if the nonprofit fails to meet its social purpose or misuses its funding.

Mapping what you need on your board: Journalism boards have traditionally included strong journalists, leaders of whatever community the publication is serving, individual philanthropists, and representatives of partner organizations. News organization boards typically have conflict-of-interest policy statements that include the understanding that board members do not and cannot have any input on editorial decisions. Some boards also have guidelines on whether board members can be politically active as individuals; they should not be active in partisan politics in any way connected to their nonprofit roles.

Give and get: Most board members either are giving financially or getting money for the organization by enlisting other financial supporters. Board members are your strategic partners in helping guide you to meet and execute your mission, helping you think about your field and where your mission fits into it. They make introductions to help you scale up and form partnerships. They drive the overall arc of the organization but should not be involved operationally especially as time goes on. Early in an operation, board members may be volunteers who provide services, but as the organization grows they become less hands-on.

Sustainability and succession

Start-up guides are much needed to help set up a nonprofit (or for-profit) newsroom and get it up and running, but sometimes the guides don't say how long the start-up period lasts. Over the years, some start-ups with deep initial funding are functioning well and growing within a year or two. Some nonprofits never seem to emerge from the start-up period, struggling from year to year to pay staff and find more funding. Some call it the nonprofit "hamster wheel". As part of a start-up strategy, it's good to think of what success will look like and what to do if it can't be reached, which is often get acquired by another nonprofit or simply close.

One last topic that is becoming more important, even during the start-up phase, is what kind of "succession" plan does the newsroom have. Founders and executive directors move on to other jobs, burn out, or age out. Supporters, donors, and foundations like to know that if something happens to the founder and/or leader, the organization will go on. Most founders do want the legacy of a continuing, healthy organization although I have met some who can't give up control and would rather the organization die than go on without them.

Advice from a leader of one of the most successful nonprofit newsrooms

Dick Tofel was president of ProPublica, the largest nonprofit newsroom in the U.S., for eight and a half years and directed its business operations for 14 years. He shared his experience and lessons learned in a widely read article in the Columbia Journalism Review in 2021.

He began by noting that he built a nonprofit newsroom from 25 to 160 people and grew the annual budget from $10 million to $36 million. He broke his article into sections based on frequent questions he had been asked.

One was how much money is needed to start and he stressed that it is the key question to ask when trying to start an organization. He wrote,

> In my view, it's a mistake to begin operations without at least 18 months of spending on hand, and two years is even better. This is hard, and quite likely daunting. But I believe it's the better part of valor.

Many newsrooms have begun one year or less with the founder spending the founder's savings while raising money, but in recent years this approach has become of the standard.

Tofel did note, ProPublica had the advantage to begin with three years of funding guaranteed, and we were well aware of our unusual good fortune.

Tofel also outlined the kinds of donors that give to nonprofit journalism, listing them as "institutional foundations", "high net-worth individuals" – or rich people, and small donors, and described the pluses and minuses of each kind. He also looked at what motivates giving to nonprofit newsrooms and he reviewed what "metrics" there are for measuring as success, writing,

> That is why I always try to stress that a conversation about metrics should begin as one about mission. As noted earlier, the most important thing for a successful nonprofit of any sort is a clear mission. By that, I mean a simple and direct statement of what you are in business to do—and, by implication if not explicitly, what you are *not* trying to do.

In addition, he answered the question of how fast a nonprofit newsroom grows with this answer: "In two phrases: as quickly as necessary; and, given that, as slowly as possible". He stressed making sure to have the funds for the journalism while acknowledging the need for business support, but noted:

> At the same time, however, never forget that business operations are support structures. There is no prize for making them bigger or fancier or more costly; they are a means, not an end.

Tofel covered several other topics in his valuable article, including donor transparency, earned income, and balancing editorial and funder priorities, but he also focused on building a successful board. He said the founding donor and first chairman of the board of ProPublica had "two basic rules for directors, and two for board meetings". One rule was

> Directors, most of all, had to be people other directors would look forward to coming to meetings with; as the flip side to that, they must not be the sort of people who make colleagues want to avoid

> meetings. No amount of possible support could overcome this consideration for him.

For meetings, one of the rules was that "ever session every session have at least one meaningful business discussion, both intrinsically interesting (with ample supporting materials distributed in advance) and genuinely important to the company".

Tofel continued

> Beyond that, he felt strongly that each meeting should include an opportunity to hear about the work from front-line staff, ideally people the Board had not met previously. We refer to this part of the meeting internally as the "show and tell," but don't let the name deceive you: these sessions are a significant part of the attraction of a nonprofit journalism board…

THREE LESSONS FROM A FOUNDER

Lorie Hearn, founder, CEO, and executive director of inewsource, the successful nonprofit investigative newsroom in San Diego said in an interview there were a few things she wished she had known when she did the startup of inewsource.

* I started a newsroom believing if you did good journalism, people would give you money. Rarely true. You have to ask.
* I wish I had hired a business colleague to join me in launching the nonprofit. I needed a business plan, not just great reporters.
* If I were to do this today, I'd conduct listening tours to find out what the community wanted from a local news outlet. I wouldn't just trust that as an editor I knew best.

Appendix B

HOW TO KEEP UP WITH THE CHANGES IN JOURNALISM

The changing models in journalism are frequent and swift in the 21st century, but there are ways to keep up with them. There are digital magazines on journalism, university institutes and labs, research centers, foundations, and bloggers who change models and often are creating them. Here are a few of those organizations.

The American Journalism Project https://www.theajp.org/

The American Journalism Project was co-founded by John Thornton, the founder of the Texas Tribune, who raised $50 million from foundations and donors to create an organization to support nonprofit newsrooms covering local news. It gives out business capacity grants to nonprofit newsrooms, provides business training, and contributes to other local news initiatives. One of its helpful sections on its website is news and insights, which captures the organization's latest activities, lessons learned in running nonprofit newsrooms and other insights.

American Press Institute https://www.americanpressinstitute.org/

The American Press Institute describes its mission as advancing "an innovative and sustainable news industry by helping publishers understand and engage audiences, grow revenue, improve public-service journalism, and succeed at organizational change". It obviously covers a wide range of topics, but highlights useful surveys, journalism methods, and business strategies.

Columbia Journalism Review https://www.cjr.org/

A constantly engaging digital magazine whose articles stay up on current issues and developments in journalism, but also provides an archive of material about many topics of the industry with a recent focus on local news, covering the pandemic and covering climate change. It really is required reading for journalists and journalism students.

Editor and Publisher https://www.editorandpublisher.com/

It once seemed that this magazine would fade with the legacy media it covered, but it has been reinvigorated over recent years and it covers all phases of industry, especially focusing on owners, the business side, and revenue and with a lot of coverage of ongoing transformation to digital.

Institute for Nonprofit News https://inn.org/

This is the place to start to keep watch on the surge in nonprofit newsrooms in North America, to learn how the business and network and to find an increasingly rich number of resources and studies. It also runs an annual conference and has many webinars.

The John S. and James L. Knight Foundation https://knightfoundation.org/

The largest foundation devoted to journalism in the U.S. is not only a grant-making foundation, but also one that includes significant support for newsrooms, training, studies on news and communities and information and democracy, convenings on media and current journalism issues, research on the news industry and a plethora of other topics. It is a living library of what is going on in journalism.

The Local Independent Online News Publishers https://www.lionpublishers.com/

Local Independent Online News (LION) Publishers is a professional journalism association for independent news publisher that provides training and research on local news, with specific resources for both nonprofit and for-profit local newsrooms. It gives special emphasis to covering neglected and disenfranchised communities that have significant diversity saying they have a vision of "a world where thriving, independent news organizations provide equitable access to inclusive and impactful news and information".

The Local News Initiative at the Medill School at Northwestern University https://localnewsinitiative.northwestern.edu/

Its self-description shows its mission is to be on the cutting edge of changing models of journalism: "With local journalism in crisis, Northwestern University has assembled a team of experts in digital innovation, audience understanding and business strategy. **The goal:** reinvent the relationship between news organizations and audiences to elevate enterprises that empower citizens".

Media Nation https://dankennedy.net/

Dan Kennedy, a long-time journalist and media commentator, produces a feisty, insightful blog with news and commentary on the latest trends and issues in journalism. He has focused on newspaper ownership and also on the transformation of local news.

Nieman Journalism Lab https://www.niemanlab.org/

Published by the Nieman Fellowship Program at Harvard, this is a stellar online magazine that has vibrant writing on current trends and issues of journalism, including the business of journalism. It often has guest writers who are experts in the field. It has sections on business models, mobile and apps, and reporting and production among others.

Online News Association https://journalists.org/

The Online News Association says it's the world's largest digital journalism association. A membership organization says its mission is to inspire and support innovation and excellence in digital journalism. ONA has always concentrated on providing emerging tech, innovation, revenue, and business models. It networks both for-profit and nonprofit entrepreneurs and has resources on its website and an annual conference.

Pew Research Center https://www.pewresearch.org/topic/news-habits-media/

The well-respected Pew Center does surveys and studies of many topics, but its journalism section – News Habits and Media – provided invaluable overviews of the state of the news industry, trends in news, and surveys of audiences. It is the place to begin for statistics for the news profession in the U.S.

Poynter Institute https://www.poynter.org/

The Poynter Institute made the transition over the last two decades for being a center of training in ethics and leadership to becoming an institute that also houses the international fact-checking network, does work on media literacy, and provides other kinds of training for journalists. Its new section does an excellent job of tracking the latest issues in journalism, including changes in business models.

The Reynold Journalism Institute at the Missouri School of Journalism https://rjionline.org/

The institute has become one of the leaders in promoting innovation and new methods in journalism and also has fellows who work on innovative projects. It has "an innovation focus" section on its website that is particularly useful for finding new digital reporting tools and also an applied research section.

Thomson Reuters Foundation https://www.trust.org/

For international coverage of journalism trends, issues, and projects, the foundation's website is a necessary destination. The foundation describes its approach as: accurate and balanced news coverage is critical to informing public opinion, revealing previously undocumented stories, exposing abuses of power, and holding authority to account. The law is fundamental to establishing and protecting the rights of individuals and to upholding free, fair, and informed societies. "As the corporate foundation of Thomson Reuters, our unique expertise combines the power of journalism and the law to advance media freedom, foster more inclusive economies, and promote human rights".

INDEX

Note: *Italic* page numbers refer to figures.

Abbott, Kimberly 170, 171
Abernathy, Penny 37, 38
absentee ownership 33–35, *35*
Accelerator Program, FJP 105
accountability journalism 5
ACLU mission statement 174–176
ad-supported journalism 157
advertising revenue 1, 6, 10, 30, 36, 52, 76
advocacy groups 167; advocacy newsrooms 169; co-publishing 170–172; NGO journalism 171; for solutions 181–183
African media 172
Agenda Watch 119
Alden Global Capital 23, 24, 33, 48
"Alerts" page 126
Alvarez, Sarah 124–125
America Amplified 154
American Civil Liberties Union 168, 174–177
American Community Newspapers 89
American Jobs Plan 180
American Journalism Project 9, 76, 80, 83, 85
American Journalism Review 32
American Press Institute 193
American Public Media (APM) 7, 158
American Society of News Editors 27
Amnesty International 168–169, 173
APM *see* American Public Media (APM)
Arizona State University 134, 141, 146
Arnold Ventures 77
Arnolt, Michael I. 147
artificial intelligence 120, 126
Associated Press study 126
Atlantic Monthly 23, 75
Aucoin, James 169

audience location 125–126
automation 122–123, 126

Baldwin, Peter 79
The Baltimore Banner 84–85
Barstow, David 146
The Beacon 86
Benioff, Marc 75
Benton, Josh 117
Bergman, Lowell 146
BerkeleySide 58
Berman, Sarabeth 83
Bezos, Jeff 28, 74
Biden, Joe 180
"Big Local News Project" 119, 128
Big Tech 92, 131–132; funding for 104–107; support of 91–92
Birnbauer, Bill 55; *The Rise of Nonprofit Investigative Journalism in the U.S.* 54
Blank, Steve 45, 46, 47, 48, 49
Block Club Chicago 93, 94, 112; American Journalism Project 116; annual subscription price 115; community areas 113; decision on coverage 112; donations 116; freemium model 115; Kickstarter campaign 114; in live 114–115; low-income residents 116; offering of news 113–114
bloggers 100
blogs: at beginning 100–102; to newsrooms 51–53
Bloomberg/Mining News 123
Borger, Jorn 51
Boston Globe 74
Brady, James 3, 28
Brandeis University 146
Breaux Symposium 2, 3, 10, 12, 13
Brown, Malachy 131
Brown, Tracy 153
Buckmaster, Jim 35
Buffett, Warren 74
Bureau of Investigative Journalism 180
Burke, Daniel 25
business: investments 71; for revenue and sustainability strategies 99–100; rule for newsrooms 98–99

CAP *see* Common Agricultural Policy (CAP)
Capital Cities 25
Capital News Service (CNS) 142–145
Capitol News Connection 63
The Cardinal News in Roanoke 85
Cardin, Ben 59
Cascade Public Media 163
Center for Community News 150–151
The Center for Cooperative Media 103
The Center for Government and Public Integrity 20, 180, 186
The Center for Investigative Reporting 52, 54, 61, 190
The Center for Public Integrity 3, 8, 52, 54, 55, 61, 63
CherryRoad Media 89, 91
Chicago Public Media 153, 165
Chicago Sun-Times 152
Chicago Tribune 23, 24
citizen journalism 16, 35
City Bureau 128
civic journalism 15, 34
classifieds 46
Clegg, Ellen 25
climate change 180
Clinton, Hillary 16
clustering 31–32

Cluster Munition Attacks in Ukraine 178
CNS *see* Capital News Service (CNS)
collaborations: cost-saver and revenue generator 102–103; nonprofit newsrooms 17–18; in reporting 59
collaborative journalism 159
collective journalism, funding for 103
Colorado Public Media 9, 166
Columbia Daily Tribune 140
Columbia University 146
commercial broadcast journalism 26; content and reach of 2
Common Agricultural Policy (CAP) 174
communications: with funders 196–197; with grantees 193
community 126
community-backed start-up 87–88
community foundations 83–86
Community News Organizations (CNO) 81
Community Newspaper Holdings Inc. (CNHI) 89, 90
Computation + Journalism Conference 121
computer-assisted reporting *see* precision journalism
conflicts of interest 191–192
Congress 156
consequentialism 172
Constructive Journalism 169, 180–181, 181–183
The *Conversation* (Web site) 147
cooperation, nonprofit newsrooms 17–18
Coppin, McKay 23–24
co-publishing 170–172
corporately owned newsrooms 15
corporate ownership 33
Corporation for Public Broadcasting 20, 92, 154
corruption index 168
Courier-Journal 31
Covid-19 pandemic 128–129; digital newsrooms 14
Craig's List 21, 35, 36
creating news products 131–132
credibility falters 15–16
cross-border investigations 18
Cross, Sue 17, 55, 56, 165
crowdfunding campaign 94
CrowdTangle 132
cybersphere 121

DAFs *see* donor-advised funds (DAFs)
dailies 41
Daily News 48
The Daily Springfield Citizen 85–86
data: analysis and visualization 123; data-driven stories 123
data-driven journalism 2, 16–17, 28, 124, 157
data-driven news 120, 128
data journalism 122
data library 123
Democracy Fund 76, 110
democratic society, cost to 43–44
Descript 127
digital advertising 14, 36, 131
Digital First Media 23
Digital Foundation Lab 132
Digital Growth Program 108
digital news 39
digital online technology 2
digital subscriptions 152
Digital Third Coast 2
DNAinfo 93, 94

Doctor, Ken 29, 30; "*Newsonomics: Twelve New Trends That Will Shape the News You Get*" 27
DocumentCloud project 123
document collection 122
Documenter project 128
donor-advised funds (DAFs) 82, 189
donor policies 190; conflicts of interest 191–192; financial transparency and donor acceptance policy 190–191
donors: nonprofit newsrooms 18–19
dot.com crash 26
Downie, Leonard 26, 135, 140
Drizin, Julie 158
Dube, Jonathan 51
Duke Media Conference 10

Eastern Europe: nonprofit investigative centers, creation of 11
editorial ethics: journalism organization 199
editorial independence 194, 195
education, funders principle 195
Efforts to Ban Gender and Sexuality Education in Brazil 178
"The Elements of Journalism" 190
"Emerging Nonprofit Media and Donors Index" 81
ethical challenges 186–188
Ethics and Excellence in Journalism Foundation 76
"Ethics for the New Investigative Newsroom: A Roundtable Report on the Best Practices for Nonprofit Journalism" 186–187
evidence-based content 120
Expanding News Desert 37

Facebook 21, 47, 104, 105, 106, 107, 132
Facebook Journalism Project (FJP) 105
fact-finding journalism 16–17
family-owned newspapers 30, 31
family-owned newsrooms 15
fascism 169
financial transparency and donor acceptance policy 190–191
First Look 76
The Flatwater Free Press 86
Flourish 127
Footnoted 68, 101
Ford Foundation 8, 76
for-profit digital news: revenue stream for 100
for-profit digital sites 42
for-profit news organization 7–8
for-profit newsrooms 8, 57–58; collaborations among nonprofit and 18; collapse of 14; plans 99
Fort Worth Report 84
foundation funds 7–9, 15
foundations 18–19, 76–77
Frank, Laura 13, 161
Freedom of Information 123
freemium model 101
Free Press, Detroit 176
Freivogel, Margaret 161–163
Frontline 157
funders: communications with 196–197; guidelines for 193–195
Fund For Nonprofit News At The Miami Foundation 82
funding 4, 7, 9; for big tech 104–107; for collective journalism 103; detail and context for 78–80; tracking 77–78; transparency as standard 82–83
"Funding Journalism in the Digital Age" (Kaye and Quinn) 117
funding sources 187
"Future of Media: Truth, Privacy and Power" 78

Galloway, Anne 69
Gannett Co. Inc. 31, 40, 148–149
Gates Foundation 77, 82
Gelernter, David 121, 122
ghost newsrooms 37–44
GIJN *see* Global Investigative Journalism Network (GIJN)
Gilbert, Jeremy 120
Glaser, Mark 56, 57, 59
global financial crimes 168
Global Investigative Journalism Network (GIJN) 10–12, 53, 121, 173
Global Witness 173
Google 21, 47, 92, 104, 105, 132; and newsrooms 107–108
Google Alerts 127
Google News Initiative 103, 107, 108
Google News Initiative Labs 107, 132
Google News Initiative Startups Program 107
government funding 187
government investment 91–92
government revenue 109–112
government support 20–21
Graves, Stephanie Lulay 93, 94, 112
Great Recession 2008 12, 35, 169
Greece's Use of Migrants as Police Auxiliaries in Pushbacks 178
Green, Dan 170
Greenpeace 172, 173–174, 179–180
Green Peace 168
Griggs, Tim 70
The Guardian 14, 29
"Guidance on philanthropic funding of media and news" 193
Guidestar 101
Gulban, Jeremy 91
Gulf States Newsroom 159
Guyette, Curt 176
Hall, Andy 106, 108
Hamilton, Jack 4
Hamilton, James T. 3, 4, 5, 52
Hansen, Elizabeth 160
Harrison, Patricia 158
The Hartford Courant 34
Harvard Business School index 180
Harvard index 81, 82
Harvest Public Media 158
Hearst, William Randolph 75
hedge funds 23, 29, 40
Henry, John 74
Horvit, Mark 133
Howard Centers for investigative journalism 146
Huffington Post Investigative Fund 7–8, 52, 63
Human Rights Organization 168, 172
Human Rights Watch 177–178
Hunter, Mark Lee 173–174

Ibargüen, Alberto 77
independence, funders principle 194
independent journalism 196
Indiana University 147
IndiaSpend 131
indigenous people 167
inequities 44
Injustice Watch 165
INN *see* Institute for Nonprofit News (INN); Investigative News Network (INN)
INN Index 55–56, 60, 61, 83
the Innocence Project 146
Institute for Nonprofit News (INN) 9, 11–12, 50, 51, 53, 54, 60, 76, 83, 95, 96, 99, 103, 161, 186, 189; individual giving to members 62, 64; member newsrooms 11, 22, 190; revenue sources for

members 62, *63*; standards and network 189–190
integrity 194
Intercept Brasil 167
Internal Revenue Service 7, 20
International Consortium of Investigative Journalists 55, 129
investigative centers 146–147
investigative journalism 154, 165, 168, 174–177, 177–178
investigative journalism fund 57–58
investigative journalists 2
Investigative News Network (INN) 3
Investigative Reporters and Editors (IRE) 123
The Investigative Reporting Project 7, 52, 146
IRS Form 990 Schedule B 191
The Island 360 45; big tech and social media 47–48; changes during pandemic 49; disappearing classifieds 46; events 49; getting printed 48; importance of legal notice revenue 47; special role in local news coverage 45–46

Jobs, Laurene Powell 75
John S. and James L. Knight Foundation 137, 150 *see* Knight Foundation
Jonathan Logan Family Foundation 147
journalism 121, 127; brands of 15; government support for 20–21; organization, editorial ethics 199; pooling funds for 80–82; professors 134
journalism labs 129–130
journalism programs: within higher education institutions 136–137; as teaching hospitals 134–137
journalism schools 133, 134, 135, 138
journalism students 134, 135, 140
Journalism Without Profit (Konieczna) 54
journalists 120, 121; artificial intelligence 127; co-publishing 170–172; data library 123; and greenpeace 173–174; web and social media 122

Kansas City Star 25, 28–29
Kaplan, David 10
Kaye, Jeff: "Funding Journalism in the Digital Age" 117
Kebbel, Gary 120
Kennedy, Dan 25
Killings, Abductions, Torture, and Sexual Violence Against LGBT People by Armed Groups in Iraq 178
Knight and Walton foundations 103
Knight Chair 120
Knight Commission report 157
Knight Foundation 8, 18, 54, 62, 65, 76, 77, 83; 2020 (year of nonprofits) 56–59 *see* John S. and James L. Knight Foundation
Knight Journalism Lab 130
Konieczna, Magda 55; *Journalism Without Profit* 54
Kramer, Joel 8

LaFleur, Jennifer 129
Langeveld, Martin 33
"The Last Days of Civic Journalism: The case of the Savannah News" (Nip) 34
Leder, Michele 68
legal notice revenue 47
Lemann, Nicholas 134
Lenfest, Gerry 81

LenFest Institute 78, 81
Lewis, Charles 3
libertarian newsrooms 180–181
Liberty Group Publishing 89, 90
lifestreams 121–122
limited liability companies (LLCs) 96, 98
Links.net 51
Lionheart Holdings 89
listenership 160
LLCs *see* limited liability companies (LLCs)
Lloyd, Henry Demarest 170
Local Independent Online News (LION) Publishers 9, 59, 101–102; and project news Oasis survey 64–66
Local Independent Online News Publishing Association 96
Local Journalism Project 154
Local Journalism Sustainability Act 110
Local Media Association 105
Local Media Association Covid Relief Fund 57
The Local New for Houston Project 85
"Local News Experiments Project" 108
local news, through student work 147–151
Logan Center for Urban Investigative Reporting 147
Logan foundations 76
"Losing the News: The Decimation of Local Journalism and the Search for Solutions" 43
The Louisville Times 31
low-income families 124–125
low-profit limited liability company (L3C) 6, 7, 9
MacArthur Foundation 76
mainstream media index 78
mainstream newsrooms 29–30, *31*
market failure 12–14
Marshall, Josh 67
McChesney, Robert 110
McClatchy 28, 33
media hybrids 6
Media Impact Fund 77, 84
Media Impact Funders 18
media industry 75, 136
MediaNews 33
Meltwater 127
member newsrooms, INN 11, 22, 190
Merholz, Peter 51
Meyer, Philip 12–13, 24
Miami Foundation 82
Michael I. Arnolt Center for Investigative Journalism 147
Michigan Democracy Watch Project 176
Microsoft 92, 105, 108–109, 132
Minneapolis nonprofit newsroom 6–7
MinnPost 62
Minow, Susan: "Saving Journalism" 110
MinPost 55
Mirror Worlds (Gelernter) 121, 122
The Missouri method 139–141
mobile device strategy 120
mobile media platforms 120
MobileMe&You conference 120, 121, 126
mobile news 120, 121
mobile newsstream 122
Mother Jones 52, 54, 170
MuckRock 123
Murdoch, Rupert 26–27, 29, 80
Murphy, Thomas 25

National Institute for Computer-Assisted Reporting (NICAR) 121, 139, 140

National Public Radio (NPR) 154, 156, 158, 160, 187, 188
network television 2
New America Foundation 136
New England Center for Investigative Reporting 7, 138
New Jersey Spotlight 62
Newmark, Craig 35, 77
"New Models for News" 2, 3
news: automation and text 122–123; automation efforts 119; consumer-oriented approach 124; data-driven stories 122–123; deliver information 125; digital news 120; lifestreams 121–122; text for 123–125; web free 121–122
News 21 134
news-academic partnerships 148, 150–151
News Desert project 14, 158
news deserts 37–44
News Deserts project 89
NewsMatch program 8–9, 81, 82
"*Newsonomics: Twelve New Trends That Will Shape the News You Get*" (Doctor) 27
news organizations: communications with funders 196–197; editorial independence 195; transparency 195–196
Newspaper Association of America 36
newspapers: circulation and revenue decline 30, *31*, 40; classified advertising 36; competition 35–36; consolidation 40–41; loss of 38–39; ownership 32; staff, decline of 34, *35*, 40
Newsroom-Classroom Hybrids at Universities: Student Labor and the Journalism Crisis (Olsen) 134–135
newsrooms: blogs to 51–53; business rule for 98–99; Google and 107–108; individual buyers of 19; loss of 42–43
Newton, Eric 76, 137, 138
New York Magazine 16
New York Public Radio 163
The New York Times 74, 131, 167, 175, 181
NGOs *see* non-government organizations (NGOs)
NICAR *see* National Institute for Computer-Assisted Reporting (NICAR)
Nichols, John 110
Nieman Labs 33, 117, 130
Nieman Reports 170, 171
Nip, Joyce Y. M.: "The Last Days of Civic Journalism: The case of the Savannah News" 34
NJ Spotlight 165
non-government organizations (NGOs) 170–171, 173
501(c)(3) nonprofit 191
nonprofit data 122
nonprofit investigative centers 9, 11
nonprofit investigative newsrooms 2
nonprofit news network 86, 189
nonprofit news organization, donation to 111
nonprofit newsroom movement 80, 185, 187
nonprofit newsrooms 1, 3, 8, 42; cooperation and collaborations 17–18; donors and owners 18–19; ethics for 184; evolution of 61–64, *63*, *64*; growth of 10; perils 19–20; plans 99; rise in 53–55; role for 4; start up of 9; sustainability 22
North American Sponsorships Lab 107

Northwestern University 146
NPR *see* National Public Radio (NPR)

Oasis Project (Project New Oasis) 64–66, 98, 101–102
objectivity, definition of 185
The Ohio Local News Initiative 85
Olsen, Gunhild Ring 137, 139, 146; *Newsroom-Classroom Hybrids at Universities: Student Labor and the Journalism Crisis* 134–135
Omidyar, Pierre 76
online database 127
online journalism blogs 52
online public service newsrooms 52
OpenCorporates 129
Open Society Foundations 18, 76
Otter.ai 127
Outlier 123, 124; method and delivery system 125; non-profit news project 123; text findings 125
Outlier Media Editorial Policy 199
Overholser, Geneva 4
owners/ownership: detail and context for 78–80; nonprofit newsrooms 18–19

Pacific News Service 63
Paris climate agreement 180
PBS *see* Public Broadcasting Service (PBS)
PEN America 43, 44
Pew Research Center 14, 30; Journalism Project at 141
Philadelphia Inquirer 19, 37
Phillips, Cheryl 128
Picard, Robert G. 1–2, 3, 13, 24, 29
place-based knowledge 126
PMF *see* Popular Mobilization Forces (PMF)
Pocantico Declaration 3, 9, 103
politco 117–118
Popular Mobilization Forces (PMF) 178
positive spillovers, defined as 5
Powers, Matthew 171
precision journalism 16–17
Press-Gazette 37
print advertising 14
printing press: building in digital age 28–29
print journalism 1
private equity funds 40
professional news reporting centers 135–139
Project News Oasis 64
The Project on Excellence in Journalism 30
ProPublica 123, 128
Public Benefit Corporation 58
Public Broadcasting Service (PBS) 7, 153, 155, 158, 159
public journalism 15, 34
public media 7; broad reach 153–154; increase local resources 157–158; local coverage criticism 154–157; public broadcasting support 156
Public Media Merger Playbook 160, 163
Public Radio Audience Task Force Report 156
public radio, financial support for 156
public radio stations 156
public service journalism 11–12
public television stations 157
The Pulitzer Center for Crisis Reporting 62
Pulitzer, Joseph 75

quality control 15–16
Quinn, Stephen: "Funding Journalism in the Digital Age" 117

Rausing, Lisbet 79
readership, decline in 27
Rebuilding Local News 108–109
receiving and giving money: guidelines for 192–197
"The Reconstruction of American Journalism" 66, 68
"The Reconstruction of American Journalism Report" 154, 157
refundable tax credit 112
regional new barons 88–91
Report for America 103–104, 109
Restivo, Ryan 125, 126
revenue, diverse streams of 95–96; business 98–99; diverse streams of 95–96; Report for America 103–104
Ricketts, Joe 93, 94
The Rise of Nonprofit Investigative Journalism in the U.S. (Birnbauer) 54
The Roanoke Times 85
Robert R. McCormick Foundation 76
Roberts, Steve 171
robust statehouse news bureau 142
The Rockefeller Brothers Fund 76
Rocky Mountain Investigative News Network 62
Romanian Center for Investigative Journalism 11
Roseman, Emily 160
Rosenthal, Robert 29

Sabella, Jen 93
Salahi, Lara 147, 148
Salt Lake Tribune 58
Sam Adams Alliance 56, 180, 186
satellite technology 131
"Saving Journalism" (Minow) 110
Sawyer, Jon 8
Schmidt, Eric 159
Schmidt, Wendy 159
Schmitz Weiss, Amy 126, 131
Schudson, Michael 26, 135, 140
Schulman, Bob 32
The Schuster Institute for Investigative Reporting 146
Scripps Howard Foundation 146–147
scrolling 122
The Seattle Times 19
self-serve portal 46
service journalism 124
Shute, Benjamin R., Jr. 3–4
Singleton, William Dean 32
Slim, Carlos 74
small for-profits 96–98
Smith, Christina 147
social media 16, 127; big tech and 47–48; management 127; organizations 15
Social Pilot 127
Solutions Journalism 169, 181, 182
Solutions Journalism Network 77, 82
Soros, George 19
South, Jeff 142–145
spatial journalism 129–130, 130–131
spatial narratives 126
"spotlight membership program" 96
Stabile Center for Investigative Reporting 62, 63
Stanford University 119
Star, Steve 25
Star-Tribune Media Company 74
start-ups proliferate 75–76
statehouse bureaus 133, 141–145
stations, business model 160
Stearns, Josh 110
St. Louis Beacon 62, 161–163
St. Louis Public Radio 161–163

Stoeffler, David 86
Stonbely, Sarah 103
storytelling on mobile media platforms 120
streaming concept 122
student statehouse program 142–145
Stymied Reforms in the Maldives 178
suburban communities 39–40
Sullivan, Andrew 51
sustainability 158; nonprofit newsrooms 22; and organizational health 194–195

Talking Points Memo (TPM): blogs 52; from blog to news organization 67–68
The Tampa Bay Times 37
Tang, Terry 175
tax credit 110–112
tax-deductible donations 57
Taylor, Glen 74
teaching hospitals 134–137
tech giants 21–22, 36–37
tech-savvy 21–22
Temple University 147
The Texas Tribune 62, 96
text findings 125
text messaging, news 123
text news alerts 125–126
The Accountability Project (TAP) 129
Thornton, John 76
time-based structure 122
Time Magazine 75
The Toni Stabile Center for Investigative Reporting 146
Toomey, Shamus 93
TPM *see* Talking Points Memo (TPM)
traditional mass-market newspaper: self-destruction of 13
traditional media 17, 143–144, 167
traditional news industry 61
traditional newspaper: transitioning to nonprofit 7
traditional newsrooms 15, 176; continued consolidation and collapse 32–33; decline of 24–26
Transactional Records (TRAC) 128
transcription service 127
transparency 188–189, 195; news organizations 195–196; with public 193
Transparency.org 168
trimming 31–32
the Trust Project 197–199
2020 (year of nonprofits) 56–59

Underwood, Doug: "*When MBAS Rule the Newsroom*" 25
Unearthed 172, 179, 180
United States' Lack of Regulation Fuels Crisis of Unaffordable Insulin 178
university journalism programs 133, 141
University of Maryland 141, 146
University of Missouri School of Journalism 139
University of North Carolina 148
University of Vermont 150–151
university statehouse bureau 133–134
university students: local news through 147–151
U.S. Census data cooperative 128
U.S. journalism, traditional model 1
U.S. public broadcasting 153
U.S. public media 157

VCU Capital News Service (VCU CNS) 143–145
Vermont Digger (VTDigger) 69–72, 73, 96
Vermont Journalism Trust 69, 191–192
Virginia Commonwealth University 142
The Virginian-Pilot (Newspaper) 144
visual investigations 131
visualization tools 126
Voice of San Diego 62
Vt. Digger 191–192

Waldman, Stephen 21, 111
Ward, Stephen 184, 186
The Washington Post 28, 74
watchdog coverage 5, 6
watchdog.org 180, 186
WBEZ station 152, 153, 160
web free 121–122
weblog 51
weeklies: on ads and services revenue 41; digitally on daily basis 41
"*When MBAS Rule the Newsroom*" (Underwood) 25
Who's Reporting Africa Now? Non-Governmental Organizations, Journalists, and Multimedia (Wright) 172
Wikipedia 79
William and Flora Hewlett Foundation 76
Wired Magazine 121
Wisconsin Center for Investigative Journalism 7, 55
Wisconsin Watch 108
WNET 62
Woolley, Buzz 77
World Wide Web 17, 51
Wright, Kate 172
Wright, Nykia 152, 153
Wyncote Foundation 76
Wynn, Matt 86, 87